Wild and Free

Published by AA Publishing (a trading name of AA Media Limited, whose registered office is Fanum House, Basing View, Basingstoke, Hampshire RG21 4EA; registered number 06112600)

© AA Media Limited 2018

A CIP catalogue record for this book is available from the British Library.

Editor: Donna Wood
Art Director: James Tims
Page layout: Elizabeth Baldin
Colour reprographics: Ian Little
Cover design: Lee-May Lim

Maps created using relief shading from Mountain High Maps® Copyright © 1993 Digital Wisdom®, Inc

ISBN: 978-0-7495-7846-6

A05344

Printed and bound in China by 1010 Printing Group Limited

Illustrations by Elizabeth Baldin
art@elizabethbaldin.co.uk

Wild and Free

Easy escapes from city life

Dominic Couzens

Contents

Introduction

This book has been written to inspire people to get outside and explore the natural world. It doesn't matter much how or when; the important thing is to get out there. Much of Britain's outdoors is a free resource. The fresh air, countryside and wildlife are available now, today, and all year round. In a relatively short travel time, people in most parts of the country can immerse themselves in some impressive wildness, where the enjoyment is in looking, in being there and in exploring round the next corner.

At the sites within these pages you can wander with a good chance of seeing some interesting plants and animals. This isn't a walking guide, although many of the sites are great for rambling or hiking; its purpose is to show you places that are blessed with an abundance of birds or mammals, insects, amphibians or flowering plants, or a combination of them all. You can walk, of course – but hopefully your attention will be hijacked by something that is moving, calling, blooming or festooning.

These locations have been chosen with several criteria in mind. They are all free to enter, they all have good wildlife for at least part of the year, and they are all within a couple of hours' drive of a large town or city (see the chapter opener pages for details). Many are off the beaten track, or at least low profile, without signposts or a website, and that is a deliberate choice. One of the great joys of Britain is its profusion of unheralded nooks and crannies, often barely appreciated by locals, let alone by visitors from further away. Many of these sites are nature reserves, lovingly preserved and looked after. They deserve more recognition.

All the locations included here are good for wildlife, but they don't all provide sightings on a plate, nor do they necessarily provide any facilities such as cafés or loos. The best plan is to bring a picnic and plenty of water so that you can roam wherever the fancy takes you, but for those who like to stop off somewhere for lunch, details of a nearby pub, mostly from the AA-recommended list, have been included.

On the whole, large, well-known reserves with visitor centres and hides, where the birds and mammals seem to have tags on them – and some plants actually do – have not been included. Wonderful though such places are, they don't usually provide the 'wild' experience, where you can feel close to nature but detached from other people. Inevitably, though, a few places like this have found their way into the book, particularly within the more heavily populated parts of the country.

Although all the sites are free to enter, you cannot always leave your vehicle for free. Many have car parks where you either must pay or leave a donation. It would have been preferable to have included a hundred good wildlife sites where it was easy to park and pay nothing, but this proved impractical, not least because things change very quickly and an owner might suddenly decide to impose a charge. But it is also too restrictive, reducing greatly the number of places to choose from.

The book is designed to be broad in scope in several ways. First, it covers as much of England, Scotland and Wales as possible, so that everybody in those countries will have at least one or two sites within relatively easy reach. Second, it includes as many different types of wildlife as possible. This is quite difficult, because most nature reserves are maintained for easy-to-spot things such as birds or flowers. Some places in this book are famous for less heralded plants or animals such as mosses or beetles or fungi, and it is hoped that, on occasion, visitors will notice these. Third, not all the places are at their best just in summer, but hopefully at other seasons too. Each site description includes a selection of seasonal wildlife highlights covering the whole year.

Whether you use this book for a day out, a holiday diversion or a two-hour lunch break doesn't matter, and whether or not you actually see anything special on your visit is, in some ways, immaterial. If it gets people outdoors enjoying a few new places in Britain, it will have fulfilled its primary purpose.

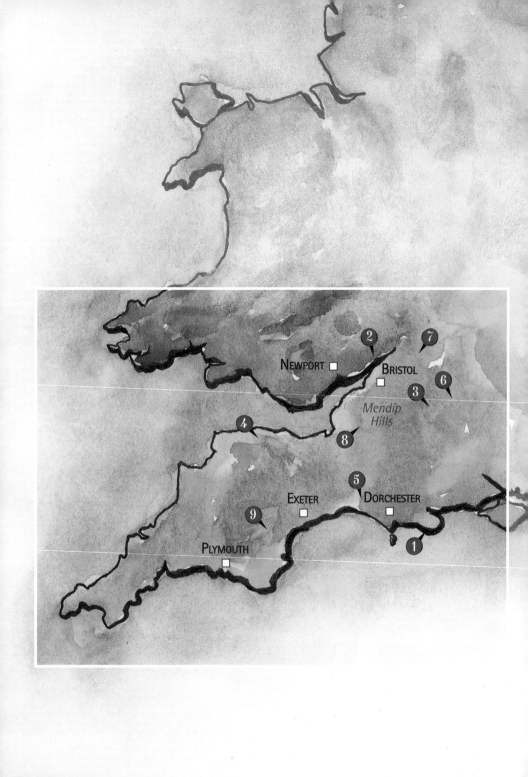

Southwest England

1 Dancing Ledge

Best of the Jurassic Coast

Durnford Drove, Langton Matravers, Swanage, Dorset BH19 3HG

Grid ref SY997783

Directions B3069 to Langton Matravers; car park is at south end of village

Lunch stop Square and Compass, Worth Matravers, Swanage, Dorset BH19 3LF

This short stretch of the Jurassic Coast offers you almost everything: marvellous views over the English Channel whatever the weather, lots of wildlife, an adventurous scramble, an unexpected swimming site, some tasty forage and a dose of history.

Park at the end of Durnford Drove and from there it is a quick trot across the fields to Spyway Barn, a listed building dating from the early 19th century, once a haunt of smugglers. Just beyond, the commanding view of the sea is overwhelming, and both ravens and peregrines, together with the abundant jackdaws, ride the breezes at the top of the steep slope. In spring and summer, look down at your feet, because the limestone soil hosts many unusual plants such as the rare early spider orchid in profusion in April and early May. Look too in July for the Lulworth skipper, one of Britain's rarest butterflies.

In fact, the next step requires you to keep looking down, because you'll be dropping to what looks like the cliff edge and the Southwest Coastal Path – it is very steep and easy to lose your footing. Stonechats and linnets are abundant on the slope, as are whitethroats in the summer. Take time to admire the chalk grassland plants you pass on the way, such as salad burnet, yellow rattle and cowslip.

By the time you reach the bottom of the slope, you are likely to be able to make out small, bobbing shapes on the sea. There is a seabird cliff here, and for much of the year it is possible to watch shags and guillemots swimming,

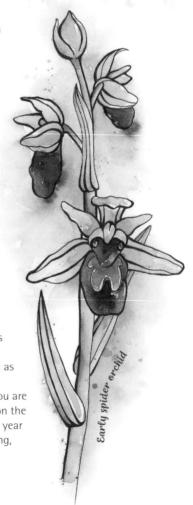

Early spider orchid

10

sometimes with razorbills among them. Dancing Ledge is most famous, though, for its puffins, which can be seen here from late March to July. There are nothing like the numbers in northern Britain – only a handful – but these birds are the nearest to London. They are small and easy to miss, but they are often just offshore.

The interest is far from over, because at the bottom of this slope there are steps down on to Dancing Ledge itself, a man-made shelf constructed by the quarrymen of the Purbeck stone to help them load their vessels. The sea dances in a particular way here, or perhaps the shelf is the approximate size of a dance floor – take your pick for the origin of the name. Beside the slightly uneven and crumbling steps grows a tasty piece of forage, rock samphire, with its fleshy leaves and a delicious, slightly salty taste.

The Ledge is a favourite place for rock-climbers and for coasteerers, and there is another surprise in the form of a small swimming pool blasted out of the rock on the orders of the head of the nearby prep school about a hundred years ago. It was used by pupils for an early morning dip, which they may or may not have been grateful for. These days it can still be used, but swimming in the sea itself hereabouts can be dangerous and is not recommended. Look out to sea instead, where the birds sometimes come in very close and even dolphins are occasionally seen. On land, rock pipits breed and, in winter, you might see a black redstart.

The rocks in the area hint at a more dangerous type of wildlife: the Jurassic Coast, as you might guess, was once roamed by dinosaurs, although the most important finds have been of marine giants such as pliosaurs. Dozens of important fossils of many types have been unearthed near here, including some of the earliest mammals ever found.

Once you have enjoyed the Ledge, return up the steps to the Southwest Coastal Path. Here you can turn right or left to prolong your walk, or venture back up the slope to retrace your steps. Please note that it is much steeper on the way back up than on the way down – or at least it appears to be. It's a hard slog, anyway.

Seasonal highlights

Spring
Puffin, early spider orchid

Summer
Chalk plants, Lulworth skipper

Autumn
Whinchat, warblers

Winter
Stonechat, black redstart, gulls

All year
Raven, peregrine, shag

Puffin

2 Lancaut

Shore to woodland in a few paces

Lancaut Lane, Chepstow, Gloucestershire NP16 7JB

Grid ref ST539966

Directions East on A48 through Chepstow and over bridge, north on B4228 through Tutshill and Woodcroft, left beyond Broadrock down Lancaut Lane

Lunch stop The Riverside Wine Bar, 18A The Back, Chepstow, Gloucestershire NP16 5HH

On the last 20 miles of its journey down to the Severn Estuary, the River Wye meanders drunkenly through a series of heavily wooded limestone cliffs. One of its most dramatic swerves is around the Lancaut 'peninsula' just north of Chepstow, where a westward and then an eastward turn has almost created an island. The peninsula has a delightful cut-off feel. There was an Iron Age fort here and a medieval settlement, possibly a leper colony, but these have long been abandoned. An 11th-century church stands in ruins.

This scenic spot is dominated by the river and the cliffs that tower over it, while some of the best wildlife is found in the woodlands. Just a few miles from the mouth of the Severn, the Wye is tidal, and at some points on the peninsula the natural transition from woodland to saltmarsh is so abrupt as to be covered in a few paces, a situation almost unique in Britain. One of the oddest experiences you can have at Lancaut, albeit rarely, is to be scanning the river from the middle of woodland and to see a seal's head bobbing up. Indeed, even porpoises have apparently been recorded here.

Although it is possible to approach the peninsula by road (Lancaut Lane), it is much more satisfying to walk from Chepstow and follow the Lancaut Loop. Park in the bustling Welsh town, go across the bridge into England, follow Offa's Dyke north, and then, at a green-painted mansion called Pen Moel, ignore the path right and instead go under a small wooden bridge into Lancaut Nature Reserve. Within a mile or so, suddenly you are swallowed up under the quiet canopy of oak, field maple and yew, and in a different world.

Follow the steep path down through this ancient woodland. You will be concentrating on keeping your footing, but this is an exceptional place for plants. Your eyes might be drawn to the bluebells in spring, and the violets and wood anemones, but the stars are the shrubs. The scarce small-leaved lime grows here, together with the wild service tree, but for sheer rarity value the shrubs known as whitebeams make botanists grow weak at the knees. Several species, including the round-leaved whitebeam and the

Symonds Yat whitebeam, occur in the Wye Valley and nowhere else in the world.

You quickly reach a patch of boulder scree and, as you descend, eventually you find yourself below the 250ft cliffs at Wintour's Leap, a popular climbing spot. The cliffs along this stretch of the Wye are excellent places to see birds of prey, including peregrine falcons, which breed here. They are present all year, along with buzzards. Keener bird of prey enthusiasts will look for goshawks, larger versions of the sparrowhawk, which breed in the nearby Forest of Dean. Red kites often drift over, too, so it is worth keeping a sharp eye on the sky.

The path follows the river closely and winds round onto the peninsula. Check the rocks for wildflowers, including the brilliant red valerian, pink-coloured lesser calamint and shining cranesbill. The beach is tidal, so you might be close to the water or seeing banks of mud. Either way, be sure to take a quick look at the small fringe of saltmarsh, where, in summer, sea aster grows, along with several other salt-tolerant plants.

There will be birds around the river – cormorants, which breed near here, and perhaps goosanders, long-bodied diving ducks. You would be lucky to see mammals, although otters and even polecats live in the area.

Having reached a clearing beyond the old quarry, the public footpath takes you up past the ruins of St James's Church, which hasn't had a roof since 1865. It ascends towards the farm, past a bench where there are excellent views over the Wye. If you turn right here you can follow Lancaut Lane past the old fort and back to Offa's Dyke, where you retrace your steps.

On the left of the lane, though, on the northern edge of the peninsula, is another woodland, Ban-y-Gor Woods (still in England), also a nature reserve. A track leads past exceptional flora (350 plant species have been recorded). There are beeches and yews, with small-leaved lime and whitebeams again making up the understorey, and hazel, which provides habitat for a good population of dormice. A very impressive range of ferns occurs here, with strange names like hard shield-fern, hard fern, scaly male fern and maidenhair spleenwort. The moss flora is also excellent – well over 50 species of moss and 12 of liverwort – although few people pay it much attention. In such a place, there is really too much else to see.

Peregrine falcon

Seasonal highlights

Spring
Whitebeam flowers, bluebell

Summer
Red valerian, shining cranesbill, ferns

Autumn
Wayfaring tree, yew berries

Winter
Cormorant, common seal

All year
Peregrine, goshawk, raven

3 Morgan's Hill

Deeply rural chalk downland

Between Blackland and Bishops Cannings, Calne, Wiltshire SN11 8PZ

Grid ref SU025671

Directions South on unnamed road through Blackland towards the A361; park on left at picnic area

Lunch stop The Lansdowne, The Strand, Calne, Wiltshire SN11 0EH

This is the kind of place that you dream about on cold winter days, or yearn for when you are overseas. Quintessentially English, with a lovely view to the north of the Wiltshire Plains, it is an area that is unsung and yet is brim full of wildlife. On any day, you can walk for several miles without touching a single public road (at least 7 miles in a broad circle including Cherhill Down).

You begin your walk at the Smallgrain car park and picnic area (SU020671), which is just to the north of the North Wilts Golf Club entrance along the minor road from Blackland, a village just south of Calne, to the A361 and Bishops Cannings. If this sounds complicated, it is – this is a deeply rural location. There is an excellent broad track up towards the hill which goes past a couple of fairways and then up the gentle slope; you can see the distinctive ring of trees on Morgan's Hill just above. Along the lane, look out for some of the birds that are here all year round: yellowhammers, always perched proudly on posts or bush-tops; linnets, the males with crimson-red breasts in the summer; and skylarks, which will probably be hovering low over the grassy down to your left. You might well see buzzards here, using the up-currents of air, and ravens with long, diamond-shaped tails. If you hear a croak from high above you, the latter is what is making the noise. On the fields here you might also see some partridges. The grey partridge is becoming quite rare in much of England, but it is sometimes seen here.

As you make your way towards the hill and see the distinctive scalloped ridges of the escarpment, you will hardly fail to notice that the ground mineral hereabouts is chalk. This is why the Wiltshire Wildlife Trust manages a small chunk of the hill, beginning half a mile from the car park. Chalk downland is very special habitat, particularly rich in flowers and butterflies, and in the last few decades it has decreased enormously in overall acreage. The remaining areas are precious.

Stunning though the area is at all times – it is part of the North Wessex Downs Area of Outstanding Natural Beauty – the hill is most enchanting in spring and summer, when the flowers are in full bloom and the butterflies fuss around them. Much is made of the fact that, on good chalk, you can find dozens of plant species on a square yard of turf. When you see the sort of profusion that is here, you can believe it. In the summer there are blooms everywhere, including kidney vetch, cowslips, primroses, wild thyme, horseshoe vetch, common rock-rose, marjoram, purging flax, salad burnet and dwarf thistle. And these are just the common species. There are a number of rarer gems, not least the fabulous autumn gentian, which is not only more purple than your usual gentian but also flowers later, from July. Other rarities include round-headed rampion, found in profusion on the 5th-century Wansdyke, a ditch on the reserve's southern border, meadow saxifrage and marsh helleborine, the latter an orchid that isn't usually found on chalk downland.

If you wander towards the old chalk pits to the east there are more orchids including lesser butterfly, fly, bee, frog, musk and pyramidal. Several of these names are fanciful descriptions of the shapes of the flowers, often making the plants sound bigger than they are. Several are small and inconspicuous, so good luck.

Throughout the summer Morgan's Hill is excellent for butterflies and other invertebrates. Less common butterflies include Adonis blue, brown argus and marsh fritillary, but on a fine day you will see plenty without worrying what they all are. After a short time of botanising, you will probably need a walk. Proceed to the eastern end of the reserve, via a look in the scrub and woodland, and wend your way along the Wessex Ridgeway as far as your fancy takes you. There are views to die for – indeed, the hill is named after a man called John Morgan, who went to the gallows up here in 1790, to evident local notoriety.

Not many people wander around Morgan's Hill in winter looking for wildlife, but in recent years doing just this has proved worthwhile. There are flocks of small birds, such as finches and meadow pipits, and their attendant hunting birds of prey, such as sparrowhawks, and even merlins and peregrines. Red kites are becoming more common, and kestrels hunt for mice and voles all year round. You will be quite lonely up here on chilly days, but who knows what you might find.

Seasonal highlights

Spring
Cowslip, primrose, Mother Shipton moth

Summer
Round-headed rampion, orchids, Adonis blue

Autumn
Autumn gentian, thistles

Winter
Merlin, red kite

All year
Yellowhammer, partridge

Yellowhammer

Overleaf: Morgan's Hill

15

4 Pinkworthy Pond
A remote pool on Exmoor

Goat Hill Bridge, near Pinkery Centre for Outdoor Learning, Simonsbath, Somerset TA24 7LL

Grid ref SS724404 (for parking off B3358)

Directions Off the B3358 between Challacombe and Simonsbath

Lunch stop The Royal Oak Inn, Withypool, Somerset TA24 7QP

The road leading towards this site might look wild enough on its own for many visitors, with its open moorland vistas between the villages of Challacombe and Simonsbath, both of which sound like they come straight out of a Thomas Hardy novel. But things become a lot wilder once you're off-road. This isn't a walk for the faint-hearted, particularly on one of the many Exmoor days when the weather can't decide between wet or very wet, when the mist cloaks the hilltops and there is a real chance of becoming alarmingly lost. Not many people come here, and you can see why.

Nonetheless, as you park beside the road just south of Goat Hill Bridge, the plateau to the north beckons you. The River Barle meanders down, luring you to follow it, to adventure. You shouldn't resist.

Quite simply, the track up towards Pinkery Centre for Outdoor Learning (it says 'no entry' but this is just for vehicles) leads to the remotest part of Exmoor, up to the notorious boggy and thrilling area known as The Chains, around the 1,500ft contour. This is rough country, usually soaking, and you wouldn't wish to be stranded overnight.

It is probable that you have already seen two of Exmoor's most famous inhabitants on your car journey, but, if not, keep a lookout for them as you go. The famous Exmoor ponies have been around on the moors since the Domesday Book was completed in 1086, and probably for a great deal longer. They are a powerful, stocky breed that are kept out throughout the winter months and are allowed to roam wherever they wish. Red deer have probably been here for thousands of years. The largest land mammals in Britain, these also go where they please, and you might come across a herd anywhere. In contrast to the ponies, which are managed and owned, they are wild animals.

Every step of the walk up to The Chains takes you further away from comfort and familiarity. You quickly pass the Outdoor Learning Centre (apparently the highest educational establishment in the country), almost surrounded by the last trees you will see for a while, cross a field (look out for two uncommon ferns: adder's-tongue and moonwort), and there you are, on the open moor.

Heather and wispy purple moor-grass proliferate, and the abundance of rushes and sedges reflects the universal dampness. There should be plenty of small birds around, unless you are coming here in the depths of winter. Stonechats – small robin-like birds with smart dark heads and white collars – are likely to call 'sack' at you from a bush-top; you might possibly see their close relative, the whinchat, with a pale stripe over the eye and an apricot-coloured breast. Linnets, with their brilliant crimson fronts, are common, but the bird that will probably dominate is the meadow pipit, a small bird that gives a panicky 'sip-sip' call as you flush it from the vegetation. It is brown and streaky, not unlike a miniature thrush.

Continue up the track and the plateau looms above you. If visiting between March and July, you should hear the fabulous, ecstatic bubbling call of the curlew by now, a fast-declining wading bird that breeds here. The snipe also nests in the blanket bog; on summer evenings you might hear the rhythmic bleating it makes to defend its territory, as if a sheep were bleating from the air. These are special birds. Perhaps a ring ouzel will be singing like a lost, melancholy song thrush, adding to the chorus of rarity.

If ever the word 'melancholy' summed up a place, it is here. As you reach the plateau summit you come across this wholly unnatural body of water, created in about 1830 by damming the headwaters of the River Barle. About 3 acres in extent, it is 30ft deep and popular with wild swimmers. It has been here long enough to seem part of the wilderness. Ducks drop in and it hosts some interesting watery plants such as floating club-rush, least bur-reed and marsh lousewort. In summer the pretty ivy-leaved bellflower dots the banks. On the nearby moors you can hardly miss the ranks of aptly named cottongrass (actually a member of the sedge family).

Nobody knows why the pond was created, but the tragic tale of a local farmer has passed down the generations. Richard Gammin was a young widower who tried to woo a village girl to marry him and help look after his 10 children. When his overtures were rejected he threw himself into the pond; his body was recovered only after they drained it.

Thus Pinkworthy Pond has become part of Britain's ghost-hunting scene, looking for Gammin and others who have perished on the moors. Ghosts aren't guaranteed here, but you will return with a dose of the wilderness, and all the better for it.

Seasonal highlights

Spring
Curlew, snipe, stonechat

Summer
Marsh lousewort, ivy-leaved bellflower

Autumn
Grasses, heather

Winter
Meadow pipit, dipper

All year
Exmoor ponies, red deer, ghosts

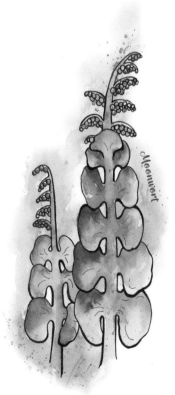

Moonwort

5 Powerstock Common

Lose yourself in deepest Dorset

Near Barrowland Lane, Dorchester, Dorset DT2 0EJ

Grid ref SY547974

Directions From Toller Porcorum, follow High Street out of village for 1.2 miles then turn right to car park near bridge

Lunch stop The Spyway Inn, Askerswell, Dorset DT2 9EP

This site really is nestled in deepest, darkest Dorset. You half expect that you might wander the woods and come across an abandoned cottage full of elves or fairies, but there is at least a chance of spotting another rare and flighty animal, the wild boar, as well as deer, badgers and lots of bats. The real delight here, though, is the sense of being lost in nature. Beware – this can happen literally. I have several times mislaid my bearings in the woods and meadows and stumbled around in circles.

Oddly, though, one of Powerstock Common's most prominent features is very much man-made. It is the cutting of an abandoned railway, part of the line from nearby Maiden Newton to Bridport that closed down in 1975. There are a few outbuildings still standing in a state of eerie disrepair, but the track remains as an excellent path running from the railway bridge close to the car park, then for a mile right around the northern edge of the 284-acre nature reserve. In places this track has high, scrubby embankments festooned with herbs and visited by an impressive variety of butterflies.

The soil here is chalky so you can look out for plants such as common spotted orchids, which are at their best in June. Bee orchids are found here, too, and cowslips are abundant, along with marjoram and other herbs giving off a suitably aromatic hue.

Other than the railway cutting, the reserve is a real maze of woodland, patches of grassland and scrub, and small ponds. If you follow the well-marked Long Trail you will cover the full range. After the embankment, the route leads into a mixed woodland of hazel, ash, oak and other trees. Here is evidence of centuries old coppice-with-standards woodland use, with spread-out oaks as the tall standard trees and an understorey of hazel beneath, which was cut at intervals for a variety of rural uses, including fencing. This land use on damp soil encourages a profusion of flowers to grow, especially in spring. The whole area is famous for its bluebell woods, and Powerstock Common has one of the finest displays you will see anywhere. Wild garlic also grows in large clusters, giving off its powerful scent.

The path wends left, goes uphill and opens out to grassland, where cattle graze in the winter. This area has been clear felled of conifers and a number of ponds dug, leading to a remarkably flourishing amphibian population. Frogs, toads and all three British newts occur in these waters, as well as a variety of freshwater invertebrates.

The damp grassland here and elsewhere attracts the most famous butterfly on the reserve, the rare marsh fritillary, and people will come from far and wide to see it in the damp meadows here. The caterpillars feed on the plentiful devil's-bit scabious plant and the adults are on the wing in late May and early June. Other butterflies worth looking out for include silver-washed fritillary, speckled wood and grizzled skipper, and on a good day in summer you could easily spot more than 10 species. These open areas with tall trees are good for a dingy-coloured bird with an excellent song: the tree pipit. The males launch themselves into the air from a tree, go up a few feet as they sing, and then glide back down to a branch with wings open and tail raised, looking for all the world like a paper aeroplane.

The whole common is excellent for birds all year round, and right from January to July the woods and hedgerows resound to birdsong. On a late winter morning you are certain to hear the drumming of woodpeckers, in spring the blackcaps simply yell at you, and there are always robins singing. Look out for bullfinches, yellowhammers and marsh tits (in the deciduous woodlands, not marshes), all three declining species that are holding their own here.

Powerstock Common has a habit of keeping its treats hidden in small nooks and crannies. It is a place where you stumble upon things, keep being surprised and drawn that little bit further in. Even after many visits you never quite discover all its secrets.

Seasonal highlights

Spring
Bluebell, marsh fritillary, narrow-bordered bee hawk-moth

Summer
Newts, tree pipit, devil's-bit scabious

Autumn
Nuts, fruits, fungi

Winter
Woodland bird flocks, chaffinch, winter thrushes

All year
Marsh tit, bullfinch, roe deer

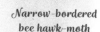

Narrow-bordered bee hawk-moth

6 Savernake Forest

A treasure hunt for veterans

Grand Avenue, Marlborough, Wiltshire SN8 3HW

Grid ref SU210684

Directions From Marlborough go east on A4 for 1.5 miles, through two pillars on to Grand Avenue (Forest Hill entrance)

Lunch stop The Lamb Inn, The Parade, Marlborough, Wiltshire SN8 1NE

It is a given that a forest will have trees, but not many have trees like this place. Some of the oldest in Britain grow here, twisted by the passing years into strange shapes that look like sculptures. Take the Big Belly Oak, the most famous of all. This sessile oak tree, aged between 1,000 and 1,100 years old, has an enormous 36ft girth and its big midriff and relatively small branches make it look as though it was planted upside down, with its roots flailing upwards. You can hardly miss it if you drive along the busy A346 between Marlborough and Burbage. What better sight could summon you into this huge forest?

The trees are so revered here, and so ancient, that some have names and about 20 have plaques in front of them. Many are well worth paying homage to, including the huge Cathedral Oak, another monster of 1,000 years, and the King of Limbs with its multiple broad branches coming up from near the base. The Duke's Vaunt Oak was apparently a favourite of Edward Seymour, brother of Jane Seymour, who became King Henry VIII's third wife. Rumour has it that the king set eyes on her for the first time in Savernake. You can get a guide to the trees and a map at Postern Campsite, where there is also a car park and toilets, off the A346 south of Marlborough. There are even walks run commercially to tick off all the named trees – tree twitching.

Although Savernake is the only privately owned forest in Britain (owned by the Earl of Cardigan), it is freely accessible. The easiest way to enter is to turn in from the A4 at Forest Hill, east of the town, just beyond the hospital. Follow the road into the Grand

Muntjac deer

Spring
Birdsong, firecrest,
marsh tit

Summer
Bats (including
barbastelle), foxglove

Autumn
Fungi, deer, chestnuts

Winter
Rare lichens, mosses

All year
Ancient oak, beech,
sweet chestnut

Avenue, a remarkable avenue of beech trees 4 miles long; drive along here, park in any layby and walk wherever the fancy takes you. If you drive far enough you reach Eight Walks, a spot from which, you've guessed it, paths diverge in eight directions, each at 45 degrees to the other. Take your pick as any one will be a delight.

Not surprisingly, the ancient trees (2,600 oaks in all, 2,400 beeches and a few hundred sweet chestnuts) make up their own special habitat, so there is always something to see. The forest has one of the best displays of fungi in Britain, with an incredible 1,100 species, many of which are rare. One of its specialities is the magpie inkcap, which has a black cap with white spots. The fungal bloom occurs in the autumn, so it peaks at the very same time that the trees are showing their best colour. A fungus foray in Savernake in late October is both colourful and delicious. Incidentally, the fact that the area is designated as a Site of Special Scientific Interest (SSSI) is because of its exceptional lichens, found on the bark of old trees. It is also very good for mosses, although not many visitors realise this. These are at their best in January and February.

Although Savernake is good for birds, some of the better species are difficult to find: the hawfinch, for example, is famously shy, and the lesser spotted woodpecker is a vanishing sprite. You are likely to hear or see the more common woodpeckers, green and great spotted, plus a variety of other woodland birds such as nuthatches, treecreepers, jays and tits, including the marsh tit. In the conifer areas look or listen out for crossbill, siskin and firecrest.

Even on a short visit, you should spot a mammal or two. Grey squirrels are typically abundant, and four species of deer occur in the forest – roe, red, fallow and muntjac – of which the fallow, with its white bottom split by black tail, is the most common. However, the mammalian gems of Savernake are the bats, drawn by the ancient trees. No fewer than 13 species have been recorded here, one of the highest totals in Britain, and including rarities such as the black-coated, fluffy barbastelle. The Wiltshire Bat Group runs periodic trips into the forest and the nearby Savernake Tunnel to count bats, and enthusiasts are welcome.

However, if you do see a bat flitting over you at the end of your visit, it could be a very rare species. Savernake Forest is that kind of place.

Barbastelle bat

7 Siccaridge Wood

Much more than just bluebells

Church Lane, Sapperton, Cirencester, Gloucestershire GL7 6LQ

Grid ref SO947033

Directions Take the A419 east through Stroud and Chalford, turn north at Chapmans Cross to Sapperton, then walk from Church Lane

Lunch stop The Bell at Sapperton, Sapperton, Gloucestershire GL7 6LE

This is a local gem of a woodland, famous for its displays of bluebells in the spring. However, it has far more to offer than an ephemeral blue haze. Plenty of unusual plants and animals are found here, and it is also a stone's throw from a remarkable unnatural wonder.

Siccaridge Wood cloaks a ridge in the Frome Valley not far from Stroud. When you are visiting, it is best to find the village of Sapperton, park near the church and then approach on foot along the towpath of the Thames and Severn Canal. As you walk west, the wood is on your right, up the slope, and there are plenty of paths you can follow to enjoy the place and its many corners.

Siccaridge Wood (the name means secure ridge) is an ancient woodland, meaning that it has been part of the countryside since at least 1600. This longevity has a profound effect on what can be found here, principally meaning that biodiversity is higher than in more recently planted woods. Here you can play detective finding the plants that are indicators of antiquity: the bluebell is one, along with wood anemone, early purple orchid and wood sanicle. The general flora is one of the best features of this wood, and in the spring and summer there are masses of flowers everywhere, including the lovely yellow archangel, the peculiar herb-paris, the recognisably scented wild garlic and the rare and local angular Solomon's seal. One of the biggest attractions occurs close to the broadest ride through the wood, Morley Ride, a flat ride halfway up the slope (accessible from the Sapperton–Tunley road bordering the site). In late May, in a small glade just off the track, there is a display of the romantic-sounding lily of the valley, with its big fleshy leaves and delicate, bell-like ice-cream-white blooms which hang in small clusters.

Don't keep your eyes entirely fixed on the ground, because the wood plays host to a good variety of common birds. Look out for nuthatches and woodpeckers, and a variety of tit species. Nightingales have bred in the scrub in the past, but now a loud voice from the thickets in spring is more likely to belong to a blackcap or song thrush.

Seasonal highlights

Although the wood is long-established, this does not mean that it is untouched by people – quite the reverse. Instead it has been a working woodland, from which timber has been regularly extracted and some trees coppiced, especially hazel. Other trees have been planted, leading to a rich variety – it's a good place to test your tree identification skills. Look out for the rich variety of understorey shrubs, too, which include spindle, guelder rose and wayfaring tree. In autumn and winter these have different-coloured fruits: shocking pink, garish red and a red/purple mixture respectively.

Overall, much of the joy of the reserve is found in scrambling past the vegetation on the paths and steps, many of which are pretty steep. At the bottom of the hill is a disused canal, now overgrown. Take care on the towpath – it is muddy and slippery in places, and the locks are deep and treacherous. Frogs and other aquatic animals have moved into the pools of water, but make sure you don't do the same.

It's just about worth pointing out that the wood is excellent for small mammals, although you are only really likely to see a grey squirrel on a normal visit. In addition to the abundant bank vole and wood mouse, the much scarcer yellow-necked mouse (like a wood mouse on steroids) occurs here, and will often forage nocturnally in the treetops. Still more arboreal is the hazel dormouse, for which the wood is a major stronghold. Boxes are provided for these sleepy rodents (they hibernate between September and April) and the mammals are regularly counted. Both roe and muntjac deer are somewhat easier to see, but tend to hide in the thick parts of the wood.

At the end of your wildlife walk, you should make time to pay homage to a local curiosity. As you return to Sapperton along the towpath you will pass the entrance to a large tunnel. This is the Daneway Portal to the Sapperton Canal Tunnel, completed in 1789 after five years of construction work. It was, for a while, the longest tunnel of any kind in England.

lily of the valley

26

8 Westhay Moor

Otters, and birds in droves

Dagg's Lane Drove, Westhay, Wells, Somerset BA6 9TX

Grid ref ST457437 (for car park)

Directions Take the B3151 through Westhay, turn first right after Westhay Bridge (Westhay Moor Drove), then drive on for 1 mile

Lunch stop The Swan, Cheddar Road, Wedmore, Somerset BS28 4EQ

The Somerset Levels are fast becoming one of England's best-known wildlife sites, and in truth you could drop in almost anywhere around here and see plenty of stuff. The most famous spot, Ham Wall, celebrated for its enormous winter starling roost, has become a very popular place for visitors. So why not try Westhay Moor, Ham Wall's little brother a shade to the north, which has much of the same wildlife but not the crowds?

After parking in the Westhay Moor car park, there's a path (Dagg's Lane Drove) that runs in a northerly direction across the moor, with a lake on the left. At the end of the lake, next to a bird hide, there is a path to the left which goes across to the next drove (London Drove). A network of tracks and hides now provides your entertainment. All the Somerset Levels habitats are here: lakes formed by extraction of the heavy, peaty soil, fields, paths, large reedbeds and patches of damp woodland, including alder, birch and Scots pine. There is also a raised bog here, good for plants and a rare habitat this far south.

The area is excellent all year round, with birds invariably the liveliest feature. In the summer, reed buntings and reed and sedge warblers sing incessantly from the marshes and their edges, while great crested and little grebes, coots and various ducks are on the open water. Marsh harriers often pass overhead, flying slowly and at moderate height, their wings raised in a V, looking for ducklings and other easy food. If they spot something they will suddenly tumble down and make a grab. The rare bittern is also here, but much easier to find – or at least to hear – is the cuckoo. Once common over all of southern England, the cuckoo is declining fast, but the large numbers of their favourite host species, the reed warbler, attract them here.

Shoveler duck

Seasonal highlights

Spring
Reed bunting, cuckoo

Summer
Dragonflies, reed and
sedge warblers

Autumn
Redwing, fieldfare,
lapwing

Winter
Starling roost, bittern,
wildfowl

All year
Otter, great crested grebe,
Cetti's warbler

Birds abound in the winter too, when ducks flock here from northern Europe to escape the continental freeze. On the lakes you are likely to see a good variety, including shovelers, with their enormous bills used for filter feeding, gadwall with their sober plumage, nervous teal, elongated pintail and showy wigeon. The best area to find them is along London Drove, where Ten Acre Lake sometimes plays host to diving ducks such as goosander and goldeneye. It is also a good spot for one of the Somerset Levels' star birds, the great egret. This tall white heron, much the same size as our familiar grey heron, is very rare in Britain but a regular here.

The woods can be surprisingly good in winter, with siskins and redpolls, wintering chiffchaffs, goldcrests and a range of tit species. Just because the wetland sites are interesting, you shouldn't ignore the wood and scrub. In the fields, lapwings are common, winter thrushes such as redwings and fieldfares are always about, and, if you are lucky, you might find wintering Bewick's and whooper swans in the fields next to the car park.

You've probably heard that otters have made a comeback in many parts of Britain in recent years, albeit as the usual shadows passing by night. Here in the Somerset Levels, however, they are common and you have a genuine chance of seeing one, even during the day. The droves across the moor are straight, allowing you to see a long way in front, and quite frequently otters will run across these paths to give you glimpses. You can also sometimes see them in the lakes and ponds, their rather square heads bobbing quizzically above the water.

Otter

28

9 Yarner Wood

Dartmoor's finest in a nutshell

Yarner Wood, Bovey Tracey, Devon TQ13 9LJ

Grid ref SX784788

Directions Take B3387 to Haytor; after 1 mile fork right and follow this road for 1.5 miles

Lunch stop The Cleave, Lustleigh, Newton Abbot, Devon TQ13 9TJ

The charms of Yarner Wood, on the edge of Dartmoor, have been known for a long time. It was bought by the Nature Conservancy in 1952 as England's first National Nature Reserve. These days the protected area has been extended to include adjacent Trendlebere Down, and the combination is star-studded. Here you will find the classic Dartmoor mix of ancient hilly sessile oak woodland next to rough open moorland: two walks in one with completely different atmospheres and wildlife.

It is best to use the car park at Yarner Wood as your base to start as it has public toilets and an interpretation display. Have a look at the stream, too, which can attract birds such as grey wagtail and dipper. If you take the short loop nature trail in reverse order, you will follow through the beech trees uphill towards the observation hide, where in the autumn and winter hanging feeders attract an impressive variety of woodland birds. You soon enter into the high oak wood for which the place is famous. The trees here are simply festooned with mosses, lichens and ferns. There are more than 100 species of lichens in this single wood, 65 mosses and 15 species of ferns, including the rare hay-scented buckler fern and Tunbridge filmy fern. The mosses and lichens are at their best in the winter, when it is even wetter than usual. In autumn, a good variety of fungi adds to the impressive flora that is often overlooked.

If you visit in the spring and early summer, the sessile oaks resound to the noise of birdsong. There are three species that draw birdwatchers here like a magnet. The easiest to spot is a flighty black-and-white bird known as the pied flycatcher. This bird breeds mainly in the reserve's many nestboxes and is easy to see when singing near the nest hole. It has a smart white front and, as its name implies, makes fly-catching sallies into the air to catch food. The second star is the delightful yellowish-coloured wood warbler. It is harder to see, but on a spring day its loud shivering song, which sounds a little like a spinning coin coming to rest, echoes through the brilliant glades. The third species is the very rare lesser spotted woodpecker, which you might spot in the alder groves near the car park, but you would be lucky to see this elusive gem.

From the hide, continue west and follow the signs to the old copper mine (Yarrow Mine). It was in service from 1856 to 1867 and at its peak employed 50 men. The mine shaft goes down 330ft. The scene must have been a great deal less peaceful in the 19th century than it is now.

Go back west from the copper mine, take the shortcut along Yarner Stream and find your way back to the beginning of the long nature trail. If you are walking in summer, look out for butterflies such as silver-washed fritillaries in the glades. They are one of 33 species of butterfly recorded here, along with an even more impressive 600 moths. These figures partially reflect the long history of study that has been made by enthusiasts over the years.

From the beginning of the long nature trail, follow the signs back to the car park. You can now either take the car or walk along the minor road out from Yarner Wood and then left towards the bottom of Trendlebere Down, where there is a small car park on the bend. Here is the other delight of Dartmoor – the open landscape with heather and birch, western gorse and ubiquitous purple moor-grass. The down is actually part of a much larger area of moorland that embraces the Haytor area to the west.

Many paths criss-cross this common land, where you are as likely to meet horses or cattle as you are other people. If you follow the road uphill you experience the transitional area between Yarner Wood on your left and the open moor; in the summer this is excellent for birds such as tree pipit and nightjar. The more open areas hold something of a surprise because the rare Dartford warbler occurs here, in one of its westernmost localities in Britain. It is hard to see except on a fine day, when these very small, dark, long-tailed birds perch on the gorse-tops.

If you can, walk right up to the top car park, where the views over South Devon extend right to the coast. It is worth the slog. And what could be more different to the deep woodland glades that you experienced earlier?

Seasonal highlights

Spring
Pied flycatcher, wood warbler

Summer
Butterflies, moths, nightjar

Autumn
Rowan berries, fungi

Winter
Tit flocks, finches, treecreeper

All year
Woodpeckers, nuthatch, dipper, grey wagtail

Pied flycatcher

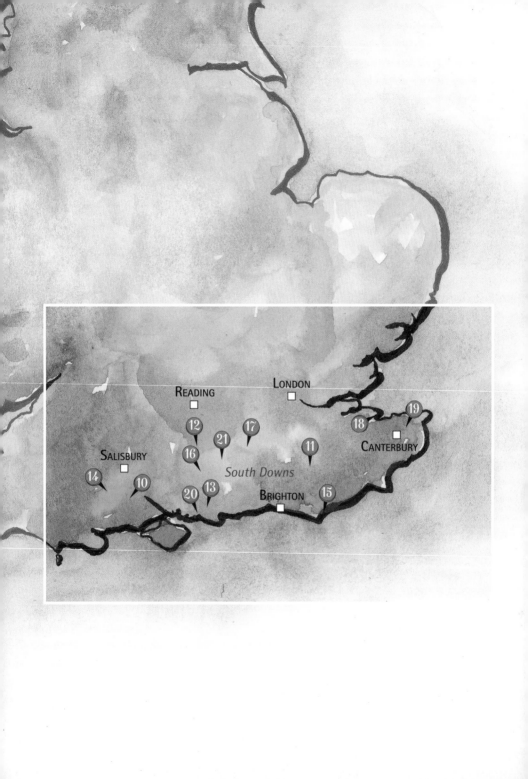

READING

LONDON

12

17

21

SALISBURY

16

11

18

19

CANTERBURY

South Downs

14

10

20

13

BRIGHTON

15

Southern England

10 Cadman's Pool

Immerse yourself in a fairytale

Between Linwood and Fritham, New Forest, Hampshire SO43 7HL

Grid ref SU229122

Directions From Fritham, turn right towards Linwood; the car park is on the right

Lunch stop The Royal Oak, Fritham, Lyndhurst, Hampshire SO43 7HJ

This site is in the quiet part of the New Forest, north of the A31 trunk road that cuts the National Park in two. Although Cadman's Pool is well known to locals, few tourists visit. It helps that it isn't signposted.

Yet here the fabulous forest is at its richest. For example, almost all the special birds of the region – redstart (summer), wood warbler (summer), firecrest and hawfinch, for example – can be seen here, along with an excellent range of plants and insects. And within five minutes of walking downhill from the car park you find yourself completely immersed in the sort of woodland that is described in dark fairytales: tall, uneven, with lots of old and fallen trees and seemingly no end. Deer skip just out of sight and ponies will often wander past.

New Forest ponies

This is not a walk to take lightly. The ground varies in places from boggy to waterlogged, but that is part of the appeal. You will need wellington boots and a map, the latter because if you get lost you could genuinely walk for miles before finding a road or dwelling, which might be more adventurous than you intended. Binoculars are essential, not just for birds and deer, but also to view dragonflies in the summer.

A good route is to drop down the hill until you reach a stream at about SU224123, which varies from a trickle to a torrent depending on recent rain. Turn right and follow the stream as far as Dockens Water, one of the New Forest's longest waterways, then turn left, negotiating the stream, mud and puddles until the trees thin out. If you've brought a picnic this is the spot to stop to eat it, on the north edge of Holly Hatch enclosure (a timber area fenced off to protect the trees from animals; there are 100 of them in the New Forest). There is a bridge here across Dockens Water, and you can enjoy the junction of forest, bog and heath. It is a good place for flowers such as bogbean, and in late April or May there is always a cuckoo calling, an uncommon sound these days in southern England. In high summer the brook is heaving with dragonflies and damselflies, and big butterflies like white admirals may well swoop by as they patrol the woodland.

If you then walk anticlockwise around Holly Hatch and Broomy enclosures, you will almost certainly have the forest to yourself. In the autumn and winter particularly, the moors and bogs round about give an austere feel to the landscape. You could be in Brontë Country. In winter, rare birds of prey including merlin, hen harrier and the songbird-from-hell great grey shrike can be found here. In late autumn you often hear the fallow deer groaning and gurning: a soundtrack to damp, darkening days.

The circuit around the enclosures takes you past isolated Holly Hatch Cottage and round back towards where you started. Take a look at the variety of trees on this walk, including batches of deciduous larches, spruce and, in Anses Wood, beech.

Children will love Cadman's Pool itself (it was built by a Mr Cadman, one of the forest officials, and has nothing to do with nearby Cadnam), where you can paddle and feed the ducks or geese. People also leave food at the car park's edge for many small birds (you can see marsh tit and nuthatch here). For the real adventure, though, you need to go down to the woods.

Seasonal highlights

Spring
Cuckoo, tree pipit, woodlark

Summer
Dragonflies, hobby, redstart, wood warbler, grayling

Autumn
Superb tree colour, deer rutting

Winter
Brambling, redwing, fieldfare, hen harrier, great grey shrike

All year
Fallow deer, ponies, woodpecker, hawfinch (albeit tricky)

11 Eridge Rocks

Rock climbing in deep woodland

Warren Farm Lane, Eridge, Tunbridge Wells, East Sussex TN3 9JG

Grid ref TQ554355

Directions Take the A26 south from Royal Tunbridge Wells

Lunch stop The Nevill Crest and Gun, Eridge Road, Eridge Green, East Sussex
TN3 9JR

This is a truly peculiar place. Imagine taking a woodland walk in the south of
England – near Royal Tunbridge Wells, no less – and finding something akin to
a village hidden in the jungle. You would hardly expect it. Yet here, just 4 miles
south of the large, busy town, is something equivalent: an outcrop of huge
rocks hidden within an ordinary-looking wood. The word outcrop doesn't do it
justice. It is a ridge of vast, looming sandstone blocks, 135 million years old,
some of them 30ft high. The place is a magnet for climbers and, as is customary
with the hobby, they have given their favourite rock faces names: *Equilibrium
Wall, Tower Girdle, Heffalump* and, bizarrely, *More Cake for Me*. Casual visitors
are advised against climbing these soft Cretaceous sandstone cliffs with their
deep fissures and weird shapes, many topped with ancient gnarled trees such as
holly, beech and yew. That fails to take account of how tempting it is to do just
that, to lose yourself in a childish impulse, hidden in your enchanted forest.

To be sure, Eridge Rocks are worth visiting just for their delicious oddness.
Yet this is a superb nature area, too, a Site of Special Scientific Interest (SSSI).
It is most celebrated, as it happens, for something that most people ignore – a
real enchanted 'forest', if you will, albeit one that is no taller than a few inches.
For these north-facing eminences are often damp, sometimes dangerously so
for climbers, and provide ideal habitat for ferns (the rare Tunbridge filmy fern is
a highlight), mosses and liverworts. Quite a number of species characteristic of
more northern parts of the British Isles occur here in the deep south. If you
were a serious bryologist you wouldn't want to miss the liverworts *Calypogeia
integristipula* or *Bazzania trilobata* (which can cover whole walls), or Scott's
fork-moss *Dicranum scottianum*. Many nature enthusiasts don't realise that
Britain, with its damp climate, is one of the best places in Europe for mosses and
liverworts. Another advantage is that these lower plants are at their best in
November and December, a downtime for higher plants.

You reach Eridge Rocks by going down the A26, which runs between
Tunbridge Wells and Crowborough. A couple of miles out of Tunbridge Wells is
the small village of Eridge Green, with its pub The Nevill Crest and Gun. A short

distance beyond is a right turn called Warren Farm Lane, by a church, and you follow this to a small car park, which is more or less at the base of the rocks. It is the entrance to a 100-acre reserve. The rocks were choked with rhododendrons until bought by the Sussex Wildlife Trust in 1997, and it has taken much work to open the place up.

The woodland that girdles the rocks is ancient, at least 400 years old. These sorts of woodlands have a richer flora than more recent plantings, and one of their signature species is the bluebell, which abounds here in late April and turns the understorey an ethereal blue. The combination of the rocks and the bluebells in one short walk, along with primroses and other spring plants, is pretty special.

If the strange rock garden isn't enough for you, almost immediately beyond the outcrop to the north is another reserve, Broadwater Warren, managed by the RSPB. Bought in 2007 as a conifer plantation, this large area of winding, muddy paths is being restored to heathland by extensive clearance. In place of the often sterile coniferous landscape, heather and gorse are reappearing, along with special birds such as nightjar and woodlark, and animals such as adders, butterflies and a good variety of bumblebees. There is even a newly dug pond to increase the biodiversity. Since the warren is right next to the rocks, it's worth extending your walk into this area.

Broadwater Warren, now managed for newly thriving wildlife, is inspiring, but it cannot compete with the star quality of the site next door.

Seasonal highlights

Spring
Bluebell, primrose

Summer
Bumblebee, butterflies

Autumn
Holly berries, ferns

Winter
Unusual mosses, liverworts, ferns

All year
Strange rock formations

Adder

12 Greywell

Nationally important fenland

The Street, Greywell, Hook, Hampshire RG29 1BY

Grid ref SU718513

Directions From J5 of the M3 take the A287 south and turn right on Hook Road to Greywell village

Lunch stop The Hogget Country Pub and Eating House, London Road, Hook Common, Hampshire RG27 9JJ

This is one of the shorter excursions in this book, to a place of rare charm. A scarce example of fen, a marshy habitat on neutral or alkaline soil, Greywell is nationally important for its plants and invertebrates. Hidden away in the farmland and downland of north Hampshire, it has an appealing scruffiness and wildness, and showcases the crystal clear waters of the chalk-fed Whitewater River.

Park anywhere along the main street of Greywell village, unimaginatively called The Street. From here you can admire the glorious old houses along the street, each very different, invariably well kept. The village was originally a Saxon hunting settlement and is mentioned in the Domesday Book. Your first task is to head for the gorgeous rural church, St Mary the Virgin, which is usually open to enter. This flint and stone structure is Norman in origin, built in the 11th century and restored in 1870. The first bird you are likely to see on your walk is the distinctive weathercock, but if you visit in autumn the churchyard, full of yew trees, is likely to be busy with berry-guzzlers such as blackbirds and mistle thrushes.

Go through the churchyard and you will soon encounter your first muddy section of path, of which there will be many. Wellingtons are almost essential here. However, relief comes fast in the form of a boardwalk along the Whitewater, from which you can admire the glistening, brooding waters with their abundant pondweeds and other aquatic vegetation. The water is so clear that you can easily see the bottom, and if little grebes are about, which they often are, it is possible to watch these plump birds as they dive underwater. Water voles, too, revel in these clean waters. The surrounding alders and willows are good for birds, including reed buntings and Cetti's warbler.

After a short while you will find yourself at the delightful mill, with its old, rusted waterwheel. You could turn right and almost immediately left to follow the footpath over the fields (look out for yellowhammers), but treats are in store if you keep the mill on your right and walk along the edge of the long pond. Coots, mallards and sometimes, in winter, gadwalls are here, while the damp

Long-tailed tit

woodlands to your left are good for long-tailed tits, siskins, bullfinches and chiffchaffs. The short stretch brings you to the corner of a reed bed and ahead, in the wood, a rookery. This is fun at all times of the year, but especially in early spring, when the birds are refurbishing their nests and are making all sorts of comical noises. Take the footpath on and then turn sharply left, taking you back through a gate and into a long meadow, with the wood on one side and fields on the right. It is often gloriously muddy here, a graveyard for walking boots. There might be yellowhammers and finches in the field, and buzzards and red kites are likely to fly over. ing encroachment of the scrub.

A little way down on your left you can turn left and go through the wood (the Wallace Memorial Reserve) to the big village green at Greywell. Or alternatively, carry on down to the road and turn left in front of the pumping station. In summer this whole area is excellent for a number of unusual plant species, including marsh helleborine, marsh lousewort, marsh fragrant-orchid and lesser tussock-sedge. Lower plants also abound here, including a rich flora of mosses and liverworts and ferns such as marsh fern, which is common.

As you cross the Whitewater River, either in the reserve or along Deptford Lane, look out for grey wagtails and kingfishers. Just before Deptford Lane meets The Street, a footpath to your right leads to the Basingstoke Canal at the eastern portal of the Greywell Tunnel. The tunnel is 0.7 miles long and disused because of several past roof collapses, but it is a Site of Special Scientific Interest (SSSI) due to the perfect habitat it provides for roosting bats. It is the largest winter bat roost in the country, with the second highest number of Natterer's bats in the whole of Europe. You cannot visit the bats without a licence, but you will still see plenty here on summer and autumn evenings.

The towpath leads to Odiham Castle, now ruined, from where King John set out to meet the noblemen at Runnymede to sign the Magna Carta in 1215. But that is another story, and another direction entirely.

Seasonal highlights

Spring
Ragged robin, reed bunting, long-tailed tit

Summer
Marsh fern, reed warbler, swallow

Autumn
Linnet, yellowhammer, Natterer's bat

Winter
Red kite, kingfisher, lichens

All year
Little grebe, alder, rooks

Reed bunting

13 Kingley Vale

Dark yews and bright downland

Downs Road, West Stoke, Chichester, West Sussex PO18 9BE

Grid ref SU825088

Directions From Mid Lavant, turn west on Downs Road towards West Stoke; car park is beyond West Stoke House

Lunch stop Horse and Groom, East Ashling, West Sussex PO18 9AX

Not many people in Britain have experienced being inside a forest of yew trees. That's because hardly any exist. Yew was the wood of choice for longbows in the battles of the Middle Ages, meaning that large numbers were cut down, leaving only those grown specially in churchyards, usually as single trees. The result is that a forest of yews is staggeringly rare, and the one at Kingley Vale, hardly enormous, is not just the largest in Britain, but in Europe too.

The yew forest here isn't just worth visiting for its rarity, though, because wandering around the gnarled, weathered stumps and stooping, ancient

branches is a unique experience, quite unsettling and eerie, particularly in the evening. But even on a sunny day entering the wood is like opening the door of an old house and venturing into the dimly lit interior. Yew is an evergreen with dense foliage, cutting out the sun and darkening the woodland floor. There is always the temptation to tread softly.

The yews are among the oldest plants in Britain. The ones here are known to be at least 500 years old, and some may be up to 2,000 years old. The largest have a girth of up to 16ft. They are native trees and, in the autumn, they produce red berries (technically known as arils) that are eaten by thrushes and other birds, despite the seed coating being deadly poisonous to us.

To get into the vale, you need to use your feet. The nearest parking area is the National Nature Reserve car park at West Stoke, some 15 minutes' walk from the entrance along an unremarkable footpath through farmland. The vale is soon visible flanking the hill (Bow Hill) ahead of you. Some of the best yews are straight on through the obvious, marked gate.

There is a lot more to see in this 395-acre nature reserve than just the trees, not least a very impressive chalk flora, most noticeably where the trees open out on

Yew tree berries

Seasonal highlights

Spring
Coal tit, skylark, whitethroat

Summer
Chalkhill blue, yellow meadow ant, common spotted orchid

Autumn
Mistle thrush, fieldfare, juniper

Winter
Fallow deer, roe deer, linnet

All year
Yew, woodpeckers, goldcrest

the east side, and also along the public footpaths flanking the woods. For instance, 11 species of orchid have been recorded, including the strange bee orchid, with its flowers that are shaped and coloured like a bee, supposedly to attract visiting pollinators to mate.

Chalkhill blue butterfly

The butterflies can be spectacular, too. Amazingly, no fewer than 39 species have been recorded. One of the highlights at Kingley Vale is the chalkhill blue, a species that is very common here in July and August, but is generally restricted in this country to southern England. The male is powdery blue and the female chocolate brown. The caterpillar lives at the base of a foodplant, horseshoe vetch, and attracts yellow meadow ants with sugary secretions on its body. The ants provide a measure of protection in the grassland.

It isn't unusual to have huge numbers of ants in south-facing chalk grassland as the insects thrive in the warm turf. While the ants protect the blue butterfly larvae they are themselves eaten in vast quantities by their greatest enemy, the green woodpecker. This big green bird with a red crown and yellow rump spends much of its time on the ground licking up ants with its long tongue. It is common here and you are likely to hear its loud, laughing call. Other birds found at Kingley Vale include abundant skylarks and pheasants, along with marsh tits and other woodland species. Watch out for buzzards and, increasingly, red kites overhead.

If you visit the chalk downland and scrub at the bottom of the hill, sooner or later you will find the hill itself irresistible, and feel compelled to climb. It is worse than it looks, particularly towards the top. However, it is well worth it, and not just for the view. Kingley Vale encompasses 14 scheduled ancient monuments, including Bronze Age burial mounds from around 3,500 years ago, and most of these are up here. Perhaps there was a yew forest too back then? We shall never know.

14 Martin Down

Throwback to a time of profusion

Sillens Lane, Martin, Fordingbridge, Hampshire SP6 3LP

Grid ref SU058192

Directions In village of Martin turn down Sillens Lane

Lunch stop The Rose and Thistle, Rockbourne, Hampshire SP6 3NL

Martin Down is one of the largest areas of uninterrupted chalk downland in Britain and has the distinction of not having been under the plough for centuries. Fifty years ago that wouldn't have been usual, but today it is exceptional.

The down lies on the border of three counties – Dorset, Hampshire and Wiltshire – and is only 10 miles from Salisbury. The countryside isn't spectacular; rather it is sleepy, with gentle rolling hills and sweeping open vistas of long grass. In summer the grassland heaves with life; in winter things quieten down, but it is still a place to escape the 21st-century rush.

Yellowhammer

It is easy to spill on to the down straight from the car and admire the diversity in seconds. There is a car park off the A354 (Salisbury–Blandford) road, and another at the end of Sillens Lane, in the village of Martin. Within a few seconds of leaving the car, you enter a very different world. There is no fixed route here, so go where you please as long as you follow the many paths. The ridge of Tidpit Down flanking the east of the grasslands will help you to keep oriented.

The charms of the site are mainly at your feet, as the whole area is quite exceptional for flowers. The lack of a history of cultivation means that *hoi polloi* types of grass are put at a disadvantage by the lime-rich soil, allowing all manner of herbs to flourish. On any summer's day, there are colourful patches everywhere, some mauve and purple, some yellow, others off-white. The names are as evocative as the blooms themselves: ox-eye daisy, greater knapweed,

Seasonal highlights

Spring
Warbler song, turtle dove, nightingale

Summer
Orchids, dark green fritillary, small blue

Autumn
Flocks of larks and buntings, migrant birds

Winter
Flocks of rooks and jackdaws, raptors

All year
Skylark, yellowhammer, partridge

yellow rattle and jack-go-to-bed-at-noon (goat's beard), and if you are not careful you might step on bastard toadflax. Botanists could spend days here in the summer and never get bored, but for most visitors the inspiration comes from the wonderful display of colours and forms. Everybody, though, loves orchids, and in June it is possible to see eight species, or even more. A speciality is the rare burnt-tipped orchid. Orchids are found around the site, but by far the best location is Bokerley Ditch (or Dyke), a Bronze Age or early Iron Age defensive ditch and boundary on the western edge.

Butterflies frequently star alongside wildflowers, and here at Martin Down they do so in style. In mid-summer, these colourful insects can simply swarm in the sort of numbers that in the past were familiar, but are now a thrilling novelty. The most exciting highlight is the dark green fritillary, a great brute of a butterfly with bright orange wings and a distinctive gliding flight. Not far behind in charisma is the gorgeous Adonis blue, as brilliant as the electric blue of a kingfisher. Other interesting butterflies include marsh fritillary, marbled white, grizzled skipper and small blue.

Patches of scrub around Martin Down act as a magnet for birds all year round. It is hard to visit at any time without seeing a yellowhammer, one of our few bright yellow species, and this fast-declining character is genuinely common here. So is the skylark, another resident bird easily detected by its habit of hovering high in the sky, pouring out its shrill, flowing song. Contrary to popular belief, skylarks sing almost all year round, even in January, so a winter's visit can be accompanied by perpetual birdsong, to complement the chilly wind that blows across the open grasslands.

There is another bird here that epitomises Martin Down, and that is the turtle dove. Several pairs breed here, in one of its last outposts in the county of Hampshire, where it was once common. Countrywide the turtle dove population has fallen 96 per cent since 1970 – another tale of what was once everywhere that is now hardly anywhere.

15 Pevensey Levels

Species-rich low-lying marshland

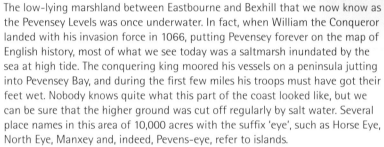

Castle Road, Pevensey, East Sussex BN24 5LE

Grid ref TQ646048

Directions In Pevensey, follow signs to the castle

Lunch stop The Farm @ Friday Street, 15 Friday Street, Langney, East Sussex BN23 8AP

The low-lying marshland between Eastbourne and Bexhill that we now know as the Pevensey Levels was once underwater. In fact, when William the Conqueror landed with his invasion force in 1066, putting Pevensey forever on the map of English history, most of what we see today was a saltmarsh inundated by the sea at high tide. The conquering king moored his vessels on a peninsula jutting into Pevensey Bay, and during the first few miles his troops must have got their feet wet. Nobody knows quite what this part of the coast looked like, but we can be sure that the higher ground was cut off regularly by salt water. Several place names in this area of 10,000 acres with the suffix 'eye', such as Horse Eye, North Eye, Manxey and, indeed, Pevens-eye, refer to islands.

Over time, the land was reclaimed with a series of drainage ditches. The village of North Eye was abandoned, for reasons unknown. For centuries the area flooded regularly in winter, providing wondrous habitat for wildlife; in the 1960s this happened less often as the land was tamed by pump drainage. Much of what we see today is very flat farmland, a mixture of grazed pasture and arable land, interlaced with a large network of ditches and reedy margins. There are hedgerows, some alder scrub and meadows and a few pools.

The charms of the Pevensey Levels are not always obvious on a single visit. It really takes repeated efforts to appreciate the area and see the wildlife that it has to offer. However, few would dispute its wildness, particularly on a cold winter's day when the frost covers the ground and nothing stops the biting winds. It can be magnificent.

There are various ways to get in, but the easiest and most obvious is to walk part of the 1066 Country Walk, which conveniently starts at Pevensey Castle, where there is a car park. The walk is well signposted, and it quickly takes you under the treacherous A27 and into the Levels, along the Pevensey Haven channel. From here you can walk into the village of Rickney and return a different way through Chilley Farm, or you can even carry on into the depths of the Levels towards Herstmonceux. The circuit is best completed in the summer, when the ditches will be replete with vegetation and invertebrates and the

scrub and grass will be alive with activity. Pay particular attention to the dragonflies and damselflies – 21 species are found here and some are uncommon, especially the variable damselfly, on the wing in May, June and July.

Some unusual plants and animals thrive here. Four very rare species of pond snails occur in the lime-rich waters, each with superb names: the little whirlpool ram's-horn, shining ram's-horn, the large-mouthed valve snail and the false orb pea mussel. Another speciality is easier to see, the fen raft spider. Britain's largest spider, with a white or cream stripe each side of the thorax and abdomen, females can grow bodies up to 1 inch long and the leg span reaches 3 inches. They hunt from perches on the edge of the water, snapping up surface hunters such as pond-skaters and insects that fall into the water accidentally. These spiders occur in two other sites in Britain, but they are widespread on the open ditches of the Levels.

Among the profusion of plants growing around the ditches there are some uncommon ones such as arrowhead, flowering rush, greater spearwort, narrow-leaved water plantain and sharp-leaved pondweed. A summer walk will be a botanical delight.

Birdwatchers will tell you that the Pevensey Levels can be a great bird area, but surprisingly difficult to work. The best parts are protected within nature reserves (one managed by Natural England, the other by Sussex Wildlife Trust) which do not allow free access because the birds are easy to disturb in such an open habitat. This means that, while you do come across excellent breeding species such as marsh harrier, yellow wagtail, redshank, snipe and lapwing outside the reserves, they aren't easy to find. On any walk you will find commoner species such as reed and sedge warbler, reed bunting and sometimes kingfisher.

In winter, though, the whole area is good for birds of prey, and in harsh weather there are occasionally influxes of geese or swans from continental Europe. At this time of year, it is worth trying a different area of Pevensey, by parking near White Dyke Farm, near Hailsham (TQ610088), and exploring the Horse Eye Level. Here and in other areas, on a sunny day, it is possible to see merlin, hen harrier and peregrine – and ravens may be attending their nests on the pylons. As the afternoon light fades, the odd short-eared owl might well appear, too, quartering the fields for voles and making the effort worthwhile.

Seasonal highlights

Spring
Snipe, redshank

Summer
Variable damselfly, fen raft spider, snails

Autumn
Yellow wagtail, lapwing, flowering rush

Winter
Merlin, peregrine, wigeon

All year
Snipe, pond life, water plants

Fen raft spider

16 Selborne

Discovering Gilbert White's village

Zig-Zag View, High Street, Selborne, Alton, Hampshire GU34 3JT

Grid ref SU742335

Directions From Alton take the B3006 south to Selborne; park behind The Selborne Arms pub

Lunch stop The Selborne Arms, High Street, Selborne, Hampshire GU34 3JR

Britain is overflowing with historic sites, but none quite like Selborne. A castle may have grazes from arrows in its stonework, but here the resonance is natural, not caught up in human affairs. You can walk the woods hereabouts and listen to a chiffchaff singing in the place where it was first recognised as a separate bird species. You can dodge the rain on the same date as a local thunderstorm was recorded more than 200 years ago, and you can touch the wood of a yew that lived for a thousand years.

It's all because of a famous book, *The Natural History and Antiquities of Selborne*, written by the village's most famous resident, the Reverend Gilbert White, and published in 1789. A series of letters recounting the natural history and village life of the parish where White was curate, it is a beautifully written and intimate picture, not of politics and kings, but of rural life covering the period 1767–87. White was unusual at the time for his meticulous observation and recording, for looking and wondering without prejudice. He is sometimes remembered as the father of ecology. The book struck such a chord that it has never been out of print.

Marbled white butterfly

The beauty of a visit to Selborne is that you literally follow in White's footsteps. For example, the curate and his brother cut a path up a steep-sided hill to Selborne Common from the village in 1753. The famous Zig-Zag Path is still there, maintained by the National Trust, and it begins just behind the main visitors' car park. Much of what you see in terms of wildlife on the Zig-Zag will be very similar to what Gilbert White saw in the 1700s, the same sorts of flowers, birds and insects – some of the trees will be the same individuals. You will get puffed as you climb up. The view from the top of the Zig-Zag on Selborne Hill has definitely changed, with more buildings, and there is even a giant golf ball-shaped dome. But the lines of hills will be the same as they always were, and it is a stirring vista.

To sample a little solitude, however, it is well worth going back to the village, paying homage to White's modest gravestone in the cemetery of St Mary's Church and then going down the slope beyond the churchyard. The path takes you over Oakhanger Stream and almost immediately there is a meadow on your right and a slope covered in beech wood on your left. Here, for the next half-mile or so, is a small piece of paradise. The meadows are ragged, overgrown and lively, brimming with colourful blooms and butterflies in the summer. The woods are dark and quiet, except for the soothing songs of woodpigeons (five coos) and stock doves (two-and-a-half coos), and the cheerful whistles of nuthatches. Two hundred years ago wood warblers used to nest in the beech woods, but they have been lost as breeding birds in the last few decades. Look out, though, for spotted flycatchers in the woods and gardens. Common in White's time, they are still here, despite a decline in southern England and elsewhere.

Follow it far enough, and the path leads into a meadow that you walk through, and you will soon see a new feature that wasn't around previously. The brook has been dammed and the result is some delightful ponds that are shallow and often overgrown with amphibious bistort and other water plants. The waters play host to moorhens, swans and occasionally, a new addition to the bird fauna, the mandarin duck, an introduced species from the Far East which has spread here only recently.

Bug enthusiasts will love this area. In season, marbled whites and ringlets are all over the meadow, feeding on black knapweed and other herbs, while on the ponds are such dragonflies as black-tailed skimmer and banded demoiselle. On a warm day everything moves briskly and makes the atmosphere buzz.

Retrace your steps, or proceed to the edge of the far pond, turn right and right again. It is often muddy and gloomy in these woods, but it isn't far back to the village. When you get back, look at the Wakes Museum, in Gilbert White's old house, and at his garden. As you do so, and as you listen to the collared doves cooing (first recorded in Britain in the 1950s), muse on how much has changed and, in fact, how much hasn't.

Seasonal highlights

Spring
Chiffchaff, blackcap, swallow

Summer
Spotted flycatcher, marbled white, house martin

Autumn
Woodpigeon, goldfinch, enchanter's nightshade

Winter
Marsh tit, buzzard, grey wagtail

All year
Beech trees, yew, collared dove

17 Sheepleas

Surrey's Coronation Meadow

Shere Road, West Horsley, Leatherhead, Surrey KT24 6EP

Grid ref TQ084514

Directions From West Horsley turn left (south) down Shere Road, then drive half a mile to the car park

Lunch stop The King William IV, 83 The Street, West Horsley, Surrey KT24 6BG

The Surrey Hills area of the North Downs, just south of London, is full of nooks and crannies and untidy corners, and quite a few of them deserve to be in a book like this. However, none of the others were proclaimed in 1913, by eminent scientists, to be the 'finest piece of botanical and entomological land within 30 miles of London'. If that was the case then, you can imagine how important Sheepleas Nature Reserve is now, after so many decades of house building and land intensification.

Sheepleas received another accolade a hundred years later, in 2013, when it was crowned the Coronation Meadow for Surrey. This was a project created by Prince Charles to select a wildflower meadow in each county for the 60th anniversary of the coronation. Here it is a locally famous meadow full of cowslips, 5 acres in extent, that attracted the attention, and this alone makes Sheepleas worth visiting, at least in late April and early May. It isn't just that cowslips are an intense shade of buttery yellow, and thus the whole field turns this colour; it's the curious shape of the flowerhead that makes them special. At the end of a straight stalk, the flowers erupt in all directions like a fountain, and they droop slightly so that the flower looks like a yellow firework that has just exploded. Every one is slightly different, and the effect is magnificent.

The cowslip meadow on the east side of the reserve isn't the only display of flowers: it turns out that Sheepleas is something of a show-off location. At the same time as the meadows host cowslips, the nearby woodland gives a mean display of bluebells, and when all this spring unsubtlety fades, a more varied riot of blooms takes over. The soil here is chalky, and so the calcareous favourites are here, such as marjoram, eyebright, milkwort, wild thyme, common rock-rose, yellow-wort and various orchids, notably lots of the purple-hued pyramidal orchid and pink-flowered common spotted orchid. Less common species include wild basil. In short, throughout the flowering year, from late March until October, there is always something colourful to see. By the way, you might also notice the old stumps of trees in some of the fields. Most of these were beeches felled in the Great Storm of 1987.

Seasonal highlights

Spring
Cowslip, bluebell, glow-worm

Summer
Orchids, rufous grasshopper, silver-washed fritillary

Autumn
Deadly nightshade berries, fungi

Winter
Brambling, siskin, mosses

All year
Hornbeam, wild cherry, beech

One particularly intriguing species that is generally uncommon but easy to find here is deadly nightshade. Many people confuse this plant with a very common purple- and yellow-flowered relative known as woolly nightshade, which has red berries. Deadly nightshade is a tall, branched perennial which has sinister, bell-like deep purple flowers, in which a large black berry forms. These berries look a little like cherries, and the confusion can be fatal. They contain an alkaloid toxin called hyoscyamine (and very little atropine, contrary to popular belief), and a meal of three berries has been known to kill a child.

There is more to Sheepleas than flowers, of course. More than 30 species of butterflies have been recorded, and it is particularly good for finding the tricky green hairstreak and the showy silver-washed fritillary. Glow-worms do their stuff in the spring, and there is an excellent display of grasshoppers and crickets (notably Roesel's bush-cricket and rufous grasshopper). Birds are plentiful and include marsh tit, bullfinch and a wide range of commoner woodland birds such as nuthatch and treecreeper. Common whitethroats, with their brief, scratchy songs, enliven the scrub, while at the same time blackcaps, with a richer and flutier effort, can be heard from the woodland understorey. At times the bird chorus is deafening.

One other claim to fame for Sheepleas is that it is an excellent area in which to get lost. The reserve covers 270 acres of varied habitats on steep, chalky and often very muddy slopes. The scrub, woodland and fields have a network of paths between and around them, and many look quite similar. However, the area is served by three car parks (the one on Shere Road, a turn-off on the A246 by West Horsley, is the most popular) and there are also two waymarked nature trails, one a Woodland Trail and one a Grassland Trail, so it happens less often than it used to. On the other hand, getting a bit lost can be part of the fun.

Cowslip

18 Shellness

Taking flight on Sheppey's coast

Shellness Road, Leysdown-on-Sea, Sheerness, Kent ME12 4RP

Grid ref TR051683

Directions From Sheerness take the A2500 east, then the B2231 to Leysdown-on-Sea; go straight on to Shellness Road

Lunch stop Ferry House Inn, Harty Ferry Road, Harty, Kent ME12 4BQ

It is hard to believe that a genuinely remote place could be only an hour and a half's drive from London. But visitors generally agree that Shellness, on the Isle of Sheppey off Kent's north coast, fits that description. Come here on a cold, breezy day in winter and you'll have no doubts at all.

The Isle of Sheppey sits in the mouth of the Thames Estuary where the river disgorges into the North Sea. It occupies the lower jaw, so to speak, on the south side, within easy reach of Maidstone and Rochester. Named for its many sheep, it is a real island separated from the mainland by a narrow but deep channel of the Swale; it was once the Isles of Sheppey, consisting of three islands (Sheppey, Elmley and Harty) until the channels between them silted up. There is now a permanent bridge on the west side, where once the island was served only by small ferries.

The isle is something of a throwback to a bygone era, and if you don't believe this, just go to Leysdown-on-Sea. With its amusement arcades and beach huts, it doesn't seem to have changed much since the 1950s. It's difficult to believe that it was once at the hub of what was new-fangled aviation, yet the first powered flight in Britain occurred here in 1909; the Wright brothers came to visit earlier that same year. Later, the first-ever pilot's licence was issued at nearby Muswell Manor.

You pass Muswell Manor on your way down towards what looks like the hamlet at the end of the world, Shellness, where there is plenty of free parking, except on warm summer days. The beach is adjacent, but a word of warning – it is sometimes possible to see prone lumps of blubber close by. Seals are seen here, but these lumps are more likely to be denizens of one of the UK's most improbable nudist beaches – not quite the wildlife that you have come to see. This is mildly distracting, but the beach itself is extraordinary. Not for nothing is it called Shellness – the ground is covered with countless millions of shells, cutting short the effort of beachcombing. Many of these are mussels.

The tide goes far out here, exposing the sludge, under which is London clay. Digging hereabouts has revealed a superb range of fossils, including remains of

Seasonal highlights

Spring
Marsh harrier, curlew

Summer
Ringed plover, redshank, terns

Autumn
Migrant waders, seabirds, shingle plants

Winter
Waders, short-eared owl, merlin

All year
Seashells, oystercatcher, shelduck

mammoths and straight-toothed elephants from the pre-historic Eocene epoch, sharks and shellfish. They have even unearthed a human skull.

But there is plenty of life hereabouts, especially birds, which you simply cannot miss. At low tide, through most of the year, wading birds treat the mud as a communal refectory, and there can be thousands of them, particularly from October through to March. In the summer there are still black-and-white oystercatchers with carrot-red bills, dapper ringed plovers on the shingle, and brownish-bodied orange-legged redshanks in the saltmarsh. In winter, however, waders that breed in the Arctic come to the Thames Estuary in enormous numbers. During low tide they feed on the exposed mud, and when the water rises they find safe places where they won't get their feet wet. One such site, where the birds repose, preening and sleeping, is close to the pill box (a guard post) just beyond the hamlet of Shellness itself. The most exciting activity is just before or just after high water, when with birds flying to and fro in all directions, the roost resembles a transport terminal – and is just as noisy. There will be miniature dunlins flocking at the feet of big, straw-coloured curlews. At low tide, sanderlings scamper over the sandy parts of the beach, turnstones search the rocks, while knots, grey plovers and godwits feed in the mud further out. There are moments here at Shellness when it is just you and the birds and the rest of the world is elsewhere.

There is an extra walk to enjoy for the adventurous. Just at the entrance to Shellness village a public footpath runs southwest along the seawall, with saltmarsh on the seaward side and a huge expanse of low, rough grazing marsh inland. The latter forms the extensive Harty Marshes, part of the Swale National Nature Reserve. You can make a 4-mile circuit of these marshes, looping back by the village of Harty. In winter there will be hundreds of ducks, particularly wigeon, and it's a magnificent place for birds of prey. You are bound to see marsh harrier, there's a decent chance of hen harrier and merlins and on a winter afternoon both barn and short-eared owls may be present.

You'll almost certainly have it all to yourself. This really is a lonely area, a place to disappear in. The broiling metropolis could be light years away.

19 Stodmarsh

Fabulous freshwater wetland

Lambkin Wall, Stodmarsh, Canterbury, Kent CT3 4BB

Grid ref TR221609

Directions From Canterbury follow Stodmarsh Road to the village and fork left after the Red Lion pub

Lunch stop Grove Ferry Inn, Grove Ferry Road, Upstreet, Kent CT3 4BP

Dragonfly

There are many places in Britain where human influence is hidden behind a cloak of wildness – the Scottish Highlands, which would naturally be wooded, is an example. But few sites, at least in the southeast, hide their human origin as well as Stodmarsh National Nature Reserve, near Canterbury. What is now a fabulous, extensive freshwater wetland acquired its character by virtue of mining subsidence, some gravel extraction and, latterly, deliberate habitat restoration. It is probably better now than it ever was.

And what a place it is to lose yourself in on a gentle afternoon. Much of the reserve is a sea of reed stems with their unkempt wig-like flower heads that sway in the breeze. There are also some large areas of open water, shallow pools and damp woodlands that swarm with birds and bugs and rich scrub beside the slowly meandering Great Stour. There is a continental feel to the place, with big skies and long vistas.

There are two ways to enter the reserve, from the western end near Stodmarsh village or the eastern end on Grove Ferry Road in Grove Ferry, southeast of Upstreet. There's a pay and display car park near the Grove Ferry Inn, while in the free reserve car park at Stodmarsh, found on the turn-off between the Red Lion pub and the church, the rustic toilets are something to behold. You could park here, walk to Grove Ferry and return by a different route, which is about 4 miles. The walk is always worth it.

The reserve is best known for its birds, with more than 200 species recorded, and you will see a lot at any time of year. Spring and summer are often magical. In April and May, the reed and sedge warblers sing incessantly, which means

when you lay down to sleep at night after a visit, you can still hear them chattering away in your head.

One of the features is the colourful bearded reedling, a rare songbird of rich chestnut colouration and with a long tail; it lives in family parties in the reed beds. A good place to see it is from the Lampen Wall on the opposite side to the main lake. Listen for the 'ching, ching' call first. If you are lucky you might also hear a very unusual sound, the booming call of the male bittern, a brownish heron-like bird. The sound, imitated by blowing over the open top of a beer bottle, is usually heard at twilight or at night.

The reeds also hold several breeding pairs of marsh harriers, and in June you may see the male passing food to the female, an act which takes place in mid-air, the female turning on her back, talons up, to receive it. Recently, this display has been on show from the Reedbed Hide, one of several dotted about the reserve. Another speciality in late summer is the build-up of hobbies, a bird of prey which catches all its food on the wing. It is possible to spot 10 or more together, often swooping low down acrobatically.

The hobby eats dragonflies, and it is the profusion of these turbo-powered insects that attracts them. With so many wet areas, it isn't surprising that Stodmarsh is a hotspot for them. More than 20 species of dragon- and damselflies have been recorded – the variable damselfly, a very localised species, abounds here. So does a profusion of other invertebrates, from butterflies to snails, as well as a number of rare and scarce flowers.

Autumn and winter shouldn't be neglected. The autumn brings passage migrant birds of all kinds, and the Grove Ferry end, with its lookout point, is a particularly good place for waders. In winter there is a big increase in the wildfowl population, with ducks on the areas of open water. Hen harriers and other birds of prey spend the winter here, and it is possible to see the secretive bittern. The relative dieback of vegetation might also make it easier to see a water vole along one of the ditches. A large population is maintained here.

Whatever the season, this part of Kent, so close to the large city of Canterbury, feels wild and isolated and part of an ancient landscape – as if it had been here forever.

Spring
Warbler song, cuckoo

Summer
Marsh harrier display, hobby, dragonflies

Autumn
Swallow, house martin, waders

Winter
Wildfowl, harriers

All year
Bearded tit, water vole, bittern

Variable damselfly

20 Thorney Island

A taste of true isolation

Thorney Road, Emsworth, West Sussex PO10 8BL

Grid ref SU756055

Directions From Emsworth village go over the river and Thorney Road is on the right after the roundabout

Lunch stop The Sussex Brewery, 36 Main Road, Emsworth, West Sussex PO10 8AU

There are hardly any places along the south coast of England where it is possible to feel truly isolated, but the tip of Thorney Island at Longmere Point, sticking out into the flat vastness of Chichester Harbour, is most certainly one of them. It is a 3-mile walk to get here, and a 3-mile trudge back, with no shortcuts. Much of the time you have only the myriad shorebirds for company, feeding out on the mudflats, and on a winter's afternoon a warm fireside seems a very long way away.

Thorney was a proper island until the local mudflats were reclaimed in 1870. Nowadays, however, it is a peninsula cut off by no more than a modest channel, known with a touch of exaggeration as 'the Great Deep'. But there is another sense in which you are isolated from the world here, because the island is a military base and you can only follow the Sussex Border Path around the perimeter, and venture a few steps into the 11th-century St Nicholas' Church

at West Thorney. The Ministry of Defence 'No Trespassing' signs spring up everywhere, and the coastal path takes you past some impressive metal gates with barbed wire, CCTV and an intercom, which needs to be pressed to enter (and sometimes you must quote your name and address to the voice on the other end). This all adds up to giving this walk an adventurous feel.

Choose a fine day with little wind and park on Thorney Road, in Emsworth. Alternatively you can park on the east side of the island on Prinsted Lane and do the walk in reverse. Assuming the former, make your way through the field and past the marina onto the Sussex Border Path, and very soon you will be on the raised dyke overlooking the harbour on one side and a large, flat marshy meadow on the other. Already you are plunged into a world where water and tides determine everything. If the tide is out and some mud is exposed there should be flocks of small, inky-black geese with blazing white bottoms feeding here. Brent geese come from Russia and spend the months of October to March in Chichester Harbour. They form chatty, mobile flocks and you won't fail to see them.

Anywhere along the path look for birds on the mudflats, or floating on the water on the seaward side. There will be many kinds of ducks, especially wigeon and teal, while a dozen or more wader species will be scampering over the mud or rocks. Look for curlews – big waders with straw-patterned bodies and long, curved bills – while the medium-sized noisy waders with orange bills and legs are redshanks.

Seasonal highlights

Spring
Mediterranean gull, sandwich tern, hare

Summer
Linnet, terns, stonechat

Autumn
Yellow wagtail, wheatear, whimbrel

Winter
Thousands of waders, brent geese, red-breasted merganser

All year
Common seal, little egret, hawthorn

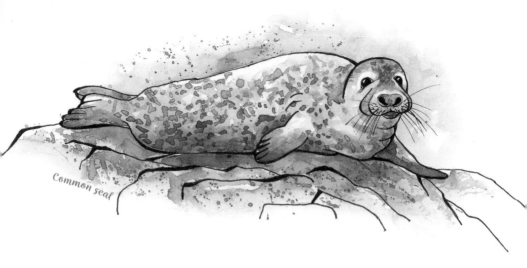

Common seal

After a few hundred yards you will see the Great Deep, the modest pool of water on your left. This often hosts birds, even avocets at times. Proceed beyond here and go through the checkpoint – there is a feeling of leaving civilisation behind. The path wends its way southward for the next few miles, at first in zigzagging fashion, then straightening after Marker Point (SU745023). Every step takes you deeper into a flat landscape of mud, sand and waves, while inland there is plenty of thorny scrub, the kind that gave the island its name.

The last thing you expect to see is a seal colony, and yet at low tide, on Pilsey Sand, this is exactly what does occur. One of the very few populations of common seals on the south coast, they don't number more than 20, but you can see them here and swimming in the channels.

By now, approaching the tip of the island, you will probably have noticed the airfield just inland. This is sometimes used as a driving track, a far cry from its busy World War II years as a centre for RAF Coastal Command, and the runways are still kept clear. Brown hares occupy the grassland, and during the winter short-eared owls are frequent hunters over the airfield, and indeed over the rest of the island. Barn owls occur too. Both species take advantage of the high population of small mammals, including the abundant field voles.

At Longmere Point you look over a mixture of shingle, sand dunes and rough pasture. There is a small and insalubrious bird hide where you can watch the birds flying back and forth around Pilsey Island, an RSPB reserve. If you arrive close to high tide, you might see streams of waders massing before roosting; because they feed on the mud, high tide is the time for resting. However, with safe, dry areas available for repose at a premium, everywhere is crowded, and it doesn't look very restful. It is noisy, too; the air is full of whistles and wails.

The return route is a bit tamer, past the settlement of West Thorney (there used to be an East Thorney, now washed away) and the church. As you continue north, you will notice the gradual appearance of Prinsted Point, where you turn back west, past Thornham Marina and the outskirts of Emsworth. You have sampled a touch of the wild; your feet will ache and you'll be glad to be back.

21 Thursley Common

A little bit of Scotland in leafy Surrey

Thursley Road, Elstead, Godalming, Surrey GU8 6LW

Grid ref SU899416

Directions From Elstead turn left (south) after The Woolpack pub and follow Thursley Road for nearly 2 miles; the Moat car park is on the left

Lunch stop The Woolpack, Milford Road, Elstead, Godalming, Surrey GU8 6HD

Thursley Common's open landscape, with heather and Scots pine trees, has the feel of a place much farther north than commuter-belt Surrey. Some of the wildlife chimes with this impression.

The common lies to the south of Guildford. If you brave the A3 trunk road south, chock full of speeding cars, turn off at the B3001 to Elstead and then go south on Thursley Lane, where you'll see the Moat car park after a mile or so. There is a pond here where people feed the ducks, and it is only as you pass through the trees that the unusual landscape opens up before you. Within a hundred yards or so you will be looking over Thursley Bog. As a wet area dominated by peat-forming plants, this is actually a mire, on very acid soil: one of the most impressive in Britain. It is a treacherous expanse of pools, marsh and masses of spongy sphagnum moss, a place that you would not wish to wander into. Fortunately, a boardwalk goes straight into the middle, allowing visitors to see the plants and revel in the unusual landscape. There are many wet-loving plants here, including hare's-tail cottongrass, purple moor-grass, cross-leaved heath and bog asphodel. The presence of cranberry is very unusual in the south of England, and it is one of the plants that seems out of place.

In these wet areas are a number of interesting breeding birds. Curlews just about hold on, in one of the few sites left for them in the southeast. Snipe also occur and so do some commoner species such as reed bunting. The bog area comes into its own in the middle of summer, though, when that spectacular bird of prey the hobby visits to catch dragonflies. The hobby snares all its prey in flight through sheer aerodynamic brilliance. To enjoy these birds diving, changing direction, swooping and accelerating over the dark waters, and then grabbing dragonflies with their feet and transferring them, mid-air, to their bill is the sort of drama you might associate with the Serengeti.

It isn't just the hobby that visits for dragonflies: human hobbyists do too. An astonishing total of 26 species of dragonfly have been recorded, and for many years Thursley Common has been ranked as one of the finest sites in the whole of Britain. It once held Britain's southernmost population of white-faced

Seasonal highlights

Spring
Woodlark song, snakes, lizards

Summer
Hobby, dragonflies, bog flowers

Autumn
Colourful heather, late dragonflies

Winter
Great grey shrike, raptors

All year
Dartford warbler, birch, Scots pine

darters, but these are thought to have died out. It still has an amazing collection, though. Heathland specialities such as small red damselfly, common hawker, keeled skimmer and black darter are all easy to find, as are the impressive golden-ringed dragonfly and the very small and inconspicuous emerald damselfly and white-legged damselfly. And that's without mentioning the species that perhaps are most searched for: the downy emerald and the brilliant emerald, both of which patrol the edge of the Moat pond. These are tricky-to-find species, and the brilliant emerald is also very rare. It occurs in only two areas of Britain: on wooded ponds in southeast England and – surprise, surprise – in western Scotland.

Being an invertebrate can be a brief existence, and on the boggy parts of Thursley Common there are sinister traps for careless waifs. Plants called sundews have unremarkable small whitish flowers, but their leaves have evolved into sticky insect traps with copious globules of glue at the end of modified hairs. When an insect lands and gets stuck, the leaves bend inwards to mire it further until escape is impossible. The plants utilise the juices of these small animals to supplement their nutrients.

If the sundews don't get them, small invertebrates fall prey to one of Britain's largest spiders. The bog raft spider has legs up to three times longer than its body and is dark brown with a pale yellow or white streak down the side of the thorax and abdomen. Unusually, it is semi-aquatic, and it hunts small insects trapped on the water surface. It can often be seen on leaves floating on the acidic pools.

Along the boardwalk, between April and October, common lizards bask and scuttle away as soon as they feel the approach of feet. They are the tip of a veritable reptile iceberg, with all six British terrestrial species thriving on the common. Sand lizards are in the drier areas surrounding the bog, along with smooth snakes, while the rest (slow worm, grass snake and adder) could be met almost anywhere, though none are easy to find.

Despite the variety of other things, most visitors to Thursley Common come for the birds. Aside from those already mentioned, stonechat and the heathland-loving Dartford warbler are present. Redstarts, nightjars and tree pipits come for the summer, while merlins and great grey shrikes often occur in the winter.

All in all, it adds up to a quite extraordinary range of exciting wildlife.

Common lizard

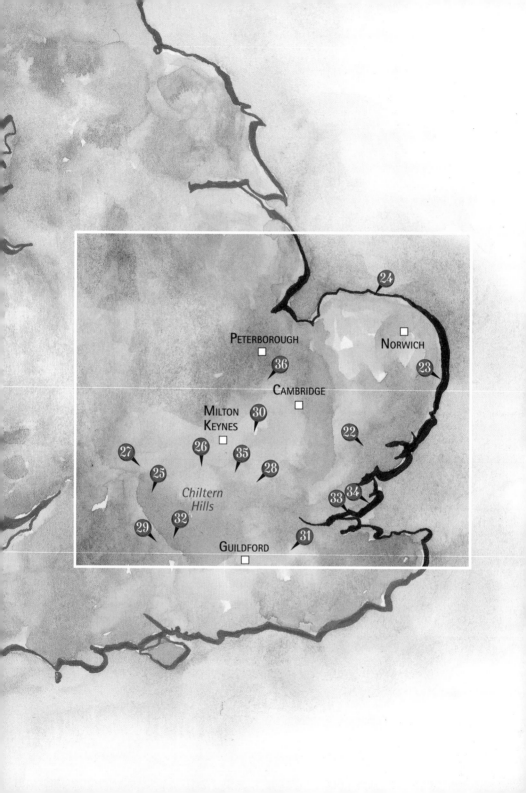

East Anglia &
the Home Counties

22 Arger Fen

Wild cherries and bluebell woods

Dead Lane, Bures, Sudbury, Suffolk CO8 5BN

Grid ref TL931353

Directions In Leavenheath village take High Road (left), to T-junction. Go left on Barracks Road to Rose Green, bear left, turn left at Dead Lane down to car park

Lunch stop The Lion, Honey Tye, Suffolk CO6 4NX

It's hard not to enjoy a walk in the rolling Suffolk countryside, but here at Arger Fen there are reasons to be cheerful beyond what you can see and feel. Not only is this a fantastic place, but it is a reflection of local people's generosity that such a space is kept at its best for wildlife.

Hazel dormouse

Whatever is in the water, it led to a flurry of donations and bequests between 1991 and 2014 from a number of local landowners, which meant that what started as a small bluebell wood in the Suffolk Wildlife Trust's care has now been transformed, bit by bit, into a substantial nature reserve of 247 acres. It covers ancient woodland, meadows, ponds, hedgerows and regenerating scrub: a delightful mishmash where you can get lost and find new corners. At a time of general wildlife retreat, a visit here is uplifting.

You park along a minor road that runs north from the slightly less minor road between Bures and Nayland. The car park has a sign saying 'Arger Fen and Spouse's Vale', and from here the waymarked trail (one of two) urges you into some tall woods with wide paths, which soon pass over decidedly undulating ground. Some of the trees you will see are genuinely substantial, including firs and Corsican pines that are leftovers from the Forestry Commission's tenure in the 1960s. However, the signature tree of Arger Fen is perhaps the wild cherry.

There are a number of huge wild cherry specimens here, some as tall as 80ft, with their horizontal bark lines and contorted bark fissures, visible all year round. From March to May these trees come out in milky white blossom, a simply superb

Bluebell

sight. Their red and pink autumn foliage is hardly bad, mind.

For most locals, the cherries aren't the icing on the cake, for Spouse's Vale, adjacent to Arger Fen, is renowned as one of Suffolk's finest bluebell woods, and a visit at the right time in April will allow you to enjoy the inland sea of metallic blue. Bluebells are generally indicators of ancient woodland, and indeed that is what this is. The woodland hereabouts has been used as common land since the Middle Ages, and you will notice plenty of signs of land use, such as coppicing – look for multiple thin stems growing from the same point. The open aspect and friable soil here are excellent for badgers, and there are several setts on site. The large trees also provide habitat for a number of bats, the rarest of which is the barbastelle.

The reserve has been added to piecemeal over the last few years, and back in the early 2000s the Hullback's Grove section was bequeathed in its state as an agricultural field. Rather than being managed *per se*, the area was simply left to its own devices, and these days it is essentially an enormous thicket: a woodland in the making. It will eventually revert to mature deciduous forest, a rare example of large-scale regeneration. The Trust has now also acquired the adjacent Pecks Piece, and plans more of the same.

Ancient hedgerows appear around the edge of Pecks Piece. They are characterised by large oak standards, and are made up of elm and small-leaved lime, as well as hawthorn; the sheer variety of shrubs on show is testament to how long this border has been present. These hedgerows host a thriving population of hazel dormice, as well as producing large numbers of berries for the birds to eat in the autumn.

The site is rich in birds all year round, but these days you can hear two species that are celebrated, but also seriously in decline. Nightingales sing their glorious songs from the coppiced sections, with a peak in April and early May, while cuckoos can be heard at the same time from anywhere around the site. To get the two in combination would be a real tonic for a nature lover worrying about Britain's landscapes. Here, at least, things are looking rosy.

Seasonal highlights

Spring
Wild cherry blossom, bluebell, nightingale

Summer
Purple hairstreak, tufted vetch, comfrey

Autumn
Bats, hazel dormouse, hedgerow berries

Winter
Siskin, lords-and-ladies, barn owl

All year
Badger, sparrowhawk, wild service tree

23 Benacre Broad

Go there while you still can

Covehithe, Beccles, Suffolk NR34 7JW

Grid ref TM521818

Directions Half a mile north of Covehithe

Lunch stop The Crown Hotel, High Street, Southwold, Suffolk IP18 6DP

Not many people make it to Benacre Broad. In contrast to the wildlife tourism fleshpots of Minsmere and Walberswick not far to the south, it is awkward to get to and has few facilities except for a single hide. So, while Minsmere attracts tens of thousands of visitors every year, and has acted as a base for the wildlife reality TV series *Springwatch*, Benacre Broad broods in its quiet corner of the Suffolk coast and has few fans. Even the Suffolk Coastal Path comes close, takes a sniff and then veers off.

So why go? Well, you will get away from the crowds, that's for sure, although there might be a few dog walkers on the beach. But the main reason is that Benacre Broad won't be with us for long – not in its present state, anyway. The Suffolk coast is fighting against the sea and losing. Sea levels are rising and erosion is taking its toll, and there are few places better to witness the salt water rubbing in its victory chunk by chunk.

You need to be slightly careful at this site, though, ensuring that you don't get cut off by the tide under the cliffs at Covehithe. The quickest way to get to the Broad is to park in the village near the ruined church (impressive in its own right), turn back inland a little, take the public footpath left and follow down narrow Smuggler's Lane to the beach near Covehithe Broad. From here it is just over a mile to Benacre Broad. Alternatively, you can approach from the north, parking at Kessingland Beach a couple of miles away.

If you start at Covehithe, it is obvious that the cliffs are crumbling at the advance of the sea. Great lumps have fallen off here, with their vegetation still clinging on to them, doomed. Elsewhere trees may be lying at crazy angles, while the cliff's sandy strata are laid bare. If you visit in summer, look out for the small holes where sand martins have dug their nesting burrows; the birds are accustomed to using ephemeral breeding sites, and it is just as well.

The cliffs end close to the Broad itself, which is just beyond the small wood up ahead. The first thing you will notice, if the storms haven't removed them since the time of writing, are the skeletons of trees which have died as a result of the advancing salinity. The second thing you are likely to notice is how thin the ribbon of sand protecting the large lake is. Benacre Broad was once filled entirely with fresh water (it's a natural lake blocked from the sea for centuries). In November 2011, however, a tidal surge inundated the broad for the first time, and altered the salinity. This now happens regularly, and eventually the sand defence will be washed away – there are no plans for sea defences here. For a few years it will be a lake, but in the near future it will be no more than an inlet. Go while you can.

The Broad is a great place for wildlife. It is one of the very few places in Britain where more than 100 bird species have been found breeding. It is a National Nature Reserve, but unfortunately the land is private and you cannot wander over it. There is a privileged path to a hide on the south side of the lake, but other than this you must view from the beach. You'll still see a great deal – marsh harriers are always here, and it is possible to see avocet, shelduck, little egret and a host of waders, which increase in variety in the autumn, when greenshank, common sandpiper and many others occur. Spoonbills also visit increasingly often. In the summer, little terns breed on the shingle beach.

As a bird site Benacre is perhaps at its best in winter. This is when wintering sea ducks and grebes often turn up looking for shelter. In a recent winter there was a great northern diver, smew and common scoter here at the same time, and the coast's proximity to the Continent means that, if geese or swans are displaced by cold winter weather, they could make first landfall hereabouts.

Other exciting winter birds are often found on the beach itself, flying back and forth among the specialised shingle flora, such as yellow horned-poppy, sea kale, sea holly and prickly saltwort. There are often snow buntings in this part of the world, which feed on the sand and shingle, looking for the minute seeds they favour. At this spot in recent times there has also been a shorelark, now a very rare bird in Britain.

The irony is that while snow buntings and shorelarks probably have a future on this stretch of coast, the Broad itself doesn't.

Seasonal highlights

Spring
Sand martin, common sandpiper

Summer
Sea kale, little tern, spoonbill

Autumn
Greenshank, sea holly, beach debris

Winter
Shorelark, common scoter, shells

All year
Tree 'skeletons', marsh harrier, reedbeds

sea holly

69

24 Blakeney Point

Wild Arctic-facing coastal spit

Beach Road, Cley-next-the-Sea, Holt, Norfolk NR25 7RZ

Grid ref TG047452

Directions In Cley-next-the-Sea, follow signs to beach

Lunch stop The George Hotel, High Street, Cley-next-the-Sea NR25 7RN

Blakeney Point is a 4-mile long sand and shingle spit that straddles the North Norfolk coast. One of the largest expanses of undeveloped coast in Europe, it faces the North Sea, with nothing between it and the Arctic pack ice. The spit is relatively flat, windy and often desperately cold. The only way to walk to the Point itself is along the unforgiving energy-sapping shingle – and then you have to walk back again, with no facilities along the way. In other words, it's heaven.

Tourists come here, mainly because Blakeney Point is beautiful and there is a seal colony and a lot of birds. Most visitors sensibly take the option of a boat trip from either Blakeney village or Morston Harbour, which is fun, quick and gives great views of the animals, which are resident. You can land at Blakeney Point, where there's a converted lifeboat-house visitor centre owned by the National Trust. But this is what tourists do. As a reader of this book you'd rather undertake the challenge of the walk, wouldn't you? You take Beach Road from Cley-next-the-Sea alongside the nature reserve and park at the small car park at the end. Walk left and, for the first couple of miles, don't be tempted back.

The trek is always magnificent, whether on a fine day in summer when you could equally be sunbathing, or on a December day when you would struggle to get back before dark. The sea always seems to be rough, inky and elemental here, especially in winter, when flocks of birds seem to be forever flying over the waves, this way and that. As you walk, the spit is narrow and the path is slightly raised so that you can see both sides, sea to the right (north) and saltmarsh to the left. Incidentally, if you walk at low tide you can have sand rather than shingle beneath your feet, which is a much kinder prospect.

There are various points along the way. After a mile of solid beach you come to a scrubbier area known as the Marrams, followed by the Watch House (often called Halfway House although it's just a third of the way), a former haunt of smugglers. Another half-mile or so and the proper sand dunes begin at The Hood, and it's the same distance again to where the head broadens out. The end of the Point is half a mile wide, the dunes can be taller than the average house, and there are several buildings including the Lifeboat House, a boardwalk from which goes to the beach, where you can see the seals; access beyond is

Sandwich tern

restricted in the breeding season. If you have reached here by foot you deserve a medal, and then another for the return.

The wildlife at Blakeney is spectacular. The seal colony can reach 500 animals, of both British species: the grey and common seal. Common seals once greatly outnumbered greys, but the tables have turned in recent years. Common seals breed in June and July, grey seals from November to January. Other mammals include hares, stoats and weasels.

Sharing the outer point with the seals is a large colony of terns, one of the best in Britain. These seabirds are similar to gulls, but more elegant and angular. Their legs are short so they waddle somewhat and rarely settle on the water. Most of the terns are Sandwich terns, about 4,000 pairs (30 per cent of the British population), while there are also little terns (about 100 pairs), common terns and Arctic terns. These birds might be elegant, but they are also fantastically noisy, maintaining a constant squealing around the colony. There are black-headed gulls here too, and in summer the cacophony is never-ending.

Other birds that breed on the peninsula are mainly waders such as oystercatchers, ringed plovers and redshanks. More unexpectedly there are several pairs of grey partridges, birds that are more usually seen in agricultural fields. Small numbers of avocets have recently begun to breed on the shingle, and shelducks are common in the dunes.

Shingle and dune are unusual habitats, with a number of scarce plants. Blakeney Point is particularly good for many of them, such as yellow horned-poppy, sea campion, sea holly, thrift, sea beet, scrubby sea-blite and several species of sea lavender. Some of these are edible, and another plant that occurs here in vast quantities on the estuarine mud, glasswort, is harvested in the summer and sold as 'samphire'.

Winter brings a changing of the guard in wildlife. Thousands of birds come from northern Europe to spend the winter at Blakeney, among them brent geese and wigeon on the marshes and snow buntings and shorelarks in the dunes and shingle. Some of these come from the High Arctic and, on a winter's day on the Point, they might just feel at home.

Seasonal highlights

Spring
Oystercatcher, redshank, wheatear

Summer
Yellow horned-poppy, terns, black-headed gull

Autumn
Sea holly, skuas, warblers

Winter
Snow bunting, wigeon, knot

All year
Grey seal, common seal, partridge

25 Chimney Meadows

Fields ancient and modern

Bampton, Oxfordshire OX18 2EH

Grid ref SP354013

Directions At Tadpole Bridge turn right and follow signs. Park in designated BBOWT car park (signposted) on left

Lunch stop The Shaven Crown Hotel, High Street, Shipton-under-Wychwood, Oxfordshire OX7 6BA

Don't be fooled by the strange name; you won't be seeing too many chimneys on this wild walk. Instead you will be admiring a stretch of the great River Thames that could almost be remote – a world away from the bustling sprawl of London, at any rate.

Coming here, having negotiated the long, narrow road to the entrance, you might also be fooled into thinking that you have found a place unscarred by time and modernity, but that would not be true. Far from being in their pristine state, these meadows have been restored from 618 acres of intensively farmed land. Back in 2003, when the farm was acquired by the local wildlife trust (BBOWT), the ground had been scarred by pesticides and overgrazing and the biodiversity had plummeted. Now it looks lush and glorious.

The meadows, within close reach of the car park, are the highlight of a visit at almost any time of year. They are at their best in high summer, when the colourful displays of wildflowers are superb. From the white of ox-eye daisies to the subtle pale yellow of meadowsweet and pepper saxifrage, and from the fiery purple of black knapweed to the flare of yellow cowslips and buttercups, these displays are a throwback to a cleaner, pesticide-free countryside. The meadows are cut commercially in the late summer for hay; otherwise the vegetation would simply rot in the winter. Some are grazed by doe-eyed Dexter cattle, sheep and horses. The management is intended to produce a wide variety of different meadows providing habitat for subtly different plants and animals.

The meadows are an excellent habitat for birds. In the wetter areas waders such as snipe, and occasionally curlew, breed. Both these species were once found all over southern England in wet grassland, but now are in rapid decline and confined to a few pockets. Barn owls hunt the abundant mammals, and birds such as reed buntings and yellowhammers feed on insects in the summer and seeds in the winter. There are two hides further along the trail, beyond the meadows, where there is scrub and light woodland and a pond and network of shallow pools have been created. Quiet viewing from the hides could produce a

Seasonal highlights

Spring
White-legged damselfly,
mayflies, cowslip

Summer
Black knapweed,
buttercup, meadowsweet

Autumn
Ox-eye daisy, teasel,
swallow

Winter
Wigeon, cormorant,
kingfisher

All year
Little grebe, brown hare,
barn owl

sighting of a kingfisher, while various ducks such as wigeon also occur here in the winter.

It isn't long before you reach a boardwalk which takes you past a large patch of scrub; in the spring you should hear the scratchy song of the whitethroat here and, if you are lucky, perhaps its less common relative, the lesser whitethroat. Bullfinches can also be seen in this section. Eventually you reach the bridge over the Shifford Lock Cut, which leads to the southern part of the reserve. However, it is best to turn right here and follow the Thames Path along the cut to the river itself. You will be accompanied by swans and ducks and, if you are very fortunate, it is possible to see water voles here, another animal that has been in steep decline in our landscape. Otters have been recorded, too, and in the larger fields there are hares.

Don't overlook the small stuff, either. On a summer visit this area will be buzzing with insect life, including dancing mayflies which, despite their name, may be seen at any time from April to August. As you might expect from a wetland, Chimney Meadows is excellent for dragonflies and damselflies, and there are one or two specialities. The localised white-legged damselfly, with its powderpuff appearance, is common along the ditches and river in late spring and at the same time, in late May and early June, there is a chance of seeing the rare club-tailed dragonfly along the Thames, a species found in very few places in the UK.

However, whatever you see or don't see on this walk, be it summer meadows or flocks of wild ducks in the midst of winter, this place will leave its mark on you. It feels a long way from anywhere and, happily, is a million miles away from the harsh agricultural desert it once was.

Little grebe

26 Finemere Wood

Emperors, admirals and royals

Quainton, Aylesbury, Buckinghamshire HP22 4DL

Grid ref SP719209

Directions 0.6 miles after Quainton take T-junction left at Grange Farm; after 0.6 miles park on verge by track on right, before pylons

Lunch stop The King's Head, Market Square, Aylesbury HP20 2RW

This very old wood was once the preserve of kings and queens; now it's only emperors that are found here. Finemere was part of the enormous royal forest of Bernwood, a vast area of woods, meadows and scrub. Kings and nobles, from Edward the Confessor to Henry II, hunted deer and wild boar here. Nowadays most 'hunters' come looking for butterflies.

Approaching by car from nearby Aylesbury, it is immediately obvious that this is a quiet corner of England. You park on the road between the quaintly named villages of Edgcott and Quainton (SP720209) and, after a short walk past fields, you enter the wood. Many local people talk about the atmosphere of Finemere; they say it really does 'feel' ancient as well as being technically ancient woodland. You don't necessarily need to see ecological indicators such as the bluebells in the spring, or the yellow archangel, early purple orchid or wood spurge, to sense the peace and wildness. The tangled scrub, fallen logs, rich ground flora, old gnarled trees and sheer variety of tree species – oak, willow, hazel, ash, birch, aspen, hawthorn – all point to the diversity of a seriously mature woodland.

But it isn't just a woodland. Right in the heart of the site is a much more open area, with rough pasture and thickets; a superb place for butterflies in the summer. Part of the wood is surrounded by meadows, too, and work is under way to clear rides connecting these to the central glade.

It is this mix of wood and open areas that encourages the butterflies for which Finemere is celebrated, so much so that many an enthusiast will be exploring the rides and glades during the peak months of June and July. On occasion, photographers have got into verbal arguments when chasing the same individual butterfly! The very rare black hairstreak is the biggest draw; all it needs for a food plant is dense, mature clumps of blackthorn, but this fussy butterfly only occurs sparsely in Britain, mostly here in the Home Counties. Not far behind is the big and spectacular purple emperor, which really does have a strong purple sheen to its wings. Hardly becoming of an emperor, it has some peculiar habits: it is drawn to carcasses and faeces, and even to urine, which

Seasonal highlights

Spring
Wood spurge, cuckoo-
flower, bees

Summer
Black hairstreak, purple
emperor, Bechstein's bat

Autumn
Long-tailed tit, grass
snake, comma

Winter
Hazel catkins, brown hare,
pheasant

All year
Red kite, midland
hawthorn, bullfinch

butterfly twitchers will gladly supply if it means attracting this elusive beauty into the range of a lens. The supporting cast of butterflies is very impressive too, with white admiral, brown hairstreak and silver-washed fritillary – each enough to draw attention on their own.

As you might expect, there are plenty of birds to see, not least red kites, which are nowadays very common in the area, as they might well have been when the royals hunted here. They are very easy to recognise, not just because of their long, forked tails, but also because the wings are held rather flat, slightly kinked down, unlike the buzzard, which holds its wings in a V. Both of these birds of prey breed, sometimes in the Corsican pines which are left over from previous forestry plantings. In contrast, two of Britain's smallest birds, the goldcrest and firecrest, breed side by side in the conifers, while marsh tits, bullfinches and occasionally turtle doves can be found in the wood and scrub.

Finemere Wood holds another secret that few visitors witness, but if you look carefully there might be clues. At certain points in the wood you can spot boxes with no obvious front entrance. These are for bats, and Finemere Wood is now recognised as one of the best places for bats in the entire country. In particular, the extremely rare Bechstein's bat, associated with ancient woodland, thrives here. It uses the boxes and old trees, and also commutes along the rides in the hours of darkness. If you do prolong your walk into a summer evening, you are very likely to see bats flying around as it begins to get dark.

Day, night, summer or winter, there is always something special to encounter here. It's a remnant of a long-lost land.

Wood spurge

27 Foxholes

Boom times in the Cotswolds

Bruern Road, Chipping Norton, Oxfordshire OX7 6QE

Grid ref SP258200

Directions From Burford take the A424 north, then the third lane on the right and over crossroads at Hill Farm; park after 1.5 miles

Lunch stop The Shaven Crown Hotel, High Street, Shipton-under-Wychwood, Oxfordshire OX7 6BA

Foxholes has long been known to the locals as one of the best bluebell woods in Oxfordshire. Visitors are easily beguiled by the ethereal blue of these woodland-floor blooms, and people come from near and far to pay homage to them in the spring. Yet the bluebell burst is only one of several annual gluts that you can experience here. There's a birdsong burst, a riot of pink foxgloves, a high summer spell of butterfly action and, best of all, some extraordinary colours in autumn.

Foxhills Nature Reserve lies in the Cotswolds, not far from Burford. Going north from the town up the A424 towards Stow-on-the-Wold, you take the third lane on the right towards Bruern Abbey and follow it down past a crossroads; a mile or so on, just after the sign to Shipton-under-Wychwood, park in the layby. A heavily potholed track to the left goes alongside the tangle of ash and maple that is Cocksmoor Copse, then reaches a car park, the start of a nature trail with badger waymarkers. You're already well off the beaten track.

The reserve lies on land leaning down from a plateau towards the brooding River Evenlode, with acidic soils on the top and base-rich soils on the downward slopes, leading to a good diversity of habitats. You will see beechwoods covering the base soils and oaks and birches on the more acidic sections, where even bilberry grows on the rides. In contrast to some woodlands, every corner and ride is satisfyingly different.

Fly agaric

Seasonal highlights

Spring
Bluebell, early purple
orchid, birdsong

Summer
Foxglove, white admiral,
speckled wood

Autumn
Fungi, bilberry, tawny owl
hooting

Winter
Red fox calling, woodcock

All year
Nuthatch, ash, beech

The bluebell explosion occurs in late April and May, with a concurrent festival of other blooms, including early purple orchids, primroses and dog-violets scattered around the wood. These early blooms bask in the sunlight that isn't yet masked by the thick woodland canopy.

The floral fiesta actually occurs towards the end of the birdsong season. This starts in earnest in January, when great tits and blue tits start up, joining the song thrushes, wrens, dunnocks and robins that have been going since the autumn. Within weeks, coal tits, nuthatches, marsh tits and treecreepers will have begun, the latter so soft and gentle that they seem like a suggestion rather than a song. These are followed by blackbirds and chaffinches in February. March witnesses the arrival of summer migrants to swell the chorus, and April still more, adding chiffchaffs and blackcaps respectively. The dawn chorus at this time of the year almost seems to make the woodland shake.

High summer sees the butterflies take over, with speckled woods dotted around in the shade. Males of this species are the butterflies you see spiralling up the rays of sun that penetrate the canopy in a kind of territorial dance. Meadow browns lilt over the open glades, while big, showy white admirals zip past like Rolls-Royces overtaking Ford Escorts on a motorway. Some of this action takes place over the colourful backdrop of serried ranks of Foxholes foxgloves.

The autumn finishes the year's blooms with a bang. Yes, of course, the leaves on the trees go red and golden, but when they fall they alight next to a floral display every bit as impressive as the flowering in the spring. From October to December is fungus season. The site has as many species of fungi – 200 and counting – as flowering plants. They aren't generally as colourful or attractive as flowers, but they exhibit amazing subtlety of hue and weirdness of form. And weirdness of name, too: take the beechwood sickener, for example, or the geranium-scented russula (well, it does have the right scent). Add to those milk caps, agarics, sulphur tufts, bracket fungi, puffballs, oyster mushrooms and even false death caps.

Don't be tempted to eat any of the fungi unless you've been on a foray with an expert. It may be hard to believe in a gorgeous place like this, but some British plants and fungi are so poisonous they can kill you. Foxholes isn't the jungle, but take care nonetheless.

28 Heartwood Forest

The real new forest

Sandridgebury Lane, Sandridge, St Albans, Hertfordshire AL4 9DQ

Grid ref TL168108

Directions Take the B651 Sandridge road out of St Albans, through Sandridge village and follow the brown signs

Lunch stop The White Horse, High Street, Southill, Bedfordshire SG18 9LD

Many of the sites in this book are famous, long-established places well known for their peaceful atmosphere and rich wildlife. Not this one. This is a new phenomenon sprouting out of the Hertfordshire countryside. Not even the name has been handed down the generations; it was coined by the Woodland Trust in honour of the fact that the forest is situated in Hertfordshire, and because some of the ancient woodland enclosed within this massive tree planting scheme contains lime trees with their heart-shaped leaves. Welcome to a completely new forest well within the commuter belt of London!

In 2008 the Woodland Trust acquired Hill End Farm, north of Sandridge, near St Albans. The 857-acre plot contained four small patches of ancient woodland amounting to 44 acres and some hedgerows, but was largely arable fields. With full marks for ambition, the Trust decided to turn the area into the largest new native forest block in England, a project estimated to last 12 years. In the winter of 2009/10, planting began, with 20,326 trees being planted in a single day on 9 December 2009. While that sounds a lot, the overall aim was, and still is, to plant 600,000 native trees. It won't all be continuous forest, so some land will be set aside for scrub, grassland, meadows and even a small 'swamp'.

The forest is a work in progress and so, to some extent, your enjoyment walking in this very new piece of wildness is too. The pockets of ancient woodland are, of course, superb, and possibly up to 1,000 years old according to measurements of some of the coppiced hornbeams. There are also veteran common limes, ash, oak, field maple and wild cherry. The best area to see these

small-leaved lime

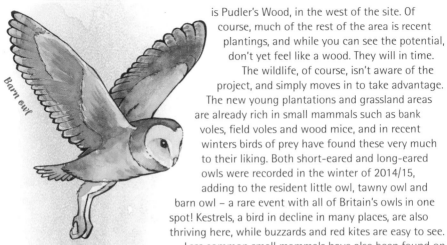

Barn owl

is Pudler's Wood, in the west of the site. Of course, much of the rest of the area is recent plantings, and while you can see the potential, don't yet feel like a wood. They will in time.

The wildlife, of course, isn't aware of the project, and simply moves in to take advantage. The new young plantations and grassland areas are already rich in small mammals such as bank voles, field voles and wood mice, and in recent winters birds of prey have found these very much to their liking. Both short-eared and long-eared owls were recorded in the winter of 2014/15, adding to the resident little owl, tawny owl and barn owl – a rare event with all of Britain's owls in one spot! Kestrels, a bird in decline in many places, are also thriving here, while buzzards and red kites are easy to see.

Less common small mammals have also been found on recent surveys, with both yellow-necked mice (typical of well-established woodland) and harvest mice (tall grass) turning up in traps. There are larger mammals too. You have a good chance of spotting a muntjac or fallow deer, while both hares and rabbits are common. It is clear that Heartwood Forest is likely to become an exceptional mammal site.

One of the best aspects of the project is that the wildlife is monitored, so while visitors can see the forest developing before their eyes, the hidden picture of wildlife populations can be equally well tracked. Butterflies are slowly on the increase – the rare purple emperor butterfly was seen for the first time in 2016. Bird populations are changing, with a noticeable increase in the number of breeding species. At the moment several birds of open country are doing particularly well, such as skylark, linnet, whitethroat and, to some extent, yellowhammer. Over the years more woodland birds, such as marsh tit and song thrush, should begin to increase in numbers.

Heartwood Forest is a great example of what can be achieved with vision and fundraising. It aims to serve people as well as wildlife, so the existing woods and many newly planted areas have plenty of access points as well as a new car park off the B651 which runs through the forest between Sandridge and Wheathampstead, a couple of miles north of St Albans. It is big enough to absorb a lot of visitors, and so it is easy to get away from the world. And if you are impressed with the site, why not sign up for the next tree planting *(heartwood.woodlandtrust.org.uk)*?

Seasonal highlights

Spring
Skylark, wild cherry, bluebell

Summer
Yellowhammer, speckled wood, rosebay willowherb

Autumn
Bank vole, tree colour, deer

Winter
Short-eared owl, brown hare, catkin

All year
Lime tree, hornbeam, maple

29 Inkpen Common

Bliss in small corners

Heads Lane, Inkpen Common, Hungerford, Berkshire RG17 9QT

Grid ref SU382643

Directions At Hungerford cross canal and railway, turn left (east) to Kintbury, then south on Inkpen Road, Blandys Hill, Pebble Hill to Rooksnest Lane

Lunch stop The Swan Inn, Craven Road, Lower Green, Inkpen, Berkshire RG17 9DX

Inkpen Common is a small piece of wildness in a bitty part of the countryside, a left-over corner in a land grab. It consists of 30 acres of heathland in a part of the world where heathland is a great rarity – which is almost everywhere, by the way, because this habitat is more threatened than tropical rainforest. It was once part of Inkpen Great Common, an expanse between Newbury and Hungerford where people had the right to let their livestock graze at will. Now only this remnant is left. It is a short walk round, but the atmosphere of any heath, especially in summer, has something special – the smell of the heather, the purple flowers, untamed gorse bushes, the boggy ground that catches you unawares. On a heath you can be next door to a housing estate and still feel far away, and this is the case here.

This particular common is 6 miles southwest of Newbury and adjacent to the small village of Inkpen. You park by the junction of Heads Lane and Great Common Road (SU382643) and paths lead into the common. Go where you will to sample a mixture of woodland, open heath, a small pond and a bog, where there is a boardwalk.

It is hardly surprising to find heaths on a heathland, and indeed there are three species here: the abundant ling, the more vividly purple bell heather and, in the moister areas, cross-leaved heath. There are also two types of gorse, the common version and dwarf gorse, so some basic botany will prove enjoyable. This is also a good site for the scarce pale dog-violet (spring) and in the summer there are yellow blooms of bog asphodel.

Look out, too, in the autumn for one of Britain's most distinctive toadstools, the fly agaric, which is easy to find here among the birches. This is the one that has a red cap with what look like lumps of icing sugar on it. If you eat this, you are likely to experience a serious hallucinogenic effect. It is best left for the fairies to dance around.

Raise your eyes and there should be plenty of birds to interest you. Marsh tits are a feature, and parties of long-tailed tits are easy to see as they move in groups between the bushes. Bramblings and woodcocks sometimes overwinter, and in summer the scrub and light woodland resound to the songs of common whitethroat and blackcap.

Even if you have completed a circuit, your exploration of the area should not end there. Should you be visiting the site between the very end of February and the end of March, there is a quite unexpected treat within easy walking distance, in the village of Inkpen itself. Follow Great Common Road south, turn right at the public footpath (which takes you beside a small extension of the nature reserve with oak and birch trees), and carry on between the plantation and the field to Inkpen village. Opposite the community centre is a cul-de-sac called Pottery Lane, and a track off this leads to another field with a wondrous display of crocuses. So good is the display that people come from miles around to see it, and there is only one other comparable display in the country.

The crocuses at their best cloak the field all the way down to a stream, and in good years there can be 400,000 blooms. They are purplish or white, and they are a marvel. The field is a Site of Special Scientific Interest (SSSI), ironically not for the crocuses, but for their supporting cast: primroses, then, later in the year, common spotted and heath spotted orchids, meadow saxifrage, cowslip, devil's bit scabious, lousewort and 25 species of grass.

Oddly enough, these spring crocuses (*Crocus vernus*) aren't native and nobody knows how they got here. Inkpen parish documents prove that they have been here for 200 years, so it is a long-forgotten mystery. At least it is an example of human intervention in the countryside having a positive effect.

Back at Inkpen Common, it is possible to follow a network of footpaths and minor roads either north to Titcombe and Kintbury, or south to join the Wayfarer's Walk at Walbury Hill. The local Wildlife Trust (BBOWT) has put together an Inkpen Wild Walk to showcase good local habitats and fine views *(bbowt.org.uk/reserves/Inkpen-Common)*.

Long-tailed tit

Seasonal highlights

Spring
Spring crocus, primrose, whitethroat

Summer
Grasses, devil's-bit scabious, heath spotted orchid

Autumn
Fly agaric, flowering heaths

Winter
Brambling, woodcock

All year
Gorse, long-tailed tit, bog asphodel

30 Old Warden Tunnel

Highlights at the end of the tunnel

Southill Road, Bedford, Bedfordshire MK44 3TA

Grid ref TL112444

Directions Take the A421 around Bedford, turn off to Cardington, take Southill Road towards Old Warden; park in layby after 2.2 miles

Lunch stop The White Horse, High Street, Southill Bedfordshire SG18 9LD

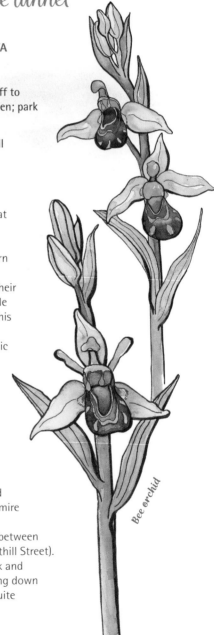

Bee orchid

When the Old Warden Tunnel was completed in 1857, the workers could have had little idea what would become of their handiwork. The tunnel was a serious engineering undertaking, built to accommodate the London, Midland and Southern Railway's main line from Bedford to Hitchin. Steam trains would have rushed through with their usual flourish several times a day, and few people would have contemplated a quieter future for this stretch of track. Yet the tunnel closed down a hundred years later, in 1963, owing to the prosaic reason of falling passenger demand. Now the tunnel and cutting are a highway only for bats, butterflies and birds, and the area is literally given over to nature.

A very small nature reserve of just over 9 acres runs from the northern end of the tunnel. There is plenty to explore here, but for those with itchy feet the reserve is next to the Greensand Ridge Walk, 40 miles of designated long-distance footpath. Once you have explored the cutting, there is plenty of countryside to admire and investigate.

You park in a small layby on the minor road between Old Warden and Cardington (Bedford Road/Southill Street). A track goes off from the Greensand Ridge Walk and towards the tunnel, which is reached by dropping down seemingly interminable steps. The entrance is quite impressive, depending how much graffiti or abandoned cars there happen to be. It is blocked off with a fence, because it contains the best site for hibernating bats in the county of Bedfordshire (it even houses barbastelles), which you might occasionally see at the tunnel entrance on an autumn evening. However, you must not enter the tunnel at any time; it is dangerous and it is also illegal to disturb the bats.

The cutting and its banks, as well as the top of the tunnel, however, can be enjoyed at leisure. There is even a small pond at the northern end of the site. The highlight is undoubtedly the display of flowers, best in the summer months but by no means disappointing in autumn, when sheets of feathery white traveller's joy (also known as old man's beard) drape over the shrubs, and when the blackthorn and hawthorn are laden with bluish-black and red berries respectively. The blackthorn also bursts into flower at the end of winter. However, to enjoy the best variety, go in June to see the intricate bee orchids, pyramidal orchids (just out), late cowslips, dwarf thistle, ox-eye daisy, common quaking-grass and spiny rest-harrow, the latter a deep shade of pink. Many of these rely on calcareous grassland which has not been spoilt by pesticides.

Delightful though the flowers are, the most impressive wildlife feature is the butterflies. In this very small cutting at least 20 species are recorded every year, and often as many as 24. The list of species is extraordinary, with even woodland butterflies such as purple emperor and wood white appearing, together with dark green fritillary and Essex skipper in recent years. Marbled whites and ringlets are seen regularly in their season, along with a host of more common species.

The berry-bearing bushes on the slopes, together with the stands of oak and ash on the margins, attract a good variety of commoner birds. It is a good place for thrushes in the autumn and winter, with parties of redwings and fieldfares passing through. Blackcaps and whitethroats sing from the hedgerows in spring and summer, and at any time of year red kites, sparrowhawks and buzzards soar over. Green woodpeckers are often feeding on the banks, attracted by the profusion of ants.

In the spring, indeed, the artificial vale is full of birdsong – a far cry from the rhythmic roars and loud whistles that would have filled the atmosphere a few decades ago.

Seasonal highlights

Spring
Orange-tip, cowslip, whitethroat

Summer
Marbled white, ringlet, ox-eye daisy

Autumn
Common lizard, hawthorn berries, warblers

Winter
Traveller's joy, fieldfare

All year
Buzzard, blackthorn, ash

31 Saltbox Hill

Richness in the footsteps of Darwin

Saltbox Hill, Westerham, Greater London TN16 3EF

Grid ref TQ407607

Directions From Westerham take A233 north to Biggin Hill; after airport runway fork left up Saltbox Hill

Lunch stop Rose and Crown, Otford Lane, Halstead, Greater London TN14 7EA

The terms 'wild places' and 'London Borough of Bromley' do not, at first sight, go easily together. However, if you are after some peace and quiet and good wildlife inside the M25, Saltbox Hill delivers remarkably well. You do have to make allowances for London Biggin Hill Airport next door, and for making your entry through residential streets, but the truth is that this tiny nature reserve, just 54 acres in extent, really is an oasis in our busy world. Somehow it has remained preserved against the southeast's rampant surge of development.

No less a figure than Charles Darwin was a fan of Saltbox Hill. The great scientist was a regular visitor for picnics, strolling across from his residence, Down House, less than a mile away. The airfield wasn't there in the 19th century, of course – neither was aviation. Darwin was undoubtedly inspired and intrigued by what he saw here in this rural valley, and today the sheer variety of plants and animals is still remarkable. Today's visitor might not share the man's genius, but can yet see some of what he saw.

Chalkhill blue butterfly

On a steep west-facing slope, the site is a mishmash of ash and beech woodland, hawthorn scrub and – the jewel in the crown – chalk grassland. This latter habitat is nationally rare and almost unknown elsewhere in Greater London. Over the years some of the grassland has been encroached by scrub, but fortunately the London Wildlife Trust is restoring some of the 15 acres that it owns. There is

Spring
Grizzled skipper,
quaking-grass

Summer
Orchids, dark green
fritillary, chalkhill blue

Autumn
Common lizard, dogwood,
buckthorn

Winter
Bullfinch, long-tailed tit

All year
Beech, ash, skylark

access at all times, either from the road known as Saltbox Hill, or from Hanbury Drive, off the A233. Several public footpaths run through the area.

If somebody were to recount a list of plants recorded on this site to a botanist, they certainly wouldn't guess their location was in the London area. Take the list of orchids, of which 10 species grow regularly. Some of these, notably white helleborine, bee orchid, fly orchid and man orchid (the last-named found only on the eastern slope), are orchid royalty, difficult to find anywhere. They are all weird and wonderful flowers: the blooms of the bee orchid, several to a stem, look remarkably like a bee visiting a purple flower, while the fly orchid has equivalent purple flowers with 'antennae' and a bluish 'thorax' – if it is meant to look like a fly, it is certainly an exotic one. Meanwhile the man orchid has a spike from which dozens of yellow mini human shapes hang down – it really is odd. The white helleborine has less elaborate cup-like flowers, coloured like vanilla ice cream.

The butterflies of Saltbox Hill are as impressive as the orchids, with an astonishing 30 species recorded. It is one of only two sites in London where the rare and fast-disappearing dark green fritillary has been seen regularly, although this species is very hard to find here. You should have some luck in season (July–September) with chalkhill blue, and careful butterfly watchers should run into two inconspicuous species: the grizzled skipper and the dingy skipper. Both look like moths, lacking the exuberant colours of most butterflies.

It would be hard not to agree that Saltbox Hill is at its best in summer, but that applies to many sites throughout Britain. Among the other highlights, common lizards can be seen well into the autumn, and in that season the changing tints of the trees are magnificent. The shrubs such as buckthorn, dogwood and wayfaring tree all produce different-coloured berries.

And, of course, there are always birds, which can be easier to see in the winter. It isn't a top-rated birding site, but there is a decent suite of common birds, such as great spotted and green woodpeckers (the latter often eating the abundant yellow meadow ants), bullfinch, long-tailed tit, nuthatch and treecreeper. Skylarks have also bred here.

Whatever you might see at Saltbox Hill, a walk is always going to prove worthwhile. That's what Charles Darwin thought, at any rate.

32 Thatcham Reedbeds

Sighing reeds and squealing pigs

Nature Discovery Centre, Muddy Lane, Lower Way, Thatcham, Berkshire RG19 3FU

Grid ref SU506670

Directions At Thatcham turn right opposite hospital onto Lower Way; Muddy Lane is 1.2 miles further on

Lunch stop The Rowbarge, Station Road, Woolhampton, Berkshire RG7 5SH

This sumptuous site within spitting distance of Newbury is a perfect example of how busy towns and wildlife havens can live cheek by jowl. You don't come here for complete peace and solitude, what with the M4, a busy railway and two market towns nearby (the other one is Thatcham). However, it is a terrific place for a very good variety of wildlife, with reedbeds, open water, woodland edge, a river and a canal to boost the biodiversity. If too many people are about, you can quickly retreat to Bowdown Woods a short distance to the south.

This area is well developed for wildlife viewing, with a spanking new Nature Discovery Centre run by the RSPB (SU505672), which has a free car park (donations requested). This has opening hours, but Thatcham Reedbeds reserve

Tufted duck

is always open, and can be reached on public footpaths instead. Whichever way you choose to go, you should be delighted at the wildlife you see.

In many ways, all visitors should be indebted to the reserve's flagship species for its original notification as a Site of Special Scientific Interest (SSSI), although you probably won't see it here. That's because the Desmoulin's whorl snail is only a maximum of 3mm long. It occurs in calcareous marshes and it is not only nationally scarce but scarce in Europe as a whole.

The casual visitor, though, will see more birds than anything else, and the whole area, with its mix of different wetlands, attracts an impressive variety of species. Viewing begins right by the visitor centre, which is perched on the side of a lake where people feed the ducks. You can mix with the public enjoying the mallards, Canada geese, mute swans, moorhens and coots, while further out there will be diving ducks such as tufted ducks and pochards, and little and great crested grebes. In the last few years there have been red-crested pochards about, too, which are probably originally escapees from a captive wildfowl collection. Incidentally, you probably wouldn't consider it a bonus, but wild brown rats often feed alongside the ducks here.

Having had your fill of the visitor area, a path leads south towards Thatcham Reedbeds reserve proper. The substantial area of reedbeds is one of the largest in inland southern England, and there are copious alders and willows lining it along the paths. In the summer these marshes resound to the rapid, complaining songs of reed and sedge warblers, together with the stuttering, hesitant song of the reed bunting and the loud volley of explosive song from the Cetti's warbler (the latter two species are also around in winter). The whole area is excellent for kingfishers – these can sometimes be seen from the visitor centre – and you would be unlucky to miss this species,

particularly in winter. The water rail, by contrast, is common but almost impossible to see; it makes a sound like a distressed squealing pig.

With so much water about, the area is excellent for fish, and some of the lakes are dedicated to angling. Bridges over streams, and the Kennet and Avon Canal, which runs to the south of most of the lakes, make good places to do some dry-land fish-watching, in summer at least. Look out for perch, chub, dace, roach and, in the shallows, the ubiquitous minnows.

Open water is quiet in summer, but busier in winter, when resident birds are joined by northern breeders taking refuge from the continent. This is particularly obvious among the wildfowl, where the populations of mallard and tufted duck are swollen and new faces include wigeon, teal, gadwall and shoveler. Far less appreciated, but still migrants, are the gulls, which are so much a part of the Home Counties landscape in winter. Black-headed gulls (which have brown heads in summer and just a speck on the head in winter) are by far the commonest, but common, herring and lesser black-backed gulls can also be seen easily.

Summer on the reserve is, of course, the time of plenty with regard to flowers and insects, both along the side of the reedbeds and the Kennet and Avon Canal. Among the blooms here are common valerian, hemlock water dropwort (a common waterside plant that is deadly poisonous), skullcap, marsh woundwort, water mint, marsh bedstraw and common meadow rue. Late summer brings a profusion of dragonflies, which provide good entertainment for visitors and food for the hobby, a bird of prey. The site is also noted for moths, with many reedbed species including obscure wainscot – which sounds suitably rare.

If you have time in your sojourn and are not enticed by a walk down the Kennet and Avon towpath, there is a small extension of the area southwards that is of interest. The area around Lower Farm, reached by going under the railway bridge, has a bird hide and a large, shallow lake. It is good for winter wildfowl and generally for waders such as lapwings and little ringed plovers. It is well worth a look, and from here you can carry on to another nature reserve, Bowdown Woods.

For a longer walk including nearby Greenham and Crookham Common, check out the Living Landscape Wild Walk One at *bbowt.org.uk*.

Seasonal highlights

Spring
Cetti's warbler, sand martin, little ringed plover

Summer
Dragonflies, common meadow rue, moths

Autumn
Lapwing, gulls

Winter
Wildfowl, kingfisher, water rail

All year
Desmoulin's whorl snail, great crested grebe, fish

33 Two Tree Island

Real nature in the urban borderland

Leigh-on-Sea, Southend-on-Sea, Essex SS9 2GB

Grid ref TQ822848

Directions Turn right to island just beyond Leigh-on-Sea station

Lunch stop The Peterboat, 27 High Street, Leigh-on-Sea, Essex SS9 2EN

Some of the sites in this book are truly beautiful; Two Tree Island, just off the bustling conurbation of Southend-on-Sea and adjacent to the heavy industry of Canvey Island, isn't one of them. It is flat, rough around the edges (and within the edges) and noisy. You can come here for solitude, but it isn't a miles-from-anywhere solitude, rather a solitude of the urban borderland. The island is only special in view of its proximity to what is next door and the contrast it provides. It does manage to present a taste of real nature, though.

If you decide that Two Tree Island could hardly be described as an Elysian haven, you should have visited a few decades ago. The entire island was a rubbish dump then, and before that it was a sewage works. It isn't a natural island, either, but was reclaimed from the Thames Estuary in the 18th century. The name arises from the fact that two large elm trees used to grow on the island and dominate the landscape, but these were blown down in storms during the 1960s. It is actually remarkable that it looks as it does now, a patchwork of grassland, scrub, reedbeds and a lagoon. It is amazing what a layer of topsoil can do. It has now been elevated to the status of being part of Hadleigh Castle Country Park.

The island is about a mile and a half long and just under half a mile at its widest north to south and is cut in two by a north-to-south road; this road begins at Leigh-on-Sea railway station and enters the island over a bridge. You park just beyond this bridge or at the end, by the slipway overlooking Hadleigh Ray, whichever takes your fancy. To the west is a nature reserve managed by the Essex Wildlife Trust, while to the east the saltmarsh is part of Leigh National Nature Reserve. These are good credentials and, indeed, the casual visitor should have plenty to see at any time of year.

There is a network of footpaths on the island, including a public bridleway. On some days, dogs are everywhere. However, if you are looking for wildlife, it is best to make a beeline for the western end, where there is a bird hide overlooking the lagoon. Astonishingly, avocets breed here. These supremely elegant black-and-white waders with up-tilted bills are not only rare, but also choosy. The fact that a small colony has set up here is a credit to birds and

Seasonal highlights

Spring
Avocet, black-headed gull, sedge warbler

Summer
Lesser marsh grasshopper, Essex skipper, carder bee

Autumn
Sea aster, sea-lavender, slow worm

Winter
Brent gooose, grey plover, short-eared owl

All year
Field vole, kestrel, little egret

reserve managers alike. When the avocets are breeding they are guarded, owing to the fact that their eggs have been stolen more than once. Other birds that breed on the lagoon and reedbeds include black-headed gulls, redshanks, water rail and reed and sedge warblers. Little egrets don't breed here but large numbers roost on the island at high tide, standing stock still and looking like discarded shopping bags.

Winter brings a new set of birds. The mudflats around Two Tree Island are rich in eel-grass, one of the few British flowering plants that grow in salt water. This plant is the staple diet of the brent goose, which breeds in Arctic Russia. Flocks of these occur just offshore and are often tame, allowing close views. The birds give a delightful mumbling murmur as they feed. Sharing the mud with the geese are a number of waders that have also come from the north. Grey plovers, curlews, knots, dunlins and redshanks are all well represented. The island is also noted for winter visits by the short-eared owl, which feeds on the field voles that are abundant on the grasslands. The much rarer long-eared owl has also been seen.

It isn't all birds. As you go round you might spot water voles in the channels or common lizards in the grassland. Insects include Essex skipper (of course), a butterfly, and also a suite of interesting grasshoppers and crickets: the introduced house cricket, the Roesel's bush-cricket, which has arrived in Britain naturally and expanded its population in recent years, and finally the lesser marsh grasshopper, which is fairly localised.

Botanically, there are some interesting plants, especially those associated with the saltmarsh, such as sea aster, sea purslane, sea wormwood and golden samphire. There are also two species of sea-lavender, which produce a delightful purplish display in summer. They include the common sea-lavender, and the lax-flowered sea-lavender, which sounds as though it doesn't flower quite as much as it should.

In short, there is something for everyone interested in natural history here. But the fact that there is anything for anyone is perhaps the most remarkable aspect of all.

Field vole

34 Wallasea Island

Thrillingly remote but perfectly accessible

Creeksea Ferry Road, Rochford, Essex SS4 2HD

Grid ref TQ966944

Directions Follow signs to Rochford then Ashingdon; go through Ashingdon on Ashingdon Road, then turn right to Canewdon; from village follow Lambourne Hall Road to Creeksea Ferry Road

Lunch stop Plough and Sail, East End, Paglesham, Essex SS4 2EQ

There aren't many places in southeast England which are full of nothing, speaking in map-reading terms. But take a virtual trip roughly northeast from Southend-on-Sea and look carefully left and above Foulness Island. Lying between the Rivers Crouch and Roach is an empty block of land with almost nothing marked on the map apart from a marina at the west end. This is Wallasea Island. Its history is as blank a canvas as its appearance, although it was once three islands and there was a small settlement with a school for a short time.

But what sets this bleak, flat island apart is its future. Wallasea Island is the chosen site of Britain's largest project to restore farmland back to 'wild coast'. The idea is that, having been farmed from since at least World War I, recently for growing wheat, the island will be returned to the type of coast that might have existed 400 years ago. Using very modern management methods, they are turning back time. There is something of an irony that a partnership of the RSPB and Crossrail, one of Britain's largest infrastructure projects (a train tunnel

Oystercatcher

connecting east and west London), will use three million tons of extracted earth to construct new sea walls and raise parts of the island to create a network of fabulous wildlife habitats, such as lagoons and islands, of the sort that existed in antiquity. This is great news, and there is little doubt that the place will become an exceptional nature reserve.

All that is very well, but how is Wallasea for a visit now? The answer is that it is currently thrillingly remote in feel, but perfectly accessible. Indeed, the RSPB are happy for people to come along and watch the transformation as it unfolds over the next 10 years or so. It is easy of access, unless there is a very high tide to cover Creeksea Ferry Road. There is a good car park and the walk along the northern sea wall allows you to feel suitably detached from the world. Having said that, it is pretty hard going in the wind and the rain.

It is a superb site for wildlife, though. Birds are the primary feature. The surrounding mudflats are visited by lots of winter wildfowl and waders, such as brent geese, wigeon, black-tailed godwits, shelducks, dunlins and oystercatchers. The flooded pools and dykes hold teal, mallard and shoveler. It is also an excellent site for wintering raptors such as marsh and hen harrier, peregrine and short-eared owl. You would be very unlucky not to see at least one of these on a visit.

Marsh harriers breed locally, and the number of nesting species is set to rise. Already, however, you are bound to hear a skylark singing on a quiet day, from

January onwards, and corn buntings and linnets help to provide the summer soundtrack with their twittering and jingling songs.

Again, though, all eyes are set on the future. The RSPB is expert at providing great bird habitat, and it intends also to help water voles and to encourage the growth of plants typical of the new habitats here at the Wallasea Island Wild Coast Project. There will be ponds and reedbeds to encourage water voles and warblers, lagoons for waders such as redshanks and avocets, and sea walls and hides to provide a network of paths. In a few years' time the eastern location of the reserve may help to attract birds that breed commonly on the Continent and rarely in Britain to settle here; birds such as spoonbill, and perhaps even the exotic black-winged stilt, with its enormously long, bright pink legs.

The project cannot help but bring widespread wildlife benefits. You might not see all that much if you visit now, but if you love your birds in particular, your imagination will run riot. And that is more than enough reason to make the trek.

Seasonal highlights

Spring
Sea clover, redshank, wheatear

Summer
Sea-lavender, small heath, painted lady

Autumn
Ringed plover, greenshank, corn bunting

Winter
Brent goose, golden plover, hen harrier

All year
Shelduck, marsh harrier, dunlin

35 Whipsnade & Dunstable Downs

Spot a muntjac or a Duke of Burgundy

Bushey Close, Whipsnade, Dunstable, Bedfordshire LU6 2LQ

Grid ref TL009180

Directions Go west through Dunstable; straight on to B489, then B4541 south to Whipsnade; follow signs to Tree Cathedral

Lunch stop The Bell in Studham, Dunstable Road, Studham, Bedfordshire LU6 2QG

This area isn't the most isolated wild place in this book. Owing to its proximity to Dunstable, it is very popular with locals and visitors at weekends and on sunny days. It is an excellent place to see different species of people – dog-walkers, picnickers, kite-flyers, long-distance hikers, joggers and even glider pilots. However, it is perfectly possible to get away from the crowds, and there is a deep pool of wildlife to enjoy.

There is a fine visitor centre on the top of the downs, but it is better to approach from lower down, because this helps you to appreciate how this escarpment rears up from the adjacent landscape like a dimple on the earth's smooth skin. The National Trust car park in Whipsnade village close to the Tree Cathedral makes a good starting point, and the extensive plantings made in the shape of a cathedral as a tribute to fallen comrades is inspiring in itself. You can greatly increase your wildlife list by walking the Ridgeway Link Path south past the perimeter of the famous Whipsnade Zoo, where wallabies and Chinese water deer can be seen and much else heard inside, but that would be cheating. Instead, take the path west out of the village and up a tree-lined track to the open downs.

These are officially called Dunstable Downs, and this southern part is the quietest. The path takes you to a steep climb up on to the top, the highest point in eastern England, and suddenly the world is below. There are fantastic views over the Vale of Aylesbury, and you can easily appreciate that this is an Area of Outstanding Natural Beauty. You don't need to see any wildlife to do so.

However, see if you can spot two types of kites. Red kites, the birds, are now common in the area and it is possible to see them sharing the airspace with human-made kites – Dunstable Downs is one of the best areas for kite-flying in the country (there's an annual festival in July). The toys are named after the birds, not the other way around.

The downs here are not all open grassland, but there are large areas of scrub and woodland, both on the tops and at the base. A splendid network of paths runs over the whole site, so it is easy to find your own quiet corner. This is a Site of Special Scientific Interest (SSSI), owing largely to its superb chalk grassland, a habitat that is now very scarce in the UK. In summer a rich array of grassland flowers flourishes, with delightful species such as squinancywort, yellow-wort, salad burnet, dwarf thistle and common rock-rose, each adding their own vivid colours. There are scarcer species to be seen too, including greater pignut, field fleawort (try saying that aloud) and the highly inconspicuous frog orchid.

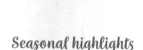

Muntjac deer

The abundant flowers and sheltering scrub make this one of the best sites in the area for butterflies. In particular, it attracts lepidopterists in search of the Duke of Burgundy, a butterfly that looks superficially like a fritillary but is actually a representative of a tropical family. It is on the wing from early May to the middle of June, and a good place to find it is to walk down the slope from the visitor centre (TL008198) to the bottom, where there are sheltered wooded gullies. Apart from Dukes, look out for dingy and grizzled skippers, green hairstreaks and the occasional dark green fritillary. On the chalky slopes are chalkhill blue, small blue and marbled white.

Along the escarpment are the remains of some ancient, medieval rabbit warrens (north of the visitor centre). The rabbit is, of course, not a native British mammal but was introduced from southwest Europe by the Normans. Initially, rabbits were kept captive for their fur and meat, housed in enclosed warrens, and it wasn't until the 18th century that they ever became common. If you see any rabbits on this walk, you will be close to one of their earliest British locations.

The same applies to muntjac deer, which inhabit the woods around here. They were first introduced to Woburn Park in 1901 and quickly spread. They are in the process of colonising much of the country.

Seasonal highlights

Spring
Duke of Burgundy, green hairstreak, skylark

Summer
Squinancywort, marbled white, chalkhill blue

Autumn
Dwarf thistle, goldfinch, field vole

Winter
Buzzard, meadow pipit

All year
Rabbit, muntjac, red kite

36 Woodwalton Fen

Cradle of conservation and wildlife

Chapel Road, Ramsey, Ramsey Heights, Huntingdon, Cambridgeshire PE26 2RS

Grid ref TL234848

Directions From Ramsey Heights village go right on Chapel Road (also called Heights Drove Road)

Lunch stop The Abbot's Elm, Abbot's Ripton, Cambridgeshire PE28 2PA

Five minutes from the small town of Ramsey, down Chapel Road, you find yourself in an ancient landscape. The Fens of England used to cover about 1,500 square miles of East Anglia, a wilderness of low-lying marsh, woodland and lakes with a comparatively sparse human population. There were seas of reeds as far as the eye could see, and large lakes and snaking rivers, with a few islands of drier ground just a few feet above sea level. That has all gone now. Ever since the 17th century various parts of the Fens have been drained in order to reach the rich peaty soil and plant it for agriculture. The drainage reached its zenith in the early 19th century, so much so that in the modern day only four tiny fragments remained of this unique landscape. Woodwalton Fen is one. Ironically, it is now the fenland that is confined to small islands in a sea of agriculture.

Walk over the Great Raveley Drain and you enter hallowed ground. There is a wide grassy level path with tall reedbeds, deep ditches and scrub either side; you feel immersed in the landscape. On any day there will be birds singing and calling, and on spring days there will be torrents from blackcaps, garden warblers and even nightingales, noisy yet tuneful, bursting with life. Reed warblers sing from the swamp and you are likely to hear their nemesis, the cuckoo, which uses this small insectivorous bird as its main host.

This is a special place. Look at the numbers: more than 400 species of wild plants have been recorded on the reserve, together with 900 species of butterflies and moths and an incredible 1,000 species of beetle (the tansy beetle is found in only one other UK site). Half of the country's dragonflies and damselflies are here, too, including the scarce chaser and white-legged damselfly. It is their abundance that is as impressive as anything; a hot summer day is characterised by the loud buzzing of dragonfly wings.

Halfway down the path is an incongruous sight – a wooden building on stilts with a thatched roof. This is Rothschild's Bungalow, where the visionary who bought Woodwalton Fen in 1910 used to come at weekends with interested colleagues to observe wildlife, attract moths with lanterns, and talk about how to conserve Britain's natural heritage. Charles Rothschild bought nearby Wicken

Fen in 1899 as Britain's first-ever nature reserve and founded the body that became the Wildlife Trusts (now with more than 2,000 nature reserves). This building is symbolically at the heart of British nature conservation.

Progress further down the path and you come to an area on the right that was never cut for peat at all, unlike most of the rest of the reserve. Here the ground is slightly more acidic and plays host to some extremely rare plants, notably the fen violet (found in only one other site in Britain), the fen woodrush (in no other sites in Britain) and a form of heath dog-violet that is unique to Woodwalton Fen. Another rarity, the great fen sedge, also grows here.

It doesn't take long before you get to the western edge of the reserve and its raised bank. Looking from here there is a large open area in front of you that is excellent for birds if you wait a while. Marsh harriers float by with their wings raised in a V, while if you are lucky you might see a barn owl or short-eared owl hunting in wavering flight low over the grass.

This is also a good place for deer. Oddly enough, one of the most popular animals for wildlife watchers at the fen is one that was never part of the ancient landscape. The Chinese water deer was introduced to Britain in 1929, escaping from Whipsnade Zoo and becoming established in the wild. However, this small deer with teddy-bear ears and no antlers is not exactly common and Woodwalton is one of the very best places to see it. Another introduced species, the muntjac deer, is common and early morning is the best time to spot them.

The view from the western bank will change over the years, because Woodwalton Fen is at the heart of one of the most exciting conservation initiatives ever devised in Britain. The Great Fen Project, set up in 2001, aims to join Woodwalton and nearby Holme Fen together by buying the land in between and managing it for nature conservation – this will include the restoration of some of the farmland to wetland. So far the project has acquired 50 per cent of the land required at 2,140 acres. The 50-year plan is to create a wetland of 9,100 acres in extent, which will include a visitor centre, cycle tracks and other amenities, as well as recreating fenland.

As you walk north along the western bank and turn right back into the fen to follow the path back to the car park, it is hard not to be excited at the prospect of habitat restoration. What is a truly ancient landscape is, now, at the heart of a very modern conservation initiative.

Seasonal highlights

Spring
White-legged damselfly, hairy dragonfly, fen violet

Summer
Tansy beetle, moths, scarce chaser

Autumn
Great fen sedge, lesser redpoll, hobby

Winter
Bittern, water vole, harriers

All year
Chinese water deer, muntjac, greylag goose

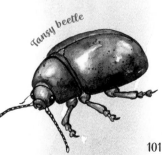
Tansy beetle

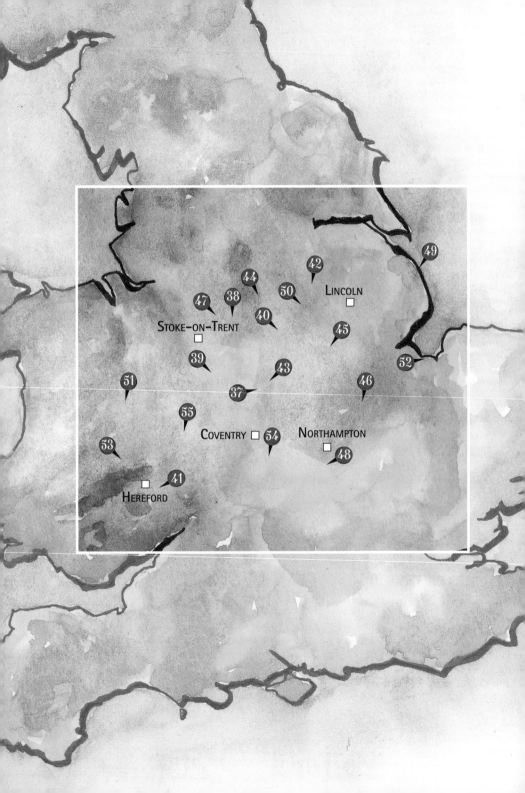

Central England

37 Alvecote Pools

An accidental haven near the M42

Pooley Lane, Polesworth, Tamworth, Warwickshire B78 1JA

Grid ref SK257030

Directions In Polesworth take B5000 (Tamworth Road) left towards Tamworth, then over canal and right on Pooley Lane

Lunch stop The Globe Inn, Lower Gungate, Tamworth, Warwickshire B79 7AT

Alvecote Pools is the perfect example of an interesting local patch. You wouldn't travel here from London, say, but regular visits from close at hand will yield an awful lot of wildlife sightings.

Fly agaric

In this part of the world true wilderness or wildness is impossible to come by. In the case of Alvecote Pools, you have to ignore the fact that the M42, with its roaring traffic, goes over the site, and that it is also right next to a railway and canal. Furthermore, there would be no pools without the Pooley Hall Colliery, which was worked between 1848 and 1965 but is now reduced to a slag heap on site. Subsidence caused by the mine and flooding of the hollows created the series of pools that we see today. The wetlands are now one of the largest and most varied in Warwickshire, and extend into nearby Staffordshire.

This site is officially part of Pooley Country Park, run by the local council. One way to approach it is to park by the visitor centre in Polesworth and take the very pleasant Miner's Trail along the canal (you can follow an audio trail to learn about the mining activities). If you prefer, you can also avoid the car-parking fee by approaching near the picnic spot by the old Benedictine abbey on Robey's Lane (off the B5000 Tamworth road). From here, cross the canal and take the path to your right before the railway track. Going further down along Robey's Lane and through Alvecote, there are more pools on the north side of the railway track.

Over time, an accidental haven has developed here, with a surprising variety of habitats in a small area (316 acres). In addition to the freshwater pools, there is the flowing water of the River Anker and the Coventry Canal, marsh and reed swamp, a couple of meadows, rough ground, some woodland, scrub and the slag heap. Quite naturally, the varied habitats lead to varied wildlife, and visitors might be surprised to hear some of the numbers: at least 300 beetles and over 100 species of spiders, for example. More than 100 species of birds are recorded annually and more than 50 breed. There is even a decent showing of mushrooms and toadstools, and the Warwickshire fungus group run a foray or two every year. The famous fly agaric, with its white-spotted red cap, is common under the birches; this one is harmful if eaten, but the blusher *Amanita rubescens* also occurs here and is delicious.

Birds are, as ever, the easiest animals to see in a site like this, and there are several notable species that breed, or attempt to breed. One of these is the shelduck, a bird that most people are more used to seeing on the coast; of similar ilk is the common tern, which uses islands in the pools. It is worth looking in the middle of summer for broods of great crested grebe and tufted duck; less common ducks, such as gadwall or shoveler, sometimes breed, too. Some waders can be added to this list, such as lapwing and oystercatcher. It is all pretty impressive. Outside the breeding season almost anything could turn up, and many rarities have done so, spotted by a dedicated band of keen birders.

Insects are also well represented in the summer, and you can hardly help seeing a good variety on a warm day. Just under 30 species of butterflies have appeared, some of which are uncommon in the Midlands, like dingy skipper and the rapidly declining wall brown. Hairy dragonflies, which are quite large but inconspicuous early-season (May) marshy specialists, have just been seen again after a gap of a few years, here at one of their very few Midlands locations. Common hawker and ruddy darter are two other of the less common species that you might find.

But really, the overwhelming impression you get of Alvecote Pools isn't about the rarities it harbours. It is instead all about the commonplace, the rich mixture of everyday wildlife that makes this sort of place an island in the sea of human busyness.

Seasonal highlights

Spring
Hairy dragonfly, grasshopper warbler, yellow wagtail

Summer
Common tern, wall brown, beetles

Autumn
Blusher, common hawker

Winter
Gadwall, shoveler, grey wagtail

All year
Kingfisher, shelduck, tufted duck

Tufted duck

38 Biggin Dale & Wolfscote Dale

Mindblowing displays of wildflowers

Hartington, Buxton, Derbyshire SK17 0AL

Grid ref SK128604

Directions From Ashbourne take the A515 towards Newhaven, then follow signs to Hartington

Lunch stop The George, Alstonefield, Derbyshire DE6 2FX

The Derbyshire Dales are part of the Peak District's gentle southeastern rump. This is the White Peak area, where carboniferous limestone takes over from the signature millstone grit of the Dark Peak to the north, where wind-lashed heather moorland gives way to sheltered, flower-rich grasslands and snaking valleys. In the northern Dark Peak you feel like an adventurer; here, in greener, kinder countryside, you can imagine tea and cakes at the end of your excursion.

Biggin Dale and Wolfscote Dale are two parts of the valley of the River Dove. If you walk from the village of Hartington, where you can park at the station, you can go down Biggin Dale and up Wolfscote Dale, getting two dales for the price of one. The walk is superb at any time of year. In the wildflower season, however, in May or June, it will blow your mind. For a longer walk you can come up from Milldale or even from Ilam (a place surely to get coffee) and you certainly won't regret a single step.

If you leave Harlington by Reynards Lane to the southeast, carry straight on when you reach the track. You cross several fields until, quite suddenly, the path swerves right, descending into Biggin Dale. Straight away you are looking at one of the area's famous ash woodlands. They cling to the hillsides and are regarded as among the best in Britain. With a casual look they don't jump out as anything special, but stand and stare within their shade and you will see that many other trees and shrubs stand alongside. There is wych elm and rowan, maple, hazel and lime – and the latter category includes both the small-leaved and the nationally rare large-leaved lime. That's just the trees. Down below is an impressive range of shrubs, such as dogwood, guelder rose, buckthorn and bird cherry. And on the woodland floor is still more variety, with a dense ground flora of dog's mercury, mountain currant and, in a few places, the strange mezereon. You have to go early in the year to see the last named in flower. It shoots out a tall spike of glorious pink blooms, but they are all gone by April.

Wow – and that's just the beginning. The limestone has much more to give the botanist and casual flower-lover yet. At the foot of the dales, in the grassland and on the scree, there are magnificent displays of flowers, some of which are rare. In April and May, early purple orchids and cowslips add a dash of pink and yellow respectively to the grasslands. And if you look carefully, particularly on the dale sides, you might find the jewel in the crown, the simply glorious Jacob's ladder, with clusters of flowers of the perfect purplish-blue. This is a common garden plant, but is here in its rare wild state, flowering from June to August. It isn't easy to find but that is part of its allure.

Lots of other unusual plants could be mentioned, among them red hemp-nettle, a very smart dead-nettle-type plant found in the scree of Biggin Dale, plus pale St John's wort and field garlic. There are many of these, as well as a host of ferns and lichens. In damp places by the river, the display of cuckoo flower, meadowsweet and marsh thistle (yes, a thistle) is a typical example of colour-co-ordinated delight, with soapy pink, soft greenish-yellow and violent purple.

The chances are that Biggin Dale will detain you for a long soak in its floristic riches, but eventually you will meet the River Dove at the bottom. Here it is worth making the short diversion to the stepping stones just downstream and the view of Iron Tors, before doubling back and forking into Wolfscote Dale. This time you'll be walking along the beck itself and, if anything, the scenery is even finer than in Biggin Dale; it is a wider view, with more grassland slopes to enjoy. Look out for the shiny green cistus forester moth on the flowers, and don't forget to look for dipper and grey wagtail on the river. Ravens might well fly over, and there are redstarts in the woodland further up. It isn't all flowers.

Well, it isn't quite, but the truth is that the flowers are the glory of the Derbyshire Dales. The walking is great, the views spectacular, the people you meet will be friendly. But the flowers elevate what is a lovely walk into something far more special.

Marsh thistle

Seasonal highlights

Spring
Mezereon, early purple orchid, cowslip

Summer
Jacob's ladder, red hemp-nettle, cistus forester

Autumn
Marsh thistle, mountain currant, dogwood

Winter
Raven, dipper, buzzard

All year
Ash, lime trees, wych elm

39 Cannock Chase

The lungs of the Black Country

Coppice Hill, Chase Road, Brocton, Stafford, Staffordshire ST17 0TN

Grid ref SJ979191

Directions From Cannock take the A34 north for 2.5 miles, go right at roundabout at Pottal Pool, left past war memorials, then 1.2 miles to Chase Road

Lunch stop The Yorkshireman, Colton Road, Rugeley WS15 3HB

There are times, such as on sunny weekends in the spring, that Cannock Chase seems so crowded with people that you might muse wistfully that a visit to a shopping centre would bring blessed relief.

That's a mirage, of course. You only have to walk a little way from any car park and you will have the Chase almost to yourself, except for a few fellow diehards. This is Britain's smallest Area of Outstanding Natural Beauty (AONB), and one of the most pressurised; they call it the 'Lungs of the Black Country',

yet at times you can hardly breathe. But this is a place to stick at it; a small effort can get you well off the beaten track.

The AONB epithet is off the mark too, as Cannock Chase could not truthfully be described as *natural* beauty. It was a hunting estate in the Norman period, but since then it has been flogged and modified enormously. The large plantations of conifers have been planted, and the agricultural land is worked, albeit with methods kind to wildlife. There are remains of industry dotted about, mostly associated with coal. And even the most cherished part as far as wildlife is concerned, the heathland (the largest in the Midlands), is a human-created habitat, caused by people grazing their livestock on poor soils and preventing the regrowth of trees. It doesn't make the Chase any less special; it simply adds to its intrigue.

Some of what is left here is certainly ancient. At Brocton Coppice, for example, some of the sessile oak trees are real veterans, being 200–600 years old. The fallow deer, of which there are about 800 in the Chase, are also thought to be descended from a herd introduced in medieval times, so their ancestors could have arrived here not long after the Normans. These deer, mainly quite dark in colour, are common around the whole site; the area around Freda's Grave, the memorial to a Great Dane dog that was a mascot for the New Zealand Rifles who were stationed at Cannock Chase in World War I, is a good place to spot them.

The heathland of Cannock is unusual because it combines some elements of north and south. The familiar heathland triptych of ling heather, bell heather and cross-leaved heath is joined by a set of plants more characteristic of

Seasonal highlights

northern Britain, notably bilberry, crowberry and cowberry. There is also a very rare hybrid of bilberry and cowberry that some people call the 'Cannock Chase berry'; this is almost the only place to find it in Britain. Gorse, bracken and birch make up the rest of the heathland habitat. This is a good place for four of Britain's native land reptiles: the adder, grass snake, slow worm and common lizard. Several interesting birds are characteristic of the heath, notably wood lark (in one of its more northern stations) and nightjar, a nocturnal bird that eats moths and beetles in the night sky. Males make a remarkable hollow 'churring' sound (like the distant engine of a two-stroke motorcycle), a most peculiar and atmospheric territorial call. Each midsummer, birders make the pilgrimage out on to the heaths to hear it.

Much of Cannock Chase is planted with pines (Scots and Corsican), which isn't a great wildlife habitat but up until recently held a remnant population of red squirrels. The various patches of deciduous woodland are much more interesting. In general, they are semi-natural oak and birch woods, with holly and, in wetter places, alders and grey willow. The older trees, some of which are very rare, make a great habitat for insects, especially beetles that require old timber and extensive tree cover.

Butterflies and moths are also here in abundance. The whole area is good, but the Sherbrook Valley deserves a special mention. This is one of the few places in the Midlands where you can find the rare and steeply declining small pearl-bordered fritillary. The valley is in the northwest section of the Chase, not far from Brocton Coppice.

In recent years, several of the car parks and visitor centres have begun to put out food for the birds, particularly over the winter, and this has enabled people to get superb views of some species that are harder to see in the wider forest. The classic case is a handsome orange-washed finch, the brambling. The feeding station at the main Forestry Commission centre on Marquis Drive (SK004153) is now stocked by the West Midland Bird Club, and is one of the sites in the county of Staffordshire to see this bird, along with yellowhammer, bullfinch and commoner birds. The bird-feeding stations are one part of the Chase that you can enjoy with the crowds.

Fallow deer

40 Erewash Meadows

Romantic flood plain with plenty to see

Stoney Lane, Brinsley, Nottinghamshire NG16 5AL

Grid ref SK450482 (Nottinghamshire); SK441517 (Derbyshire)

Directions From Brinsley pass Brinsley Lodge on right, turn left to Hall Lane and first left onto Stoney Lane

Additional access from Jacksdale Community Centre in the north (SK441517)

Lunch stop The Nelson and Railway Inn, 12 Station Road, Kimberley, Nottinghamshire NG16 2NR

This place won't be everybody's cup of tea, with the noisy A608 at its southern end, a railway next door and the looming metropolis of Nottingham just to the east. However, no fewer than two wildlife trusts have seen fit to buy parts of Erewash Meadows, a flood plain that straddles their borders. And, anyway, there is a certain romance to a place like this. D H Lawrence set several of his novels in the Erewash Valley, not least *The Rainbow*.

'Erewash' approximates to a wandering (meandering) marshy river, and this is a duly wet, slushy spot. The river has a tendency to flood rapidly, meaning that the site isn't always passable. And even when it is, you must keep to the paths around the reserve to ensure your feet remain dry.

In the middle of winter, with the skies leaden and bursting with rain, there isn't a lot of difference between a flock of wigeon flushed from a rough meadow in the Midlands and a flock flushed from a ditch in a remote corner of East Anglia or Scotland. The males of this duck make a delightful explosive whistle, which to many birdwatchers is the epitome of winter. Erewash Meadows is a good site for these and other winter ducks, including teal, gadwall and shoveler. Each of these has its own specialised feeding techniques that you can watch from the pools here. The wigeon grazes on grass next to the water, the teal in the poolside mud and shallows, the gadwall feeds on plant material in slightly deeper water, and the shoveler filters the muddy shallows for edible animal material.

There are three parts of Erewash Meadows. Aldercar Flashes are at the south end, near Eastwood, while the middle section encompasses Brinsley Meadows (there can be shooting nearby) and the northern section runs alongside the disused Cromford Canal. Aldercar Flashes are most favoured by birdwatchers; you can access them from Plumptre Road in Langley Mill and under the A610,

Barn owl

or from Stoney Lane in Brinsley, or for a longer but more salubrious walk, park on Boat Lane at Stoneyford Lodge to the north. The Aldercar end has six newly dug pools and several reedbeds. It is the haunt of secretive birds and water voles. The former includes the famously shy water rail, which is common here, and often lurks in the open under bird feeders near the Stoney Lane entrance. Snipe and even jack snipe are here in winter; if you disturb the former it will fly away, zigzagging and making a kissing call, while the latter only flushes if you nearly step on it, and flops away silently. Snipe breed here in the summer, along with lapwings, the one making a strange bleating buzz in display (drumming) and the other making ecstatic whooping calls.

In all, a remarkable total of almost 200 bird species has been recorded here, including many rarities such as the spoonbill. It is an excellent place for kingfishers, especially along the Cromford Canal, and grey wagtails too, which also like running water. Grasshopper warblers, now quite a localised species, breed here and sing their odd reeling song, like a freewheeling bicycle. You might also spot a little owl, a bird that likes willow trees and low posts, while barn owls hunt over the long, grassy meadows.

In summer, all the areas of Erewash Meadows are good for dragonflies. No fewer than 17 species have been seen, and most of them breed. Black-tailed skimmer and the gorgeous banded demoiselle catch the eye, while the rare red-veined darter has been known to appear in late summer.

Mammals include foxes and, if you are lucky, you might spot a weasel zipping across the path in front of you. They are quite common but incredibly elusive, often spending time in the holes of their favourite prey, voles. Frogs are abundant and so are their nemesis, grass snakes, although again you would be fortunate to come across these.

On any visit there will be plenty to see, particularly early in the morning. The setting is soggy and basic, but aesthetic appeal doesn't matter a jot to the creatures that live here.

Seasonal highlights

Spring
Grasshopper warbler, lapwing, reed bunting

Summer
Banded demoiselle, shoveler, swift

Autumn
Common sandpiper, blackcap, greenshank

Winter
Jack snipe, wigeon, teal

All year
Little owl, weasel, water vole

41 Haugh Woods

One of Britain's best wildlife woods

Haugh Woods car park, Herefordshire HR1 4QX

Grid ref SO592365

Directions From Hereford follow the B4224 to Hampton Bishop and Mordiford, then where the B4224 turns right, go straight on uphill to Haugh Woods

Lunch stop The Crown Inn, Woolhope, Herefordshire HR1 4QP

Just southeast of Hereford, next to where the River Lugg gurgles into the River Wye, the road uphill from the village of Mordiford goes through a large forest perched on top of the Woolhope Dome. This is Haugh Woods, pronounced in these parts as Hoff. Arriving in the Forestry Commission car park your eye might be caught by the prickly tops of thousands of conifers, resulting in the immediate sinking of the wildlife-watcher's heart. But first impressions can be deceiving. This is an absolutely top wildlife wood, one of the best in Britain.

Great tit

You'll feel better immediately when you read the notices describing the two Butterfly Trails, one to the north and one to the south of the road. Haugh Woods is the best butterfly site in Herefordshire and hosts several rare species. However, you need to work for these – don't expect them to fly to you. They are all found in the deciduous sections, where oak stands lie next to broad, herb-rich rides. At the moment the lepidopterist intelligentsia recommend taking the South Trail. Looking at information board 6 (pearl-bordered fritillary), follow the track that goes right and thus become transported into butterfly heaven. The most important species are the aforementioned fritillary (late April to June), high brown fritillary (June to August, rare) and wood white (May to June). These are the sought-after species, but on a sunny day there will be plenty of others about.

You won't immediately notice it when looking for butterflies, but Haugh Woods is also an outstanding place for moths. Most people don't bother with moths, and some are repelled by them, but the truth is that this group of insects is astonishingly diverse, and often every bit as beautiful as butterflies (which are merely day-flying moths anyway). Moths' nocturnal habits make them difficult to observe. Remarkably, about 650 species have been recorded here, 10 times

Seasonal highlights

Spring
Pearl-bordered fritillary,
wood white, wild daffodil

Summer
High brown fritillary,
moths, bees

Autumn
Craneflies, meadow saffron

Winter
Ash keys, crossbill, siskin

All year
Woodpeckers, tits,
goldcrest

the number of species of all established British butterflies. Some of these moths are rare and have contributed to Haugh Woods being given the status of a Site of Special Scientific Interest (SSSI), along with the butterflies, bees and, perhaps surprisingly, craneflies. Although a roll-call of some of the moths here might not mean much to you, the names are without doubt evocative: lunar hornet moth, cloaked carpet, barred rivulet, satin beauty, poplar lutestring, tissue, mocha, drab looper, triple-spotted pug and barred hook-tip. On a good night in July, moth enthusiasts have recorded 100 species in a single night. The Forestry Commission occasionally runs public moth events and they are recommended.

The wide, hard paths of Haugh Woods are family-friendly and ideal for pushchairs, and picnic tables are dotted about. However, there is one aspect to the wood that is less than ideal: the biting insects and ticks. It is worth using insect repellent and wearing long trousers during the butterfly and moth season.

As you wander along the rides, you will see an excellent range of flowers, although the most interesting species will, like the butterflies, take some finding. Gems like meadow saffron, which is actually a crocus of the most delicate pink on a white stem, are found in the small ash-maple segment in the northern part of the wood. It comes up in August. In the same section are columbine, herb Paris and greater butterfly orchid. Wild daffodils also grow in the northern part, next to Pentaloe Brook, and there is a small area nearby that has a decent orchid flora, including marsh helleborine.

Your failsafe for any visit, of course, is birds, which can be found in all weathers. The spring chorus resounds to the songs of great tits, chaffinches and blackbirds, as it does everywhere, but it is particularly worth coming here in February or March to have a chance of finding lesser spotted woodpecker. It makes a more even drumming sound (striking the bill very fast on a piece of wood to make the equivalent of a 'song') than the much commoner great spotted woodpecker, with a longer burst. Great spotted woodpeckers have more of an abrupt attack to the beats when they are drumming.

There are other good birds. Crossbills occur in the summer and probably breed, while marsh tits, tree pipits, wood warblers, redstarts and other small birds can be found. The area is generally under-watched, so who knows what might be lurking among the trees?

Wild daffodil

42 Idle Valley

Wetland wildlife paradise

North Road, Retford, Nottinghamshire DN22 8QH

Grid ref SK689829

Directions From Retford follow the A638 north for 1.5 miles then follow signs to Idle Valley

Lunch stop The White Horse, Great North Road, Barnby Moor, Retford, Nottinghamshire DN22 8QS

Not every industry has a history of working out in favour of wildlife, but one that sometimes does is gravel extraction. A case in point occurs here in northeast Nottinghamshire, along the River Idle, where gravel works began at the end of World War II. Gravel extraction inevitably produces pits in the ground, which fill with water, and these often arouse the attention of wildlife-watchers, especially birders. In 1989, so enamoured was the local Wildlife Trust of this artificial wetland that it bought a small piece of filled-in quarry. To cut a long story short, when Tarmac Ltd completed the works in 2012, they left 1,112 acres of lakes, meadows and wood behind for the Trust to use for nature conservation: a whole basket of goodies in a wildlife sweetshop. Thus the Idle Valley Nature Reserve was born, the largest wetland in Nottinghamshire and now of national importance.

It is hard to imagine what the site must have looked like in the early days as it is now a grand spanking modern nature reserve, no less than 3 miles from south to north, and with a magnificent Rural Learning Centre at its heart, with café and shop, plus miles of trails. The place is so big that it is like several nature reserves in one – a lake there, a wood here, marshes and fens, the river and scrubby areas. It is easy to lose the crowds and find corners to yourself, and be grateful for those with the foresight and chutzpah to turn gravel into a marvel.

The site is close to Retford, to the east of Worksop. If you leave Retford on the A638 going north, you will spot a brown sign to the Idle Valley after about half a mile. Follow the lane down through a wooden gate to a huge car park, where payment is blessedly voluntary. From here the Idle Valley is yours; you can indulge in following reserve trails or you can go where you wish. On any day of the year there will be something to see. Yes, it is all artificial. But this is the sort of artificial that even the wildlife purist can enjoy.

The Idle Valley is a paradise for birders. There are always some good things around, and often rarities, too, while the mix of habitats means there will be excellent variety. The many hides ensure that you can watch in relative comfort

in all weathers. The only problem, if it is a problem, is that you simply cannot hope to cover it properly in one day. The best birds may be in the places you left out.

Waterbirds are the speciality. The area was designated as a Site of Special Scientific Interest (SSSI) in 2002 for, would you believe, the large wintering population of coots, as well as a duck called the gadwall, a grey-brown species which feeds on vegetation – one per cent of the British wintering population can be found here. Up to 17 species of ducks, geese and swans may be on site all at the same time. Gadwall have bred, too, as have several other localised wildfowl, such as shelduck and red-crested pochard. Waders and gulls also feature. Oystercatcher, lapwing, redshank, little ringed plover and ringed plover have all bred, and even avocet has too. Black-headed and lesser black-backed gulls breed on the islands in Bellmoor Lake, right next to the visitor centre. Indeed, you can see a great deal just here, without visiting anywhere else.

Along with the bird variety (257 species have been recorded) there are inevitably masses of other forms of wildlife. Some of the impressive figures include 28 species of butterflies, 19 species of dragonflies and damselflies, and about 600 moths. There are frogs, toads, snakes, voles and an enormous variety of flowering plants. There are even some unusual pondweeds.

It would be easy to list in detail all that you might see here, but that would be missing the point. Idle Valley is not the wildest location you might visit in this book, but it is undoubtedly one of the richest. And with its recent history of industrial use, that is encouraging for the future of wildlife.

Seasonal highlights

Spring
Lesser black-backed gull, little ringed plover, lapwing

Summer
Redshank, dragonflies, turtle dove

Autumn
Gulls, great crested grebe, greenshank

Winter
Gadwall, snipe, coot

All year
Pondweeds, wildfowl, grebes

Oystercatcher

43 Kelham Bridge

A neglected beauty spot

Sence Valley Forest Park, Ravenstone Road, Ibstock, Leicestershire LE67 2AN

Grid ref SK402111

Directions From Ibstock go right on A447 (main road through town), north to Sence Valley Forest Park

Lunch stop George Inn, Loughborough Road, Coleorton, Leicestershire LE67 8HF

There are several sites in this book that have grown up out of the ashes of burnt-out industry or amenity: mine subsidence, landfill and so on. This beauty spot has an insalubrious past, too – as a place to dump sewage. Its new career, though, has seen it resurrected in style. Not only is it a local nature reserve with a river, ponds, reed swamp, scattered scrub and meadow, but it is now part of that patchwork of replanting known as the National Forest.

Kelham Bridge Nature Reserve is very small, just a 20-acre parcel of land next to the River Sence, to the southwest of Coalville in northwest Leicestershire. You could describe it as a neglected corner, and it would take seconds to drive past it and barely notice. At the same time, it doesn't harbour much that is rare. But it is precisely these sort of places that are precious. At a time when many common animals and plants are declining, it is the neglected corners to which they retreat. And this one, furthermore, is carefully managed by the Leicestershire and Rutland Wildlife Trust to promote biodiversity.

It is easy to visit. The reserve is open all the time and it won't take you long to explore a plot little more than half a mile long. Park in the Sence Valley Forest Park (also part of the National Forest, and itself worth a visit) and cross over the A447 and walk half a mile north to the entrance gate. You will see the old pumping station of the sewage works; the reserve is behind.

Almost immediately you will appreciate the essence of this site, as you look over a large reedbed. In the summer this area resounds to the songs of reed and sedge warblers, together with the jerky staccato of the reed bunting. In the winter it is full of skulking birds like moorhens and water rails, while bittern has been seen occasionally.

Not much further along are some open pools, the first two of which are overlooked by a hide made out of an old metal container (there is another hide a little way down). Look out for teal from here, and also kingfisher, which is regular. You are highly unlikely to see any mammals, except for the common

rats that attend the bird feeders by the second hide, but that doesn't mean they aren't here. Otter is occasionally seen, and two very elusive small mammals have been found: the water shrew in quiet ditches and the harvest mouse in the reedbeds.

At least one bird species that occurs at Kelham Bridge is a reminder of its sewage-works background. The green sandpiper in Britain is something of a backwater bird. It breeds in northern Europe, but comes here from late summer onwards on a non-breeding retreat. It likes ditches and vegetated streams, and isn't too fussy about the mud and edges over which it scampers. Long may it remain here.

The watery landscape is beginning to acquire a reputation for dragonflies, and so far 19 species have been found, in addition to 22 butterflies. Both figures are likely to swell, as is the list of just over 100 birds. The fact is, this is a very young reserve, and is a work in progress. You might even find something new yourself.

The 'work in progress' feel is magnified next door to the nature reserve itself, where there is a woodland restoration site managed by the Forestry Commission. Replanting of these fields began in 2006 and is carefully managed to create, as the saplings grow, a range of woodland habitats to complement the adjacent wetlands. The upper fields will be broadleaved forests of oak and ash, while those lower down are more suitable for wet-loving species such as alder and willow, two very different habitats cheek by jowl. Some of the plot has been left as rough grassland, too.

It is all a far cry from the site's toxic past.

Seasonal highlights

Spring
Sand martin, reed warbler, sedge warbler

Summer
Black-tailed skimmer, comma, small skipper

Autumn
Green sandpiper, common darter, teal

Winter
Stonechat, water rail, common rat

All year
Water shrew, reed bunting, moorhen

44 Leash Fen

Untidy rough-edged fenland

Shillitoe Wood, Fox Lane, Derbyshire S32 3YR

Grid ref SK295749

Directions From Baslow take A621 Sheffield Road northeast; go over crossroads at Clodhall Lane, fork right into Fox Lane and follow for just under a mile to car park

Lunch stop The Devonshire Arms at Pilsley, High Street, Pilsley, Derbyshire DE45 1UL

If you had to pick the least fashionable part of the Peak District National Park to visit, it would almost certainly be the Eastern Moors, just to the south of Sheffield and within spitting distance of Chesterfield. And if there was a least fashionable part of the Eastern Moors, which does include some impressive countryside, it would undoubtedly be Leash Fen. The fen is not especially attractive and it is very tough going underfoot. Much is impassable. It is, you might say, an acquired taste. But that is also its charm, and it is a good place for wildlife.

If the locals know anything about Leash Fen, it is probably in the form of an intriguing local legend. There is an old poem that goes:

> When Chesterfield was gorse and broom
> Leash Fen was a market town.
> Now Chesterfield's a market town
> Leash Fen is but gorse and broom.

No one would write a poem that bad unless there was a ring of truth in it, would they? Could there be a sunken town that lies in the bosom of the peat? It is an intriguing thought and, on a murky day when mist clouds the horizon of tall, tussocky grass, you can easily imagine a village of people emerging from the gloom.

Leash Fen lies a couple of miles northeast of Baslow, off a minor road from the A621 towards Sheffield. It is adjacent to Ramsley Moor and Big Moor to the north. If you park at Shillito Wood (SK295749) you can easily access the fen and moors in one convenient package. The wood is on the north side of the fen. It is a modern conifer plantation that has a few birds, and it incongruously contains a mysterious stone cross at least a hundred years old.

Many birders stop by Shillito Wood to look over the fen for its signature species, the short-eared owl, which sometimes breeds here but is more reliable in the winter. There are sometimes several birds – in fact up to eight have been recorded at a time – which make a glorious sight on a bright afternoon. These owls, in contrast to tawny owls, routinely hunt in the daylight, flying low over the tall, rough grass where their favourite food – field voles – occur. When they spot one they will dive or even somersault down onto it, a great piece of wildlife action. Just recently the RSPB and National Trust, who have taken over management of the East Moors area, have put up a box for barn owls, which also occur here. Short-eared owls breed on the ground.

Short-eared owl

That management is part of something of a renaissance for Leash Fen and its fellow moors. Two hundred years ago the locals tried to dry out the fen by digging drainage ditches, a job that never tamed the area but left it drying out. These ditches have now been plugged, allowing Leash Fen to become wetter and wetter, closer to its natural state. The wildlife is recovering. There are now more frogs and dragonflies; even kingfishers have been seen. Water voles have been introduced, too. This delightful mammal, which many people still know by its nickname of 'water rat' – its ears are smaller than a rat's, its tail is shorter and its snout less peaky – has suffered one of the biggest declines of any British animal, which only very recently has begun to reverse. The beleaguered animal is thriving on the beleaguered fen.

If you do visit, you might as well nod in the direction of the other Eastern Moors. Ramsley Moor is literally across the road from Shillito Wood. The immediate area is good for lesser redpoll, a small bird that is attracted to birch trees hereabouts, and look out for stonechats, too. Curlews and snipe breed on the moor and, if you are lucky, you might spot a red deer.

But neither Ramsley Moor nor even Big Moor have quite the untidy, untamed rough edges of Leash Fen.

Seasonal highlights

Spring
Reed bunting, curlew, common frog

Summer
Stonechat, dragonflies, snipe

Autumn
Lesser redpoll, field vole

Winter
Short-eared owl, great grey shrike, fieldfare

All year
Water vole, barn owl, red deer

45 Muston Meadows

A flower meadow ringing with birdsong

Woolsthorpe Lane, Muston, Nottinghamshire NG13 0FE

Grid ref SK828374

Directions In village of Muston follow Church Lane down to Woolsthorpe Lane

Lunch stop The Chequers Inn, Main Street, Woolsthorpe, Nottinghamshire NG32 1LU

This site is a great example of the delightfully serendipitous, almost random nature of wildlife viewing in Britain. You turn off a major road, take a couple of lanes, park at nowhere in particular, cross a field and suddenly, without warning, you come across a miraculous sight. On the other hand, you could turn up in winter in the same location and, frankly, not notice anything particularly different about one or two fields adjacent to the disused Grantham Canal. There might be a few yellowhammers about, and perhaps a covey of grey partridges in the corner by the hedgerow, but no clue that in the following May and June, the fields will become one of England's finest flower meadows.

Muston Meadows is, however, a National Nature Reserve, a real gem hidden away in the countryside just to the south of Muston (footpath at SK827374). In the spring and summer the neutral clay meadows host roughly a hundred species of flowering plants, a staggering variety crammed together, making them among the best hay meadows in the whole of Britain. The signature species is the lovely green-winged orchid, which flowers between the end of April and early June. It has purple flowers with narrow green veins on the hood, and each stalk has 10–20 blooms. It thrives best on unimproved pastures, those which haven't recently been fertilised or sprayed with herbicide.

The green-winged orchid doesn't just flower here, it invades. For a few weeks the serried ranks, militarily straight, overwhelm the short sward. This sets the scene for a delightful ritual, the annual counting of orchid spikes by the Botanical Society of the British Isles, when a team of volunteers goes

Brown hare

on its collective knees and, tiny patch by tiny patch, tallies up the population. At the last official count in 2014 there were 26,081 spikes of green-winged orchid, rather fewer than the year before. Hopefully they didn't miss any.

Orchids have a way of stealing the attention, and you never hear of anybody counting the spikes of yellow rattle, or buttercups, or lady's bedstraw. Even in botany, it seems, there is a celebrity culture. Yet all these plants are here, and many more, some of them notable. There is a large sward of great burnet, with its deeply red-purple globular heads, and pignut, a delicate, lacy member of the carrot family, grows here and there. Cuckoo flower grows in the wetter patches, by the canal and the ponds.

Hardly anybody bothers with grasses, apart from specialists. Yet don't we think of grasses when the thought of a meadow goes through the mind, with their wavy stems and wind-borne pollen? Grasses are flowering plants, just as much as any other; there are about a hundred species in Britain, and a third of them are here at Muston Meadows. There are quaking grasses, red fescue, sweet vernal-grass, creeping bent and crested dog's-tail among many others. Come here and appreciate them, if only for a day.

The first cut of hay meadows takes place after the orchids have stopped flowering, in June, and the short sward enables you to see the brown hares, which are a feature of the site. They have a long breeding season, and could still indulge in some 'boxing' and chasing even in the middle of summer. These turbocharged floppy-haired herbivores are the most prominent mammals here, but both field voles and bank voles take advantage of the long grass to hide away and produce a series of litters.

There are plenty of birds at Muston Meadows at any time of year, but even these are at their best in the spring and summer months. Swallows twitter as they whisk over the long grass, trying to catch large flies, and both skylarks and yellowhammers are in full song, the former from the air and the latter from a prominent perch. The yellowhammer may sing its 'little bit of bread and no cheese' ditty 5,000 times a day. The common whitethroat has a scratchy song that it delivers from the hedgerows, often among the wild roses.

There is little in the world to compete with enjoying a flower meadow with birdsong ringing in your ears. If you can do this in a quiet spot in a forgotten corner of Britain, then the experience is richer still.

Seasonal highlights

Spring
Green-winged orchid, cuckoo flower

Summer
Wild roses, great burnet, grasses, swallow

Autumn
Bank vole, field vole

Winter
Linnet, skylark, winter thrushes

All year
Brown hare, yellowhammer, willows

46 Old Sulehay

A place of startling contrasts

Sulehay Road, Peterborough, Northamptonshire PE8 6PW (nearest postcode)

Grid ref TL056980

Directions From Wansford turn right at main crossroads by church and bear left into Yarwell Road (becomes Wansford Road); at crossroads for Yarwell village turn right into Sulehay Road

Lunch stop The White Hart, Main Street, Ufford, Stamford PE9 3BH

Fancy a trip to an ancient woodland to look for oysters? That's a ridiculous idea, right? It might sound like it, but Old Sulehay Forest in Northamptonshire, a very long way from the sea, just happens to be a place where you might find seashells among the trees. They are fossils, naturally enough, from an oolitic quarry within the boundary of the forest. The fossils aren't well preserved but there are lots of them and they are easy enough to find. Even ammonites have been recovered here.

Old Sulehay itself is what remains of a much larger ancient forest, Rockingham, which once stretched from nearby Wansford all the way to Kettering, 20 miles to the southwest. In common with many ancient forests, it wasn't all woodland, but 'forest' was a legal term for a preserved hunting area. The present-day Old Sulehay nature reserve is the same. There is a patchwork of woodland, old, overgrown quarries, grassland and wetland areas divided into four discrete chunks, with a highly varied geology under each one. There is Old Sulehay ancient woodland itself, Stonepit Close quarry, a woodland/grassland called Ring Haw, and a southern section, Sammock's Hill, which is being restored as a limestone grassland and also has a small pool and reedbed. Although the site is just a few miles to the west of Peterborough, not many people visit any of these chunks and you are likely to have the reserve virtually to yourself for the day.

The ancient woodland of Old Sulehay, the most northerly section, a retired coppice of oak, ash and field maple, is a fabulous place; it sometimes reminds you of an old house, with a somewhat dark aspect and untidy corners that have been left for many a year, its 'furniture' being fallen logs and standing dead wood. In the spring, though, it lights up with a superb display of bluebells and, particularly impressively, there are vast swathes of wood anemones, with their creamy-white blooms, giving off a sharp, musky smell. Some less common plants also occur, such as the curious toothwort, a strange flower with scales instead of leaves and no green pigment. It is a parasite on the roots of hazel, robbing them of nutrients. The wood is a good place for birds, with reputedly both great and lesser spotted woodpeckers, although the latter is very secretive and difficult to see. So are the muntjac and fallow deer.

The Stonepit Close area could hardly be more different from the closed woodland. This is one of the old quarried areas. In the spring, rather than bluebells, there is a fine display of cowslips, and botanically inclined visitors should revel in some of the less common plants, such as lesser centaury, common cudweed and ploughman's spikenard. The short sward, dotted with scrubbier areas, is a terrific place for invertebrates of all kinds, of which the best known are the grizzled skipper, a moth-like butterfly, and, particularly, glow-worms. These are beetles, and the wingless female is famous for emitting a green glow from its abdomen at night, caused by a chemical reaction (bioluminescence). The females climb up stems to be an obvious target for males, which can fly and have light-sensitive eyes. Boy meets girl and the larvae feed on snails.

Ring Haw, the third segment of the nature reserve, has a combination of woodland and old quarry scrub. The quarry area has many of the same birds as Stonepit Close. Turtle dove, a steeply declining species, is hopefully still purring its soporific song out on a summer's day by the time you read this. Green woodpeckers complete the woodpecker hat-trick, feeding on the numerous ants. The wood itself is an oak–ash combination like Old Sulehay and shares many of its plants, including nettle-leaved bellflower, and also has a few of its own, such as the stinking hellebore, a plant described in the books as a 'foetid perennial'. It flowers very early on in the season, from February to April.

In the southernmost segment, Sammock's Hill, the Northamptonshire Wildlife Trust is undertaking a limestone grassland recreation project. Until recently this was an area of arable farmland, but the underlying bedrock is limestone. The project aims to use seed from nearby grasslands to transform it back to its original state.

The Old Sulehay nature reserve is certainly a place of contrasts, from deep woodland to open quarry, and with both clay and limestone soil. Yet one of its greatest contrasts is between the past and the future. The ancient woodland has been intact for centuries, while the newly seeded grassland is a project for the future.

Seasonal highlights

Spring
Wood anemone, toothwort, glow-worm

Summer
Grass snake, green tiger beetle, viper's bugloss

Autumn
Dogwood, ploughman's spikenard, yellow-wort

Winter
Stinking hellebore, muntjac, lichens

All year
Fossils, green woodpecker, nuthatch

Cowslip

47 The Roaches

Gritstone escarpment with great views

Leek, Staffordshire ST13 8UA

Grid ref SK004621

Directions Follow A53 through Leek for about 2.5 miles, then turn left to Upper Hulme, follow through village to car park

Lunch stop Three Horseshoes Inn, Buxton Road, Blackshaw Moor, Staffordshire ST13 8TW

The Roaches is a gritstone escarpment looming above the town of Leek, in the extreme southwestern part of the Peak District. It rises to 1,657ft and on a clear day you can see as far as Snowdon. But really you don't need to, because the view over the nearby hills and dales, and nearby Tittesworth Reservoir, is quite fabulous enough. There are huge slabs of sandstone beloved of climbers, and vast carpets of heather moorland that turn the area purple in the summer. Some of the rocks have strange, unreal shapes that would not look out of place in a modern art museum.

The Roaches was once looked after by the Peak District National Park Authority, but since 2013 the area has been leased to the Staffordshire Wildlife Trust for the slender margin of 125 years. This is a hint of just how good this area also is for wildlife.

You'll receive another hint if you park near Hen Cloud, at the southern end of The Roaches ridge (leave the A53 Leek to Buxton Road, turn left at Upper Hulme and park after a mile at about SK006623). In the last few years, between the end of March and the end of June, there has been a Peregrine Watch at the base of Hen Cloud, where telescopes have been set up to view the breeding peregrine falcons. These magnificent birds have been nesting here since 2008, and they are resident, but what better opportunity, and what better setting, could you have to enjoy them? They are the fastest animals on earth, easily capable of flying 100mph, even on the flat, and much quicker when diving ('stooping') upon their bird prey from above, and here you might actually see them doing just that.

Peregrines are not the only birds of prey hereabouts. Merlins occasionally breed in these hills, along with the commoner buzzards and sparrowhawks, while hen harriers have now been reduced to the status of winter visitors. The whole area is excellent for birds generally, although some of the most exciting species are difficult to find, and avoid the areas frequented by too many walkers. You won't have any trouble finding red grouse, which sometimes burst from the heather as you walk, intentionally startling you to give them a chance to escape. Curlews return to the moors from March, and their beautiful bubbling

Seasonal highlights

Spring
Peregrine, curlew, ring ouzel

Summer
Stonechat, twite, green hairstreak

Autumn
Purple moorland, rowan berries, bracken

Winter
Hen harrier, merlin

All year
Wallaby, dipper, meadow pipit

songs are somewhere between sad and joyful. Golden plovers are restricted to the remoter crags, although they might fly past as you are exploring the Roaches themselves, while snipe occur in the bogs. Among smaller birds, the commonest is generally the ubiquitous meadow pipit. Look out for stonechats and whinchats and, if you see a blackbird with white around the chest, it is the rare ring ouzel. Twite, a small streaky finch, does occur but keeps its head down. On the streams in the area there should be dippers and grey wagtails. Tree pipits breed in the plantations dotted about the area, although they are migrants and leave in the late summer.

Ironically, the animal that everybody who visits the Roaches wants to see is one that shouldn't be here at all. In the 1930s a certain Captain Courtney Brocklehurst released five red-necked wallabies into this part of the Peak District. These marsupials were of the race from Tasmania, Australia's most temperate state, and found the conditions to their liking, feeding on the copious heather. They began to breed and eventually numbered 60. However, cold winters and hunters all but wiped them out by 2000. Since then there have been very few sightings and the wallabies have become almost equivalent to one of those big cats said to be at large in wild Britain, though rather less fierce. They are probably all gone now.

Mind you, you are more likely to see them than the Mermaid of Doxey Pool, who inhabits a small tarn on the top of the Roaches. She is a local legend, but as far as your wildlife watching and your general wellbeing are concerned, she's bad news – better left alone.

Buzzard

48 Salcey Forest

Butterfly haven with treetop walkways

Wootton Road, Northampton, Northamptonshire NN7 2HX

Grid ref SP794517

Directions From the M1 J15 take the A508 south for 0.6 miles, take 1st left and follow under motorway to Quinton, turn first right past Quinton Green to forest

Lunch stop The Old Crown, 1 Stoke Road, Ashton, Northamptonshire NN7 2JN

At first sight, the idea of a large block of largely coniferous woodland next to the M1 and only 7 miles south of the centre of Northampton doesn't sound immediately appealing. However, Salcey Forest doesn't just have saving graces, it is actually a terrific place to visit. Anywhere with a 6-mile unbroken forest circuit has to have a pool of wildlife, and in this case the pool is deep.

Wood white butterfly

The area was once a medieval hunting forest, and while most of it bears not the slightest resemblance to such a place, there are some tracts that take you back in time. In the eastern part there are large blocks of mature oaks, some of which are at least 150 years old, and some may be veterans of 500 years. These parts are ancient woodland and as such have a gloriously diverse ground flora, including bluebells and primroses in season.

They attract what is generally regarded as the site's top bird, the lesser spotted woodpecker. In actual fact all three British woodpeckers breed in Salcey Forest, the others being the great spotted woodpecker and the green woodpecker. In their honour the Forestry Commission has labelled a 6-mile marked track The Woodpecker Trail. Since it follows a loop around the whole forest, you can either join it at the main visitor centre (pay for parking), or from the other car parks, for example on the road between Hartwell and the B526 (GR810828). There will be plenty of other birds along the way. At any time of year, watch out for the marsh tit (actually a woodland bird), raven, bullfinch and siskin. In summer there are some good breeding extras such as cuckoo, grasshopper warbler and garden warbler.

Seasonal highlights

Spring
Wood white, nightingale, garden warbler

Summer
Black hairstreak, white-letter hairstreak

Autumn
Tawny owl hoot, fungi, lesser whitethroat

Winter
Lesser spotted woodpecker, woodcock

All year
Ancient oaks, mistle thrush, tits

There isn't a Wood White Trail, although there ought to be, because Salcey Forest is arguably the best site in the whole country to see that languidly flying butterfly, the wood white. To be honest, it behaves a little like a sick small white, its white scales a bit off-colour and the flight distinctly lacking in zest. It is one of a magnificent array of butterflies that lift this place well above average as a wildlife haven. The wood whites first turn up in May, and are followed by a stream of excellent species, such as white admiral, dingy skipper, grizzled skipper and white-letter and black hairstreak.

Black hairstreak, in particular, is a considerable rarity. There is a large open meadow area south of the road to Hartwell and very close to the M1, and here, if you can find good stands of blackthorn bushes, you might flush

out a black hairstreak in June and early July. White-letter hairstreak can be found in the same area in July, often flying around ash trees. This hairstreak double would be a major achievement.

Once you have paid your dues to the butterflies and birds, your conscience is clear to join the tourist circuit and visit Salcey Forest's most famous attraction, the Tree Top Walkway. If you can bear the shock of seeing other visitors after the solitude of the Woodpecker Trail, this is a lot of fun, and educational too. It is a slatted walkway that slopes very gently up the incline until it is high among the forest canopy – mainly, but not entirely, coniferous. A further climb at the end takes you up to the Crow's Nest Lookout Tower. From here you can see Northampton in the distance and much of the rest of the doughnut-shaped forest, with its hole in the middle. The walkway wobbles, intentionally, to add a little extra spice, and the whole thing really is an inspiring glimpse into that mysterious world of the woodland canopy.

The walkway begins at Elephant Pond. It is now an excellent site for frogs, but was once genuinely associated with elephants. The animals were commandeered into carrying logs in the forest during World War II, and used to cool off in these waters at the end of the working day.

However, these days that sort of wildlife is definitely not guaranteed.

49 Saltfleetby– Theddlethorpe Dunes

Beach, sand dunes and saltmarsh

Rimac Nature Reserve, Louth, Lincolnshire LN11 7TS

Grid ref TF467917

Directions From Rimac village turn left over Great Eau to car park

Lunch stop Kings Head Inn, Mill Road, Theddlethorpe All Saints, Lincolnshire LN12 1PB

The official name is a mouthful: Saltfleetby-Theddlethorpe Dunes National Nature Reserve. It is a 5-mile stretch of coast potentially accessed by nine car parks, and there are three main trails and seven different named walks. If the authorities want to keep visitors away by making things complicated, then it seems to work. This is a quiet and overlooked part of the Lincolnshire coast.

It is also glorious – an elemental mixture of beach, shifting sand dunes and saltmarsh, with subsidiary freshwater pools and dune slacks, grassland and scrub. It is an open-access site, but parts are used by the Ministry of Defence for demolition work, so it is a good idea to keep away when the red flags are flying. A footpath connects the whole reserve to the landward side of the dunes. Wherever you choose to park, it won't take long until you find yourself contentedly alone.

There are two main reasons to come as far as wildlife is concerned: for the display of flowers in the dunes, and for the birds. The plants flourish in summer and the birds are best in the winter, although there is inevitably some overlap. Each part of the reserve hosts similar things, so it doesn't matter where you choose to park and walk.

Having said that, a good starting point is Rimac, off the A1031 beside the almost negligible settlement of Saltfleetby St Clement. To get to the car park you drive over the large channel known as the Great Eau. There are two official trails here, a short loop and a longer figure of eight, both well maintained for easy access for wheelchairs and pushchairs. You also have the option, red flags permitting, of walking the 1.5 miles to the sea. This is a delightful area, replete with a myriad of flowers in summer. These include large numbers of bee and pyramidal orchids, plus a host of other colourful blooms such as yellow rattle. The dunes themselves are held together with prickly clumps of marram grass and sand couch. Both trails also pass by freshwater pools with dragonflies and pond life such as newts, and on the longer walk you might be lucky enough to see a water vole.

The Rimac area also has a saltmarsh viewing platform. In summer, you can see typical plants of the habitat from here, such as the colourful sea-lavender, while you can hardly miss the noisy redshanks. However, this lookout comes into its own in winter, when the variety of birds increases immeasurably. The flats will be dotted with brent geese, muttering to themselves as they feed, together with curlews, oystercatchers and shelducks. You might also spot the odd grey seal, although nearby sites are better for these.

If you visit Rimac, you can access the other well-maintained sections on foot. A very short distance to the north is the Seaview set of trails, also reached along Sea View Road, another turn off the A1031. To the south, a little further, is the Churchill Lane set of walks, near another access point to the sea.

Anyone interested in birds should pay particular attention to the winter flocks of smaller birds on the dunes and beaches throughout this site. You are highly likely to see parties of snow buntings, white-winged visitors from the north; their flocks seem to 'roll along' as they feed, with back markers constantly flying over the front. They are quite tame and surprisingly unobtrusive. Occasionally these flocks, or those of skylarks, may contain a much rarer winter visitor, the Lapland bunting. Another speciality is the twite, a linnet-like bird that is easily overlooked. It forms much tighter flocks, and when the members fly off, they all seem to be connected to one another with invisible elastic threads.

If you happen to visit in autumn, there is a subtly different picture. The copious sea buckthorn bushes produce their orange berries, providing food for potentially large numbers of birds making landfall after crossing the North Sea from the Continent. Birds such as redwings, fieldfares and ring ouzels gratefully tuck in, and smaller birds like warblers and flycatchers use the bushes for shelter. Rarities such as red-backed shrikes and wrynecks often drop in.

Indeed, almost anything can drop in. On this long stretch of coast, there is much scope for finding something exciting. But even if you don't, the choreography of beach, wind and sky, different every moment, should make your trip worthwhile.

Sea buckthorn

Seasonal highlights

Spring
Pond skater, marsh marigold, whitethroat

Summer
Viper's bugloss, pyramidal orchid, green hairstreak

Autumn
Sea buckthorn, warblers, wryneck

Winter
Snow bunting, twite, curlew

All year
Redshank, marram grass, sand couch

50 Sherwood Forest

Richness borne of sheer antiquity

Sherwood Forest National Nature Reserve, Edwinstowe, Mansfield, Nottinghamshire NG21 9HN

Grid ref SK626677

Directions From the edge of Mansfield take the A6075 east to Edwinstowe; go left in town on B6034 to visitor centre

Lunch stop Forest Lodge, 4 Church Street, Edwinstowe, Nottinghamshire NG21 9QA

Sherwood Forest is so famous for its association with the outlaw Robin Hood and his Merry Men that you could be forgiven for wondering whether the site itself is make-believe. It isn't; it is real, and what's left of it is situated between Mansfield and Worksop, although it once stretched the 15 miles south to Nottingham. Given that the tales of the dashing folk hero arise from ballads composed in the 15th century, you might deduce that the real forest, the wooded hinterland where Robin Hood supposedly had his hideout, must be very old, and it most certainly is. Amazingly, pollen testing has proven that the area has been wooded since the end of the last Ice Age more than 10,000 years ago, and historical records show that parts of the forest are more or less as they have been for a thousand years. This is a place where you step into history.

The best part of the forest for wildlife centres around the National Nature Reserve. This encompasses the ancient Forest of Birklands (=Birchlands) and Budby South Forest just north of Edwinstowe, the site of the Sherwood Forest Country Park. It is easy to find; follow signposts from the A6075 out of Mansfield. This area contains the highest concentration of veteran trees in the whole of Europe, mainly sessile oaks. There are more than a thousand of them, and a good many are 500 years old or more. The most famous is the Major Oak, which legend would tell you provided a safe hiding place for Robin Hood when the Sheriff was on his tail. Look at it now and, despite old-age spread and some scaffolding to support its limbs, you can easily imagine somebody disappearing into the voluminous foliage of its youth. This tree is thought to be about a thousand years old.

The Major Oak has a girth of about 35ft and its branches spread out over 92ft. It is very close to the visitor centre car park and attracts many admirers. Yet if you simply wander away from it in any direction you will soon be plunged into solitude, and you will come upon many oak trees of impressive girth and antiquity. They wrinkle and stoop just as humans do, but take longer to do it.

To wander here is moving and, despite the strange shapes of the branches and the dark corners, it isn't spooky at all.

Several of the veteran oaks have been given names. The Major Oak isn't named after its size, but in honour of Major Hayman Rooke, who compiled a book about the forest's trees in 1789. Another is the famous Parliament Oak, named for the fact that King John assembled a parliament in 1212 by the tree to deal with a Welsh uprising. Not much of it remains now, but it is thought to be 1,200 years old.

A biological quirk of very old trees is that they harbour insects that are adapted to dead and decaying bark. With so little truly ancient woodland remaining it Britain, it is perhaps not surprising that such insects are often very rare indeed. In Sherwood Forest there are many species of beetles, flies, wood wasps and spiders in this category, and indeed the whole area is rich in these insects. If, on your wanderings, a fly buzzes past your nose, it has a higher chance of being rare than almost anywhere else.

The forest is superb for birds, and recently the RSPB has taken over part management of the old part of Sherwood Forest. Several rarities will immediately get birders excited: the fast-declining lesser spotted woodpecker is still found here, and the habitat is also ideal for the hawfinch, a bird with a beak so thick and strong that it can tackle cherry stones. Hawfinches are very shy and flush at the slightest disturbance, making for the treetops. The forest is excellent for siskins and redpolls, especially in the spring, while crossbills are sometimes present. Long-eared owls and woodcocks breed, too, and can be looked for on summer evenings.

The forest isn't all trees. Budby South 'Forest' is much more a wild heathland area dominated by heather, with a smattering of acid grassland. Harebells grow here in summer, once the bluebells have faded in the woodland. As well as containing another very rich, yet different suite of invertebrates, the heathland part of the forest is good for open country birds. Tree pipit and woodlark breed on the interface between wood and heath, while there is also a very healthy population of nightjars, a nocturnal bird that hunts over the open heath and woodland edge for moths and other night-flying insects.

Whether it is birds, or moths, or flies, or fungi – of which 200 species occur – the sheer richness of this area is evident even on a short stroll. This is a rare sort of richness, one borne of its sheer antiquity. You can feel it.

Seasonal highlights

Spring
Siskin, tree pipit, wood wasps

Summer
Woodcock, nightjar, moths

Autumn
Multiple spider species, rare fungi

Winter
Hawfinch, crossbill, grey squirrel

All year
Historic oaks, long-eared owl, lesser spotted woodpecker

Acorn and oak leaf

Overleaf: Sherwood Forest

51 Stiperstones

Where the Devil holds forth

Bog Visitor Centre, Shrewsbury, Shropshire SY5 0NG

Grid ref SO355979

Directions South of Shrewsbury take the A488 southwest through Pontesbury and Minsterley; after about a mile turn left to Snailbeach and through Stiperstones village to visitor centre

Lunch stop The Stiperstones Inn, Stiperstones, Snailbeach, Shropshire SY5 0LZ

Stiperstones is a prominent ridge to the southwest of Shrewsbury, close to the border between England and Wales. In fair weather it just looks like a ridge, but the slightest inclement conditions turn it into a dramatic place like the set of an adventure film.

You begin to believe in the local legend that claims that the Devil was flying back from Ireland carrying rocks in an apron (as you do), when the apron strings broke and deposited the rocks here, thus creating the Stiperstones and the soaring eminence known as the Devil's Chair. Watch out on the night of the winter solstice, too, when the bad guy returns to sit on his chair and have an audience with the local witches and other ne'er-do-wells. That wouldn't be a good time to go walking.

As it is, the jagged Ordovician quartzite rocks of the Stiperstones ridge are extremely ancient, some 480 million years old, meaning that they witnessed the Age of the Dinosaurs come and go. During the last Ice Age prolonged freezing shattered them into the millions upon millions of shiny pieces you see while walking upon them today, and caused the sharp-pointed silhouettes of the topmost crags. The quartzite apparently attracts lightning strikes, so it is worth being very careful if a thunderstorm is rolling in.

The rocks might be white and shiny, but if Natural England, in charge of the National Nature Reserve here, has its way, the rest will all be purple. The Stiperstones ridge was once a 6-mile hill of unbroken heather, but in the 1940s many commercial coniferous plantations were planted, somewhat blighting the landscape and reducing the biodiversity. So Natural England has begun the long-term Back to Purple project, restoring some of the heathland. On your visit you are likely to see some Natural England employees, albeit ones with four legs – Hebridean sheep and Exmoor ponies keeping the grass down in the new heathland. This should help some of the wildlife that already uses the heather, such as the magnificent emperor moth, fox moth, butterflies such as the grayling, and common lizards.

The whole area lies in the Shropshire Hills Area of Outstanding Natural Beauty, and visitors are well catered for. There are several car parks, and facilities in the village of Stiperstones and at the Bog Visitor Centre to the southwest of Cranberry Rock. It is a case of choosing your path if you wish to avoid other visitors. If it's a wet, cold day, they will do the avoiding for you.

It's a good place for wildlife. One of the most obvious inhabitants must be the red grouse, a game bird which lives off the shoots and other parts of heather, and has the plumage to match. On a spring morning you can often hear its display call, a noisy 'go-back, go-back' delivered in flight. On a fine day at almost any time of year you are likely to be serenaded by a skylark, and ravens are common, soaring over with a deep 'cronk-cronk'. In the breeding season the meadow pipit, a small lark-like bird, delivers a very repetitive and interminable 'sip-sip-sip...' song, and if you spot small birds perching boldly atop the heather or bracken you might find that they are stonechat (orange breast, black head and prominent white neck patch) or whinchat (apricot breast, white eyebrow). Red kites and buzzards are also common overhead.

In season, the area is excellent for flowers. Ling heather is everywhere, while a little yellow relief comes in the form of tormentil and common cow-wheat. There is an excellent moss and lichen flora on the rocks. The higher heathland has both cowberry and its near-namesake crowberry. And perhaps the most sought-after of all is the delicate yellow and purple mountain pansy, which grows in the fields towards the base of the ridge.

If you have energy to spare, a mile and a half to the north of the Devil's Chair is a remarkable area of open woodland of pure holly. You can immediately guess when visiting that this is an ancient place, owing to the gnarled shapes and broad girths of the holly trees. Some are thought to be as much as 300 years old, making them among the oldest trees in Britain. They were once cut to provide food for cattle because the leaves, although prickly, are highly nutritious.

This holly grove is a strange, evocative place, especially if you visit on a dark, misty day. You might wish to make a hasty exit.

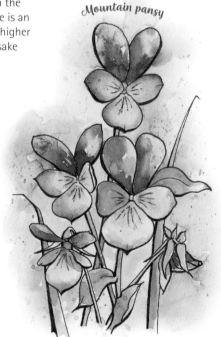

Mountain pansy

52 Sutton Bridge

Big skies and real solitude

East Bank, Sutton Bridge, Spalding, Lincolnshire PE12 9QJ

Grid ref TF492256 (east lighthouse)

Directions From Sutton Bridge, go over bridge and immediately left up East Bank

Lunch stop The Chequers, Gedney Dyke, Spalding, Lincolnshire PE12 0AJ

Go north from Sutton Bridge and you meet the Wash. This is the largest estuary in Britain, the square indentation between East Anglia and the bulge of Lincolnshire, a massive area of sea, sand and saltmarsh. It is one of the last true wildernesses in Britain. There must be thousands of places out there where no person has ever stood, because if they did they would sink and perish. On the embankments here you can find a very real solitude, looking over open expanses with nobody about. It's a place of big skies, where frequently grey cloud and grey sea meet and mingle and you can hardly tell one from the other.

At Sutton Bridge the River Nene disgorges; this is one of four rivers to empty into the Wash, the others being the Witham, the Welland and the Great Ouse. Although the Wash itself is a wild area, the rivers are not. Since Roman times they have been tamed, then straightened, and then straightjacketed with dykes and flood defences. Once the rivers meandered, now they follow tamely along cuts. But the Wash itself is the untamed morass of puked-up mud beyond, covered twice daily by the tide in an endless recycling of nutrients. The great unwashed Wash, you might say.

Around 21,942 acres of the estuary are protected as a National Nature Reserve, the largest in England, which equates to less than half of the total area. It only encompasses a small fringe of the Wash shoreline, and all the rest is saltmarsh, mud and sand. You might ask yourself why anybody would want to preserve this intertidal ooze. And that is a problem, because few people 'get' estuaries, or their value.

As it happens, estuaries are fantastically productive. In every square foot of estuarine mud there are simply thousands of organisms of three main groups: worms, crustaceans (such as shrimps) and molluscs, the last named in the form of seashells such as mussels. Some of these are edible for us, of course, and they are all edible for birds. For birds, the mud is their saviour; they can spend their lives feeding in roughly the same area every day, and the food never runs out, refreshed every tide.

It goes without saying, then, that the Wash is full of birds. This is particularly the case in winter, when thousands upon thousands retreat down to Britain from their breeding areas in the north. The sheer numbers are mind-boggling: 20,000 brent geese, 46,000 lapwings, 36,000 dunlins and 16,000 bar-tailed godwits, to name just a few. Very large numbers of many other species occur, too: birds such as pink-footed goose (from Iceland), knot (from Greenland), redshank, pintail, wigeon and cormorant. It would be pointless to give figures for them all, because this is a big area and you will only meet a small sample, but it shows what is out there on the mud. In the spring and autumn, large numbers rely on the Wash as a sort of motorway service station where they can feed during their migration.

The large numbers of birds attract a lot of the wrong kind of interest, and in winter in particular, the Wash is awash with predators, including merlin, peregrine, sparrowhawk and harriers. Short-eared owls prefer voles, and hunt along the sea wall and on the fringes of the saltmarsh. The sightings of such birds punctuating a good walk are as exciting to us as they are alarming to the chosen prey.

It is easy to dip one's toes into the Wash experience. Go north from Sutton Bridge and you will find two lighthouses, one on the west of the River Nene cut and one on the east. There are car parks on each side and you can follow west and east respectively. The east lighthouse used to be owned by the great naturalist and conservationist Sir Peter Scott, who experienced a profound conversion from keen wildfowler to nature conservationist while in these parts, transitioning from killing to preserving. A 10.5-mile trail, named the Sir Peter Scott Walk, starts at the lighthouse and follows along the top of the flood defences all the way to West Lynn, although you can cut back halfway and follow your map through the quiet, flat fenland lanes. It is a perfect way to escape the frustrations of life.

Don't let yourself get frustrated with the wildlife in this faraway place where the inhabitants are often just dots on the mud or lumps on the sand (common seals). Take binoculars with you.

Seasonal highlights

Spring
Shelduck, skylark, fish nurseries

Summer
Scurvy-grass, glasswort, redshank

Autumn
Mussels, sea aster, hoverflies

Winter
Bar-tailed godwit, knot, pink-footed goose

All year
Ragworm, common seal, oystercatcher

Oystercatcher

53 Titley Pool

Peaceful, secluded and delightful

Off Eywood Lane, Titley, Kington, Herefordshire HR5 3RU

Grid ref SO323594

Directions Turn left on outskirts of Titley towards Eywood at Eywood Lane

Lunch stop The Stagg Inn and Restaurant, Titley, Herefordshire HR5 3RL

Titley Pool is nestled in a quiet corner of a peaceful part of the country, in the west of Herefordshire very close to the Welsh border. Offa's Dyke is just over a mile away. It is one of those gems that, in normal circumstances, would be known only to locals and kept secret from the rest of the world. But in a county with very little standing fresh water, this pool and its neighbours Garden Pool and Flintsham Pool are something of a draw, accounting for a significant percentage of the total surface area of lake. Herefordshire wildlife enthusiasts come here to get their fix of such strange creatures as ducks and fish.

Pied flycatcher

The lakes are natural in origin. They are 'kettle lakes' formed from blocks of ice shearing off glaciers and creating hollows, which then fill up with water from the melted ice and keep filled with rainwater. Titley Pool has been enlarged and dammed. It is the only accessible one, the others being entirely privately owned. The Herefordshire Wildlife Trust looks after Green Wood on the south side, allowing a view of the shore, and there is a permissive path that leads towards the dam. There is one bird hide. The habitats include the lake, an island, the ancient woodland and some flowery meadows, all crammed into a small but luscious area.

You approach from Kington, which is west of Hereford and Leominster, the nearest decent-sized towns. From Kington, go north up the B4355 to Titley and turn left at the Stagg Inn on to Eywood Lane. After half a mile or so, at SO322597, turn left again and proceed down the old driveway of Eywood House (the lake is sometimes called Eywood Pool) to a car park. From here it's a short walk to the hide looking over the lake, although the paths are often very muddy.

Although there is a bit of everything here, the pool is best known for its birds. However, we are not talking rarities: Titley Pool is just a delightful place with everyday stuff. Great crested grebes are a feature, and through the summer it is possible to see their magnificent courtship displays. The two birds often fluff out their face ruffs and shake their heads at each other, and their overall reddish brown colouration is magnificent. A brilliant blue flash signals the appearance of a kingfisher, while mallards, mute swans and coots also breed. In the winter the duck population expands to include tufted ducks, pochards, teal and, quite regularly, goosander. The goosander breeds in rivers nearby, and it is unusual among ducks in feeding almost exclusively on fish, which it obtains in an underwater chase – as do the grebes. The lake's population of fish is healthy, and includes pike, perch, roach and European eel. Grey herons are also all-year-round visitors.

The lake is surrounded by a ribbon of woodland, mainly of willow, alder and birch, with some rowan. These woods attract breeding warblers such as willow warbler, chiffchaff and blackcap, which join the resident woodland birds to make a delightful cacophony in the spring. Pied flycatcher has been recorded, and could potentially breed. The alder woodland often hosts siskins and redpolls in the winter months, the birds forming tight-knit flocks to forage on the seeds.

As for other stuff, you can see some common wetland plants such as the highly distinctive bulrush (great reedmace) with its 'furry' seedheads, and a number of sedges and rushes. There is a good display of bluebells in Green Wood in the late spring and a decent range of dragonflies and damselflies. You might spot bat boxes on the trees, which are monitored regularly by the very active Herefordshire Mammal Group.

A walk in the reserve won't take you long: an hour perhaps – plenty of time to enjoy a secluded break. If you have time, return to the pub and follow the Herefordshire Trail to Flintsham, the River Arrow (which rises in Wales), Titley Mill and Offa's Dyke. The water is clean, the air is clean, the countryside beatific. What more could you ask?

Seasonal highlights

Spring
Chiffchaff, willow warbler

Summer
Perch, roach, dragonflies

Autumn
Bulrush, docks

Winter
Ducks, including goosander and pochard

All year
Great crested grebe, grey heron, pike

54 Ufton Fields

An almost perfect backwater

Leamington Spa, Warwickshire CV33 9NY

Grid ref SP378613

Directions From Royal Leamington Spa take the A425 east towards Southam; at roundabout village of Ufton, take 2nd exit south on Harbury Lane and continue past double bend

Lunch stop The Stag at Offchurch, Welsh Road, Offchurch, Warwickshire CV33 9AQ

Here's a recipe for the perfect nature reserve. Take a patch of fallow ground, furrow it enough so that there are banks and hollows, to which you add water. Leave to grow naturally, forming woodland of all different types and stages. Allow in all kinds of wildlife. Place into 77 acres of otherwise unremarkable countryside within reach of large towns and cities. And, hey presto, you have Ufton Fields, near Leamington Spa, Warwickshire.

This is how Ufton Fields came into being, albeit not intentionally. In the 1950s this spot was quarried open cast for its limestone, and then abandoned. The works left the spoil in ridges, with deep furrows in between that collected rainwater and became pools and marshes. Years of neglect allowed the site to re-wild itself, although some trees were planted. Now it is carefully managed by the Warwickshire Wildlife Trust so that the calcareous and neutral grassland areas are kept free of encroaching scrub. There is a car park, paths and even some bird hides. Even so, much of the time it is quiet and peaceful.

The wildlife doesn't mind at all that the place isn't completely natural, and whatever strand of natural history most floats your boat, you will find something of interest. Its main importance happens to lie in its invertebrates. Thousands of people flock here each year to see the nationally rare soldier fly *Stratiomys furcata* and two rare beetles. Of course, they don't really, but the site is also excellent for two sets of summery insects: dragonflies and butterflies. There are 15 species of dragonfly and 28 butterflies on the reserve list (more may have been added recently), pretty good for an unremarkable Midlands site. The more unusual species include the highly localised variable damselfly, which is one of the powder-blue ones you see flying around in mid-summer, and ruddy darter, which is mainly a southern species in Britain. The butterflies are abundant, and include marbled white (which, oddly, is related to the meadow brown and its ilk, not to the whites), the chalk-loving grizzled and dingy skippers, and small blue. The latter are all relatively scarce and declining species.

Those who are after wildflowers won't be disappointed, because there is a terrific range here in the varied habitats. As ever, the orchids, the glittering reality stars of the plant world, take much of the attention. There is a six-pack of species, namely common spotted, early purple, bee, greater butterfly and man orchids, plus common twayblade. Of these, man orchid, with its bizarre flowers like hanging mannequins, is not found anywhere else in Warwickshire. Other good chalky flowers are here, too, although they don't scoop the awards: yellow-wort, wild basil, ploughman's spikenard and cowslip are all great in their own right.

No reserve is complete without its reptiles and amphibians, or 'herps' as they are often called. Those drawn to the cold-blooded will delight in common lizard, grass snake, common toad and both smooth and great crested newts. The latter, when they are breeding, share the waters with abundant life that would make any pond-dipper happy.

And then there are birds. More than 130 species have been recorded, with scope for more. Little grebes breed in the pools, and sometimes water rail does, too, in what must be an isolated site for this secretive bird. With all the wood and scrub around, it is great for warblers such as garden warbler and lesser whitethroat, and there are siskins and redpolls in the winter. Almost anything could turn up.

Let's go back to the recipe for the perfect nature reserve mentioned at the start. There was something left out, which was 'populated with responsible dog-walkers'. This seems not to be the case, and many visitors comment on the annoying dog poo on the path or, worse, placed in bags and just left behind, sometimes hanging on bushes. Shame on these rogue dog-walkers, spoiling this almost perfect backwater for everybody.

Marbled white butterfly

55 Wyre Forest

Ancient woodland glades full of wildlife

Dry Mill Lane, Bewdley, Worcestershire DY12 2LT

Grid ref SO772763

Directions South of Bewdley take B4190 east (Cleobury Road), then third left (Yew Tree Lane); bear left (The Lakes Road) and take second left (Dry Mill Lane) to the car park

Lunch stop The Mug House Inn and Angry Chef Restaurant, 12 Severnside North, Bewdley, Worcestershire DY12 1EE

Think of the West Midlands and enormous forests don't necessarily spring to mind. But the Wyre Forest is a *bona fide* Black Country location no more than 50 minutes from the centre of Birmingham, and it is most certainly a place in which you can lose yourself and see nobody for hours. In all it covers 5,930 acres – you could fit nearby Kidderminster into it and have some space left over, and it encompasses many different types of woodland, as well as some old orchards and meadows. It is one of the largest ancient woodlands in Britain, but no square mile is quite the same.

Not only is the Wyre Forest big, it is also very special, with an outstanding diversity of plants and animals, some of them rare and localised. Few groups of creatures are not stunningly represented.

A fifth of the forest is a National Nature Reserve, while other organisations seem to have fought it out for the rest – the Forestry Commission, the Worcestershire Wildlife Trust and even the West Midland Bird Club. Wherever you go in the forest, there is the chance of seeing something special.

The forest lies on a plateau west of the River Severn, with such varying geology that one part of the wood may have a completely different atmosphere to the rest. For example, on much of the plateau the soils are acidic, and oaks and birches intermix; however, on the limestone sections there are woods of ash and hazel, with a completely different ground flora. Add in the many conifer stands, in different shades of dark green, with almost no ground flora, and you have an idea of how there are forests within the forest, pockets that are seemingly self-contained and with a separate identity.

Cutting through the plateau, more or less from west to east, is the gorgeous Dowles Brook and its valley, which is the richest part of the whole area. This is the heart of the forest, and where any visitor should head as a priority. You can walk from the Forestry Commission Visitor Centre at Callow Hill, but a quicker way is to take the B4190 road from Bewdley town centre, turning right after half a mile into Lakes Road, then continuing through the estate to Dry Mill Lane.

From the car park walk west along the brook, looking out for kingfishers, grey wagtails, dippers and even mandarin ducks! The oaks on the valley overflow with birds, and butterflies flit along the dappled shade next to the stream.

Seckley Wood, on the northeastern corner on the banks of the Severn, is another outstanding section. With a mixture of old oak and birch, plus some beeches and an adjacent cherry orchard, it is particularly good for birds, including pied flycatchers, wood warblers and hawfinches. From the top there is a terrific view of the river below, and the atmosphere is sublimely calm.

The wildlife interest is so great that it is difficult to do this place justice – if there were wildlife Oscars to give out, the forest would do well in every category. Take the outstanding butterflies award: that would go to one of the largest populations of pearl-bordered fritillaries in England, while the supporting 'actors' would be small pearl-bordered fritillary, wood white, white admiral and purple hairstreak, with special mention to speckled wood, which abounds here. On the bird front, some of the less common breeding birds not already mentioned are long-eared owl, redstart, lesser redpoll and crossbill.

You get the idea. The easiest mammal to see apart from grey squirrel is probably the fallow deer, which is very common. There are lots of scarcer ones, of course, including hazel dormouse, otter, yellow-necked mice and even polecat, although all of these are highly elusive.

Thankfully plants stay still and aren't nocturnal, so it should be possible to see a fine range on a walk through the woodland at any time of day, in any weather. Botanists will lick their lips at the prospect of finding lily of the valley, common columbine, wood cranesbill and intermediate wintergreen as well as trees of exceptional diversity.

The diversity of almost everything is exceptional. Take the 33 butterflies, 1,150 moths and 1,400-plus species of fungi. There are even plenty of reptiles (adders are a feature), club-tailed dragonflies on the River Severn and lampreys in the brook. The forest is even famous for a caddisfly; it is the British stronghold for our only terrestrial species, *Enoicyla pusilla*. The larvae of all our other caddisflies live in the water, while this one lives in leaf litter.

Having visited this amazing place, perhaps the next time you hear the term 'West Midlands' you'll think of glades full of wildlife rather than streets full of people.

Seasonal highlights

Spring
Pied flycatcher, tree pipit, wood white

Summer
Wood cranesbill, club-tailed dragonfly, pearl-bordered fritillary

Autumn
Fungi, adder, land caddis

Winter
Crossbill, siskin

All year
Fallow deer, woodpecker, hawfinch

Fallow deer

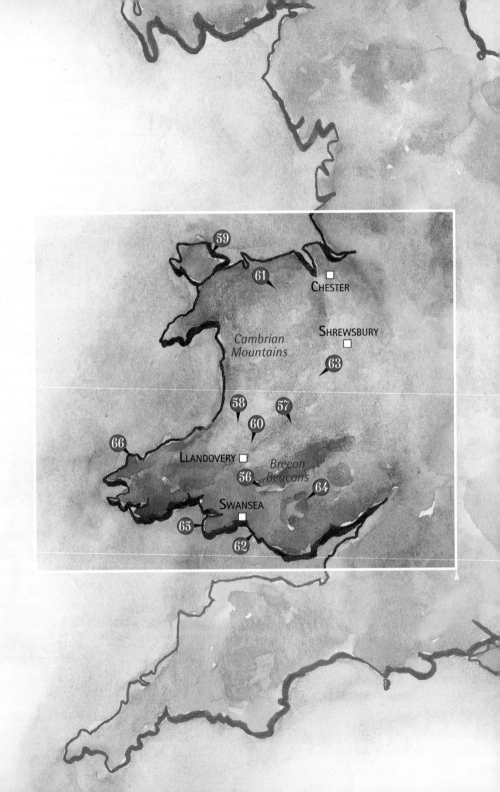

Wales

56 Allt Rhongyr & Craig-y-Rhiwarth

Hill-top nature reserve

Penwyllt, Swansea, Powys SA9 1GE

Grid ref SN852156

Directions Just beyond Pen-y-cae take right turn to Penwyllt; park after about a mile

Lunch stop The Tanners Arms, Defynnog, Powys LD3 8SF

Allt Rhongyr is a hill above the Upper Swansea Valley that is just within the southern border of the Brecon Beacons National Park. It commands delicious views over the River Tawe, as well as an excellent range of plants and birds. It lies above the attractive Victorian garden at Craig-y-Nos Country Park, where you can park if you are happy with a rugged walk.

The nature reserve is a relatively new one, acquired in 2013 by the Brecknock Wildlife Trust, although it lies right next to another, Craig-y-Rhiwarth. The Welsh names of the reserves should give you a clue what they are like to visit: *allt* is Welsh for hill and *craig* is Welsh for crag. The going can be steep and slippery, with loose rocks and scree, particularly at Criag-y-Rhiwarth. There are also grazing animals on site: ponies and sometimes cattle, and the former might take a liking to your picnic. Electric fences keep them in the correct grazing. Survive all this and you should have a fabulous wildlife walk.

Although there is some acidic grassland, most of the botanical interest arises from the limestone bedrock. Allt Rhongyr offers open slopes, while Craig-y-Rhiwarth is woodland; the former is easier to explore than the latter, but both have terrific stuff. For example, not many places host a plant that is critically endangered on a worldwide scale, but on the cliffs of Craig-y-Rhiwarth a tree known as the thin-leaved whitebeam grows among the ash trees. It is found at this site and one other, with fewer than 50 individual trees altogether.

The flowers of the limestone at Allt Rhongyr include many favourites. In the spring, you will see ranks of yellow cowslips and creeping mats of common dog-violets. The

Lily of the valley

Wood spurge

splendid bugle, which with its upright stems and multi-storied complex blue flowers pretends to be an orchid, is a feature of both grassland and woodland edge. It is in fact related to dead-nettles and mints. Later in the year, in the flush of summer, the soil by the scree and fragments of limestone pavement will be adorned with the generous yellow blooms of common rock-roses, the wispy stems of salad burnet and clusters of wild thyme, the latter giving off their characteristic aromatic scent, such a feature of chalk grassland everywhere. Other attractive plants here include the field scabious, an upright plant with dense flowerheads of the most perfect mauve imaginable. In the rockier places, particularly on the cliffs of Craig-y-Rhiwarth, grows the delightful mossy saxifrage, with its five perfect-white petals. This looks like the classic alpine flower, and cultivars are common in rockeries.

The woodland is no less diverse than the grasslands. There are stands of oak, birch and ash, some on level ground and some very steep. Allt Rhongyr has a superb display of bluebells at the height of spring, while the ash woods on the slopes of Craig-y-Rhiwarth have beauties such as lily of the valley and wood spurge.

While enjoying the flowers of this part of the world, you will doubtless be happily distracted by the sounds of the birds. In the woods, redstarts sing their slightly mournful, sighing ditties alongside more confident singers such as the robins and chaffinches that abound here, as well as willow warblers and treecreepers. In the more open areas look especially for the wheatear. Related to robins and restarts, this is a ground-nesting species, here using rocky crevices to site its nest. The male has a black mask on its head, a grey back and a creamy-white breast.

This reserve, then, has much to offer the wildlife enthusiast and, besides the views, it also once held an Iron Age hillfort at its highest point. The remains of the hillfort are found at the west end of Allt Rhongyr, next to the clifftop of Craig-y-Rhiwarth.

The main entrance to Allt Rhongyr is on the minor road to Penwyllt, off the A4067 half a mile south of Craig-y-Nos Country Park. A mile up here the road bends sharply and the entrance is to your left. If you begin at the country park, go through to the end and cross the River Tawe, then turn right following the river (the slopes of Craig-y-Rhiwarth are on your left) until a public footpath goes left at Rhongyr Uchaf. Follow it up the hill to the Allt Rhongyr reserve.

57 Bailey Einon

Total immersion in a rich woodland

Shaky Bridge picnic area, Llandrindod Wells, Powys LD1 5PD

Grid ref SO085612

Directions From Llandrindod Wells go south through town past hospital on left, left on Craig Road, straight on to Broadway and left on Cefnllys Lane out of town to picnic area

Lunch stop The Laughing Dog, Howey, Llandrindod Wells, Powys LD1 5PT

This walk won't keep you long, but it is a delightful example of total immersion into a rich woodland, one that is alongside a gleefully gurgling river – what site in Wales isn't? This Radnorshire Wildlife Trust reserve is just a short distance from the spa town of Llandrindod Wells, and it is easily possible to walk from there if you want a longer excursion.

Otherwise, drive just east of town along Cefnllys Lane. At the end of the houses take the sharp right turning uphill, and after a short while you will see a Powys County Council sign for the Shaky Bridge picnic area. In these days of health and safety, any shaky bridge would make councillors quake, so long ago the bridge over the River Ithon was made firm, but less interesting. The path over the bridge leads to the 14th-century St Michael's Church, but for the nature reserve go straight on through the kissing gate. A boardwalk takes you into the wood, and then you'll need walking boots to cope with some steep and slippery sections. However, the whole walk is only about a mile, and you can loop back halfway to cut it shorter still.

If you come at the right time in spring (late April), you will immediately be overwhelmed by the display of bluebells, a sure indicator that this is ancient woodland. However, while these are a treat, a less common sight alongside them are the imperious early purple orchids, which are rare in these parts. They are rather like big, better-decorated brothers to the bluebells, with a deep pink colour, a cluster of complicated blooms and purplish spots on their large, fleshy leaves. Their air of nobility is somewhat undermined by the smell they give off, like a tom cat. Other woodland flowers to look out for include such spring and early summer staples as greater stitchwort, dog's mercury and yellow archangel.

The wood here is composed of sessile oak and ash, with a hazel understorey, which is coppiced by volunteers. The path isn't narrow, but it often feels hemmed in and atmospheric with the abundance of vegetation in this damp climate. The reserve is excellent for myriads of mosses and lichens. It makes you feel small yet part of it all.

Seasonal highlights

Spring
Bluebell, early purple orchid, pied flycatcher

Summer
Sand martin, banded demoiselle, yellow archangel

Autumn
Willow warbler, blackcap

Winter
Lichens, kingfisher, lesser spotted woodpecker

All year
Sessile oak, swan mussel, moss-covered branches

At any time of the year the woods are full of birds, and a very impressive 40 species have been recorded breeding. This includes the increasingly rare lesser spotted woodpecker, which favours the alders by the river. This is an extremely elusive species and you might have better luck coming across Lord Lucan wandering along the trails. In the summer the dense vegetation resounds to birdsong, especially of warblers, with the shiver of wood warblers, the sweet descending scale of willow warblers, the incessant repeating of the chiffchaff, the liquid shout of the blackcap and the garbled, slightly demented babble of the garden warbler. Working all these out, in addition to chaffinches and other common resident birds, can be an overwhelming task. It could just be better to listen.

You soon come to good views of the River Ithon, and here you have the chance to see some different birds. Kingfishers are often seen along here, as are grey wagtails, dippers and also goosanders, a fast-flying, fast-fishing, fast-living duck. Sand martins nest in the banks in small colonies, and these delicate, swallow-like birds make little flatulent sounds.

You might see large shells along the river. These belong to swan mussels, which are big freshwater molluscs that can grow to nearly 8in (20cm) long. They are smelly and used by anglers as bait. More importantly, they attract otters to this stretch of river. They are sometimes seen near the Shaky Bridge, and even within the town of Llandrindod Wells itself.

You'd be pretty lucky to see an otter on this short walk in the semi-wild countryside of Wales. But you will always see something delightful, whether it be a banded demoiselle dancing over the river or a spotted flycatcher trying to catch the same. The wildlife doesn't realise that bustling Llandrindod Wells is just nearby and, during your total immersion, you might just forget it too.

Bluebell

58 Cors Caron

Large raised bog with abundant wildlife

Tregaron, Ceredigion SY25 6JF

Grid ref SN692625

Directions From Tregaron take the B4343 north out of town, drive just under 2 miles to car park

Lunch stop Y Talbot, The Square, Tregaron, Ceredigion SY25 6JL

It is always a surprise to come across Cors Caron. Lying amidst the rolling hills and sheep country of Central Wales, it is an unexpected wide plain of pale brown grassy swampland, with scattered trees. Half-close your eyes and it could be a savannah, with elephants and giraffes around the next corner.

It isn't big animal country, but Cors Caron, translated as Tregaron Bog after the nearby town, is special. It is a large raised bog – in fact three adjacent raised bog domes – formed 12,000 years ago at the end of the glacial period, when a large shallow lake formed in the valley. Over time this lake became covered with vegetation, which eventually died and built up into peat. The layers soon accumulated above the water table (hence 'raised') and became more acidic, giving rise to an unusual plant community. Apparently, this is the best-preserved peat bog in the whole of the country.

You might not easily appreciate the value of bogs, particularly the specifics of the various plant communities. However, what this site does provide is a rich variety of wildlife that everybody can enjoy. It is also a superbly accessible National Nature Reserve, managed by Natural Resources Wales, with 2 miles of excellent boardwalk, good enough to take a pushchair or wheelchair. In some ways, the smart hides and facilities are slightly at odds with a 12,000-year-old habitat, but bogs need fans, and there aren't enough of them.

So, what better ambassador for bogs could there be than an otter? One of the reasons that Cors Caron is dedicated as a Site of Special Scientific Interest (SSSI) is that otters occur here, particularly in the pools and in the River Teifi, drawn by the high populations of fish and frogs. They are never easy to see, but it is worth the effort of being in the hide at dusk or dawn, or by the river next to the bridge (Pont Einon) carrying the A485. Another special mammal that occurs, but is seen even less often than the otter, is the polecat. Central Wales has long been a stronghold for this elusive carnivore, which also has a strong association with water, predating on frogs and toads.

Birds, though, are easy enough, and there are always plenty of these around. The locals made a big effort to conserve the local red kite population here when

Seasonal highlights

Spring
Sedges, marsh cinquefoil, snipe

Summer
Bogbean, large heath, rosy marsh moth

Autumn
Dragonflies, greenshank, fish

Winter
Teal, whooper swan, willow tit

All year
Otter, polecat, red kite

Dragonfly

it was perilously low, and the fact that kites are easy to see here now is thanks to them. The bog is generally a great place for any raptor that thrives in open country, so it is no surprise that hen harriers and merlins winter here, one specialising in low, slow flight over long grass and the other relying on a dashing, low-level approach. Barn owls, which have a similar hunting style to hen harriers, take over the twilight shift.

In winter the bog is well stocked with wildfowl, including a small flock of whooper swans. However, in conservation terms it is more significant for its breeding birds, many of which are wetland specialists in decline. Curlew and snipe breed, as well as teal and water rail. Willow tits breed in the surrounding woods, as do redstarts and pied flycatchers, with a few whinchats in the bog itself.

The site has all manner of other specialities. Those who like insects will appreciate the large heath butterfly, here at its southern limit in Britain. There is also a moth, the rosy marsh moth, which was thought to be extinct in our country until being rediscovered in Wales – and it is quite rosy, too. Sixteen species of dragonflies have been found here. Botanists will be pleased with the white frilly, lacy flowers of bogbean, the yellow stars on spikes of bog asphodel, the woolly heads of the cottongrasses and the minute details of all the sedges, rushes and grasses. The white-beaked sedge is the food plant of the large heath.

With its abundant year-round wildlife, good facilities and satisfyingly wild complexion, Cors Caron is in danger of giving bogs a good name.

59 Cors Goch

Complicated little gem in a quiet valley

Tyn-y-Gongl, Anglesey LL74 8RY

Grid ref SH504817

Directions On Anglesey take the A5025 north towards Benllech. Turn left along minor road and through Llanbedrgoch; after 1 mile entrance is on left

Lunch stop The Ship Inn, Red Wharf Bay, Anglesey LL75 8RJ

This reserve is an absolute gem that is set in a quiet valley in Anglesey and is looked after by the North Wales Wildlife Trust. It is complicated to get here, complicated to work your way around, and complicated to understand how all the different parts of the landscape – fen, heath, woodland, scrub and grassland – fit together. In addition, the underlying geology is – well, you get the idea.

The Anglesey Fens, of which this is one of four, are particularly unusual because they are fed by water that has passed through the underlying bedrock of limestone, and are thus lime-rich. Most places where there is a deep layer of peat become acid bogs rather than lime-rich fens. Sixteen thousand years ago, glaciers gouged this valley out, and peat accumulated in the gouges: it is this which has now transformed into fenland. Just to add to the mix, some of the underlying rock is not limestone but sandstone, and here the soil is acidic. The result on the ground is sometimes plain to see – acid-loving heather grows next to lime-loving thyme and rock-rose – but you could be forgiven for getting confused.

No matter; if you get the chance, this is a very special place, worth getting to over the Menai Bridge from the mainland and taking the A5025 towards Benllech. Turn left along the minor road and through Llanbedrgoch; after about a mile there is an entrance to the left, through a large gate. This entrance will take you into the reserve and along to a boardwalk. There are then three routes (indicated on the display board at the entrance), one a short taster and the others much longer, taking several hours. The paths are muddy and the boardwalks are often slippery, but keep going!

The sheer variety in the reserve is astonishing. Numbers give a hint; there are 19 species of butterflies on the list (including marsh and small pearl-bordered fritillaries) and 15 dragonflies and damselflies (including the rare southern damselfly), each with their own specific requirements. And take the orchids. Orchids are the divas of the plant world: everything must be just right for them, equivalent to a famous actor who complains of being fed the wrong type of caviar. Yet here is an impressive range of species cheek by jowl. There are early

Barn owl

Seasonal highlights

Spring
Sedge warbler, orchids,
common butterwort

Summer
Southern damselfly, marsh
fritillary, grasshopper
warbler

Autumn
Heather, gorse, tormentil

Winter
Raptors, owls, wildfowl

All year
Stoneworts (freshwater
algae), rushes, sedges

purple orchids, green-winged orchids and early marsh orchids (woodland, limestone grassland, damp areas) for example, all within the reserve. Later on in the year there are lesser butterfly orchids, not in woods but in boggy areas. There are marsh fragrant orchids and marsh helleborines. Sometimes half a dozen orchid species are found virtually as neighbours, and there are 10 species in all.

This reserve is also rich in plants at the opposite end of the glamour stakes from orchids: the sedges and rushes such as saw-sedge, great fen-sedge, and black bog-rush and blunt-flowered rush. Botanists can literally immerse themselves in studying these.

Birds add a year-round dimension. There is a reasonable list of breeding species, among them lapwing, grasshopper warbler, lesser whitethroat, reed bunting, sedge warbler, stonechat and yellowhammer. Barn owls also occur, hunting by flying low over the open parts of the site. In the autumn and winter these predators are joined by marsh and hen harriers, while many water birds use both the reedy sections and the open water, such as Llyn Cadarn. Snipe are common and wildfowl use the lakes.

This is the sort of reserve where the deeper you delve, the more unusual stuff you find – hedgehog stonewort, anyone? Sometimes it finds you instead; dip your bare feet in the water and you might find a medicinal leech taking a fancy to you. If it's any consolation, the leech is a rare animal.

This is the sort of place to get stuck in!

60 Dinas

The perfect mid-Wales location

Llandovery, Carmarthenshire SA20 0PG

Grid ref SN788471

Directions From Llandovery go left by station onto A483 (New Road), then left on Cilycwm Road

Lunch stop The King's Head, 1 Market Square, Llandovery, Carmarthenshire SA20 0AB

If you were to dream up the perfect mid-Wales location, you could do no better than here. The 128-acre Dinas reserve is on a mountainside, next to a tumbling stream, encompassing a knoll covered by oaks – vivid green in spring and turning crispy brown in autumn. The nearest town, Llandovery, is almost a village, and the reserve is on a road almost to nowhere. It is peaceful yet bracing, isolated yet accessible, and the walk is mainly flat but with some adventurous sections. And to cap it all, it is bursting with wildlife. The singing birds would practically deafen you if the roar of the torrent of the rivers – the Afon Tywi and Afon Doethie, which meet here – didn't do it first.

It is a reserve of the RSPB (along with Gwenffrwd next door) about 10 miles north of Llandovery on the minor road that passes through Rhandirmwyn and on to Llyn Brianne dam. There is a car park (room for 12, which is usually excessive), an information hut, benches, information boards and even a boardwalk; all the mod cons of a nature reserve, even one so isolated. From the road starts a circular walk, which is 2.5 miles long. The first bit is along the boardwalk, next to delightful woodland by a stream, and then it is stout walking boots all the way. Further on, along the Tywi, you'll need to do as much bobbing and weaving over the rocks as the dippers that live in the torrent. While you are trying to keep your balance, look out too for the lemon-yellow underparts of the grey wagtail, and the bottom-wagging common sandpiper, both of which flourish in this habitat. The deeper stretches of river hold goosanders, so you might see these powerful ducks fly past. Kingfishers also visit from time to time.

One bird you can hardy fail to see at Dinas is the red kite, which is now widespread and common in Central Wales. In an age when people feed red kites in their gardens in the Home Counties, it is easy to forget that this magnificent bird was quite recently on the verge of extinction in Britain. There were fewer than 20 pairs in the 1960s and 1970s, all in Wales. And some of the last kites managed to hold out here. Of course, since then the bird has recovered naturally in Wales and has been reintroduced to the rest of the UK, but when you see one

Spring
Marsh marigold, pied
flycatcher, wood warbler

Summer
Gold-ringed dragonfly,
yellow flag iris, ragged
robin

Autumn
Common hawker, fungi,
chiffchaff

Winter
Peregrine, goshawk, dipper

All year
Lush woodland, red kite,
buzzard

over these hills, soaring through the sky and flaunting that long, forked tail, you should spare a thought for the local conservationists who worked hard to ensure their protection.

Red kites are not the only raptors in this gorgeous area. Buzzards are abundant, and often share the thermals with kites so that you can see the difference between these two big birds of prey. The buzzard has broader wings and a shorter tail, and when soaring it holds its wings up in a shallow V, while the kite holds its wings flat or slightly arched downwards. The wild miaow of the buzzard is easy to appreciate in the early spring, when the birds are marking out their territories. It is well worth keeping an eye out for peregrine falcons, too, which nest in this area, and even for their diminutive relative, the merlin. Goshawks occur in the nearby forests.

The treetops resound to birdsong from February until July, first from resident species such as blackbirds, chaffinches, and both marsh and willow tits. In April these are joined by smart pied flycatchers, redstarts and various warblers, including blackcap, chiffchaff, willow and wood warblers. Cuckoos arrive in May, while tree pipits sing in the open areas next to the wood. On a good day, you are drenched in tuneful natural sound. It is total immersion.

Spring and summer bring a succession of blooms, firstly of bluebells, which are everywhere, and then such delights as ragged robin and yellow flag iris in the wetter areas. The autumn is every bit as delightful, with the second big bloom of the year: fungi on the woodland floor, surrounded by burnished fallen leaves. The summer burst of insects includes a reasonable butterfly list and several good dragonflies including the common hawker (which isn't as common as it sounds) and the smart and fast-flying golden-ringed dragonfly.

Dinas, though, isn't about lists of species; it is all about being plunged into an isolated place that is far from the human treadmill, yet vibrant at the same time. This is a gem of a location, the epitome of what the Cambrian Mountains have to offer.

Red kite

61 Gors Maen Llwyd

A tapestry of interesting habitats

B4501, Denbigh, Denbighshire LL22 8UY

Grid ref SH970580

Directions 7 miles southwest of Denbigh on the B4501

Lunch stop Ty Gwyn Inn, Betws-y-Coed, Conwy, Clwyd LL24 0SG

The Denbigh Hills are a neglected corner of Wales. Just to the west lies the tourist trap of Snowdonia; Betws-y-Coed, the gateway to the National Park and Outdoor Accessories Shop Central, is only a few miles away. The mass of visitors is drawn towards the massif of Snowdon itself. If there was such a thing as a tourist shadow, Gors Maen Llwyd would be in the middle of it.

This, though, is a magnificent place, excitingly isolated, beautiful but intimidating. It is a land of open, windswept moors and conifer plantations next to the large, man-made lake, Llyn Brenig. Britain is the home of three-quarters of the world's moorland and here it is in abundance, together with a precious collection of wild things.

The Welsh name translates as 'Bog of the Grey Stone'. The eponymous rock lies just beyond the northeast branch of the lake, carried here on an ice sheet and summarily deposited when the ice melted, all alone. It is thought it has been standing on its spot for 14,000 years. It is easily reached along the path that runs next to the B4501, the road to Denbigh 7 miles to the north. There is parking along this road at SH970580 to the west of where it crosses the Afon Fechan. Another car park, next to a bird hide, can be reached by taking the minor road south at Bwlch-du a mile down to the archaeological trail by the side of the lake (SH983575). There are Neolithic burial sites here, and growing around them you might see the delicate yellow and purple blooms of the delightful mountain pansy.

Most of this 692-acre reserve, run by the North Wales Wildlife Trust, is blanket bog, but there are also areas of acid grassland, dry heath, wet flushes and conifers. It is this sort of tapestry of habitats that attracts what is probably the reserve's most celebrated bird, the black grouse.

Mountain pansy

Seasonal highlights

Spring
Mountain pansy,
whinchat, skylark

Summer
Sedges, heath speedwell,
curlew

Autumn
Weasel, great crested
grebe, red grouse

Winter
Goldeneye, goosander,
stoat

All year
Black grouse, brown hare

This game bird spends much of its time hidden among the trees, but in spring and summer, and sometimes for a while in autumn too, males gather together to display. They are a magnificent sight, with their royal-blue plumage, long, lye-shaped tail, white wing and under-tail flashes and red comb over the eye. The males make a fabulous cooing sound, interspersed with whooshing. The females are brown and barred and less exciting to look at, but, in a sense, they wear the trousers; they choose the male they like, mate only with him and then carry out the nesting duties alone. The males display from first light onwards. Red grouse occur on the reserve, too.

Speaking of displays, the black grouse don't have a monopoly on wildlife spectacles on this moorland. Brown hares breed here too, and on early mornings right through spring and summer you might see them boxing in 'mad March' style. These aggressive encounters are not, as you might think, between rival males, but are females rebuffing the unwanted advances of males. If you are very lucky you might see both displays on the same morning.

The brown hare is one of 15 species of mammals that have been seen on Gors Maen Llwyd; others include stoat and weasel, although seeing these carnivores is a matter of pure chance. For those who prefer relative certainties, you can always choose a summer day to go botanising instead. Apart from the mountain pansies, you can enjoy the bog asphodel and cottongrass on the bog, heath speedwell and harebell on the grassland, and sedges everywhere. The site is noted for sedges: there are 13 species of these grass-like flowering plants.

It is, though, the birds that stand out. Even on a casual walk in the spring or summer you should see delightful species such as common sandpiper (lake), great crested grebe (lake), skylark, whinchat, wheatear, snipe and curlew. It is an excellent place for birds of prey, too, with a very good chance of seeing red kite and half a chance of a goshawk. It is harsh in the winter in this area, but ducks such as goldeneye and goosander use the lake and can be seen from the hide.

In fact, it isn't only the birds that are amazing. Even if you see no wildlife at all you will revel in the desolation and solitude. The reserve has superb views, too, both across the Vale of Clwyd and the Irish Sea, and to Snowdonia in the west.

62 Kenfig Pool

An unexpected corner of wildness

Kenfig National Nature Reserve, Ton Kenfig, Bridgend, Glamorgan CF33 4PT

Grid ref SS802810

Directions Follow B4283 into North Cornelly; after 1.5km turn left (west) at crossroads and follow to reserve

Lunch stop Prince of Wales Inn, Ton Kenfig, Glamorgan CF33 4PR

Within sight of the Port Talbot Steelworks, one of the largest in the world, and close to the large conurbations of Swansea and Bridgend lies an unexpected corner of wildness. This is the natural lake of Kenfig Pool, set within the National Nature Reserve of Kenfig Dunes. The reserve is what is left of a vast system that once stretched from the mouth of the River Ogmore south of Bridgend all the way to the Gower Peninsula. Covering 8,154 acres, it was one of the biggest areas of sand dunes in the whole of Europe.

Dunes are an unusual habitat and they host some very particular plants and animals. Kenfig is not only a good place to find these, but to do so in a delightfully scenic and peaceful environment. There are various dune systems of different age and vegetation cover, freshwater pools ('slacks'), some reedbeds, woodland, scrub and, of course, the beach, from which you can see the cliffs of the nearby Gower Peninsula.

Shoveler duck

This is a large reserve, criss-crossed by numerous sandy paths. Many of the dunes are tall and quite similar to look at and it is surprisingly easy to get lost – which seems crazy when so much humanity is near at hand. There is a car park, visitor centre and interpretation boards dotted about, and you are free to wander as you wish. Kenfig is most famous for its orchids. At first sight you might not associate orchids with sand, but of course sand has a strongly calcareous element, with the breakdown of seashells into tiny fragments. Dunes have much in common, therefore, with inland chalk and limestone. The rain-

filled pools in the low parts of the dune system, known as slacks, additionally have the moisture beloved of marsh orchids and their allies. In all, about 15 species occur, flowering in shifts from April to August. There is an abundance of pyramidal, marsh fragrant and southern marsh orchids, together with less common species such as marsh helleborine and green-flowered helleborine, both classic dune-lovers.

The rarest orchid at Kenfig, though, is the fen orchid. Here it exists as a special dune-loving variation (the plant is normally found in fens), and Kenfig is now the only place in Britain to find this quirk. The peak time to see it is early to mid-June. It is a small orchid with greenish-yellow spiky flowers.

The fen orchid has been declining in recent years, so the Countryside Council for Wales has recently taken extreme measures to protect it. They have grubbed up some mature areas of overgrown dune and moved the sand to a new spot to ape the orchid's favourite habitat, new 'mobile' dunes. If this works it will encourage not just orchids, but other rarities that like newly formed dunes, such as the dune tiger beetle and the vernal bee. These are among a glittering array of unusual invertebrates at Kenfig. Others include the medicinal leech in the pool itself, the shrill carder bee and a weevil called *Tychius quinquepunctatus*.

Kenfig is also an excellent place for birds. The Pool attracts reasonable numbers of water birds, among them the water rail, Cetti's warbler, great crested grebe and a range of ducks. Teals and shovelers have bred. In winter there are more ducks, and the overall area is excellent for waders, including several hundred golden plovers in the surrounding fields. The beach and coast offer chances to see Manx shearwaters passing by, particularly in the summer months, and gannets, too. At Sker Point the rocky shore and beach attract turnstones, sanderlings and purple sandpipers.

Much more could be said about this site. There are many more special plants and invertebrates that could be listed, and that's without mentioning the animals of the intertidal zone. However, rather than list everything, it is probably better just to recommend that you visit this marvellous place, and see it all for yourself.

Seasonal highlights

Spring
Vernal bee (early *Colletes*), mayflies, sea holly

Summer
Fen orchid, dune tiger beetle, rock pools

Autumn
Shrill carder bee, Manx shearwater, autumn lady's tresses

Winter
Shoveler duck, winter stalkball, stinking iris

All year
Medicinal leech, Cetti's warbler, marram grass

63 Roundton Hill

Precious fragment of acid grassland

Old Church Stoke, Montgomery, Montgomeryshire SY15 6EL

Grid ref SO293946

Directions Take minor road from Churchstoke towards Old Church Stoke; avoid turning to latter, go round sharp bends and follow sign to reserve

Lunch stop The Three Tuns Inn, Salop Street, Bishop's Castle SY9 5BW

From a distance, Roundton Hill doesn't look much different to many other hills on the England/Wales border. Indeed, its neighbour, Corndon Hill, is both bigger and taller. Roundton Hill, though, is a National Nature Reserve and Corndon Hill isn't. There is a reason for this.

It doesn't sound attractive, but acid grassland is one of the most threatened habitats in Britain. Or, at least, unimproved acid grassland that has never been under the plough or reseeded is unusual. Here on Roundton Hill, a precious fragment has been preserved, and it hosts many rare and uncommon plants and fungi. This is what brings botanists and flower enthusiasts to this generally unheralded part of the country.

You need to be quick, though. Blink and you miss some of the action. Several of the hill's treasured plants are known technically as 'spring ephemerals', which means that they germinate, grow, flower and seed early and very quickly, in a matter of four or eight weeks. The thin soil on which they live soon dries out and becomes unsuitable for them. So you need to be here at least in April, when it is still cold and wet, to catch up with them.

To be honest, you might wonder what all the fuss is about, because not one of these spring ephemerals is in any way spectacular. And only one, the early forget-me-not, is even colourful, with the small sky-blue blooms typical of its relatives. The rest – shepherd's cress, common whitlow-grass, lesser chickweed and upright chickweed – are small, with white flowers. The chickweeds are particularly scarce, so you must appreciate them for their rarity.

There is a second bloom in the autumn, of fungi that depend on acid grassland. Several rare species occur on Roundton Hill, such as the pink waxcap, the date waxcap, the olive earth-tongue and the violet coral. And in the winter the site is also excellent for mosses, liverworts and lichens.

Even if these treasures weren't there, Roundton Hill would still be an excellent wild walk. To get here, if you follow the brown signs from the village of Churchstoke, they will lead you down a narrow road, over a ford and to a car park. One walk takes you back up the road towards a natural pond, next to which grows a large stand of colourful yellow monkeyflower. Frogs and newts are common here, and if you visit in summer it is good for dragonflies. Follow up the stream and into the wood and listen out for birds. Redstart, woodpeckers and tawny owl breed here, and on the slopes above so do linnet and wheatear. Ravens are a constant presence overhead.

Near the car park are some large and very ancient rabbit warrens, still very much occupied. These provide food for some mammalian predators, including fox, polecat, stoat and weasel, with buzzards also snacking on the occasional youngster as well. The other mammal highlight is bats. The hill used to be mined, and horizontal tunnels (adits) were cut into the side. Now long abandoned among the trees, these are an excellent habitat for roosting lesser horseshoe bats. These rare mites, no bigger than a plum, are uncommon in Britain, and nobody knows where the individuals that hibernate here actually breed in the summer. Natterer's, Daubenton's, brown long-eared and both common and soprano pipistrelles are also found on the reserve.

Despite all the wildlife at the base of the hill, no visit should be complete without an ascent, which takes an hour or two, following the well-marked route. There are more plants on the way up, such as mountain pansy, a profusion of common dog-violets (in spring), the splendid burning-yellow rock stonecrop, wild thyme, lady's bedstraw and, among the rocks, navelwort and a fern, the black spleenwort.

But lift your eyes upwards, too, because on a good day there is a 360-degree view of the Shropshire Hills to the east and the Welsh mountains to the west. There was once an Iron Age hillfort up here – so perhaps the ancients also recognised just how different Roundton Hill was.

Seasonal highlights

Spring
Early forget-me-not, rare chickweeds, shepherd's cress

Summer
Linnet, rock stonecrop, bats

Autumn
Violet coral, pink waxcap, black spleenwort

Winter
Mosses, lichens, red fox

All year
Acid grassland, polecat, rabbit

Common frog

64 Silent Valley

Proof of the healing power of nature

Cendl Terrace, Cwm, Ebbw Vale, Blaenau, Gwent NP23 6PZ

Grid ref SO186060

Directions In Cwm town centre turn right on to Cwm Terrace; road runs parallel with main road, and Cendl Terrace is third on right

Lunch stop JJ's, Marine Street, Cwm, Ebbw Vale, Gwent NP23 7ST

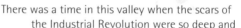

Crab apple

There was a time in this valley when the scars of the Industrial Revolution were so deep and all-pervasive that the landscape looked as though it had been flogged to death. The River Ebbw ran black, there were three huge slag heaps dominating the horizon, and smoke polluted the upland air. It was 1790 when the iron workings began, followed by coal mining at the end of the 19th century. In this area, the coal was near the surface, so it was mined from shallow pits or along horizontal adits, puncturing the hillside from the top and side and leaving gaping wounds. The footsteps of thousands of mineworkers and their working ponies pounded the ground. When the mines closed, the landscape was scarred and grey. It seemed impossible that life could return to the valley's corpse.

In fact, during the years of ravage, there were some farms along the valley near Cwm where, miraculously, open fields remained and woodland still stood, where the miners and their families could walk and relax on their occasional days off. Beechwoods grew on these hillsides at the westernmost point of their natural distribution. Some of the veteran beech trees were mature when the Industrial Revolution began. Now, more than 300 years old, they preside over a different kind of revolution.

In terms of heavy industry, the valley is indeed now silent and the wildlife is coming out of its shell. The woods of Cwm Merddog and Coed-tyn-y-Gelli, where the revolutionaries once took refuge, are now the centre of a recovering ecosystem. Even the waste tips of shale are being gently covered by the green of mosses, lichens, heather and grass, softening the contours. The air is now clean enough for beards of lichens to drape over the branches, testament to the smoke now cleared. In short, the Silent Valley is no longer choking.

Progress is such that the area is now a local nature reserve, and an impressive one at that. It has a wide range of everything – birds, mammals, flowers, trees – and not all of it is run-of-the-mill wildlife, either. The site holds a colony of the rare and declining small pearl-bordered fritillary, a glorious, showy orange butterfly that lepidopterists would go far to see. This insect, you might say, is the site's orange award for regeneration.

Every spring, the woods, which are ancient, are carpeted by a fabulous display of bluebells, as well as lesser celandines and wood sorrels. How this sight must have lifted the hearts of the miners, accustomed to so many hours in the gloom. Another common plant is the splendidly named opposite-leaved golden saxifrage. The word 'saxifrage' means 'stone-breaker', so the plant is a perfect metaphor for this post-industrial site.

The local nature reserve is a mixed bag. There is woodland, heathland, grassland and the Nant Merddog stream (a tributary of the Ebbw). Three marked trails run around the site, for all abilities, some steep and rocky, others level and gentle. The trees include alders, birch, holly, ash, hawthorn and lots of crab apples. Things to see and hear include yellow ants, common lizards and at least three species of grasshoppers – mottled, field and meadow.

But it is perhaps the birds that are the clearest sign that the land has got its breath back. In spring the chorus is superb. The green woodpeckers call with a sound like a demented laugh, the pied flycatchers sing a tuneless ditty, the redstarts sing mournfully, the blackcaps shout, the chiffchaffs are metronomically repetitive. The blackbird provides a tuneful touch of class. All this can be to a background of that famous songster, the cuckoo, so symptomatic of the countryside. It's the sound of bird heavy industry.

This local nature reserve is not a bustling place, despite being close to several centres of population. You approach from the industrial village of Cwm, and the busy A4046 to Ebbw Vale roars by. You would barely know it was there. But it is, and that in itself is testament to the healing power of nature.

Seasonal highlights

Spring
Lesser celandine, wood sorrel, chiffchaff

Summer
Common lizard, mottled grasshopper, small pearl-bordered fritillary

Autumn
Stinkhorn, tiered tooth-fungus, grasshopper

Winter
Opposite-leaved golden saxifrage, crab apple, chaffinch

All year
Veteran beech trees, green woodpecker, grey wagtail

65 South Gower Cliffs

Serendipitous natural encounters

Coastguard Cottages, Rhossili, Swansea, Glamorgan SA3 1PR

Grid ref SS414880

Directions Follow B4247 through Rhossili to where the road ends

Lunch stop King Arthur Hotel, Higher Green, Reynoldston, Glamorgan SA3 1AD

This is the sort of place where the wildlife comes to you, even if it isn't invited. You might come merely to take the dog for a walk, to find a chough interrupts you by indulging in some carefree aerobatics above your head; you might be walking with the family, and the rock pools call a halt to any progress; you could be sitting down beside the Gower Way, taking a break in a long walk, and suddenly you notice the clifftop flowers at your feet. This is a place for serendipitous encounters of the natural kind.

It is a coastline rich in all kinds of treasures: intriguing history and geology; bracing walks; one of the best beaches for miles around. The latter, indeed, is right next to where you must head to begin your exploration – the village of Rhossili. The long sweep of golden sands will tempt you as you park your car, especially on a warm sunny day or perhaps a roaring, windswept one, but for wildlife-watching purposes you are heading southwest.

The first destination might provide enough adventure for a whole day. Worm's Head is an island that is only accessible for about two and a half hours each low tide, but if you arrive at the right time (tide times are available at the old coastal lookout building, now an information centre, a mile down the wide path), it makes for an exciting challenge. You descend to the beach and then embark on a scramble over the causeway, which is made up from large, jagged rocks and boulders, interspersed with rock pools – look out too for the huge anchor embedded from an old wreck. After 20 minutes or so you reach the Inner Head, with some relief. It is easy enough to follow the path along and over Devil's Bridge, what is left of a collapsed sea cave, and then the land gets narrower and more precipitous as you get towards the Outer Head. You cannot climb to the top in the birds' breeding season (1 March to 31 August). There is a blowhole on the side of the cliff, and at times the flume reaches the top of the cliff, 150ft above the sea.

Once at the end of the Outer Head, you are a mile out. Make sure you easily beat the tide back, as it comes in very fast. People have been cut off many times before and it is a seven-hour wait for it to recede. The poet Dylan Thomas was once stranded here and wrote about the experience.

Worm's Head is, in wildlife terms, a microcosm of the Gower Peninsula. The rock pools, sea cliffs and grassland hold many of the specialities associated with the area. There are, for example, breeding guillemots and razorbills, kittiwakes, shags and fulmars on the cliffs here and further east. Puffins may occur, especially early in spring, but they don't breed. The rock pools exposed at low tide are good for the snakelocks anemone, coral weed, hermit crabs and fish called blennies. The grasslands are full of wildflowers, including thrift and both golden and rock samphire.

The chough, a member of the crow family that has red legs and a long, down-curved red bill, also occurs here, along with jackdaws, ravens, rooks and carrion crows. Choughs appreciate the very short sward grazed by the numerous rabbits.

There are many things to see if you don't walk out to Worm's Head (the name, by the way, is translated as 'Dragon's Head'). Simply follow the coastal path towards Port Eynon. There are several nature reserves along the way, such as Deborah's Hole, named after an inaccessible cave, which has a good range of flowers on the limestone here, and breeding rock pipits and linnets. The rare plants on this part of the coast include the small restharrow, spring cinquefoil, early gentian and goldilocks aster. One of the most interesting is the yellow whitlow-grass, an intense yellow plant related to cress, which in Britain is confined to 10 miles of Gower coast. It is common here but normally only found on mountains in Europe.

To be honest, whichever way you walk, you can't go wrong. And whichever way you walk, you'll probably be interrupted by something very special.

Seasonal highlights

Spring
Spring squill, yellow whitlow-grass, early gentian

Summer
Guillemot, puffin, thrift

Autumn
Manx shearwater, hermit crab, goldilocks aster

Winter
Rock pipit, eider, cormorant

All year
Chough, jackdaw, rock pools

66 Strumble Head

Marine thrills from dry land

Goodwick, Pembrokeshire SA64 OJL

Grid ref SM895412 (car park)

Directions From Goodwick follow signs on minor roads to Strumble Head

Lunch stop Rose and Crown, Goodwick Square, Goodwick, Fishguard, Pembrokeshire SA64 OBP

West Wales has an embarrassment of rocky headlands on its coast. Follow the coastline on the map and your finger practically trips over them. So, without being rude, why would you choose to go to Strumble Head, if it is only to enjoy yet another cliff walk and yet another lighthouse? Is there something special about it?

You bet there is. Strumble Head is one of those very unusual locations where you can keep your feet on dry land and see some of the true creatures of the sea. It is famous for two things: its sea mammals and its rare seabirds. When the surrounding waters are calm, you would be unlucky not to see something special. The late summer, particularly August, offers the best variety.

Almost anyone who has tried to see dolphins and whales from land knows how difficult it can be. These mammals are unpredictable in their appearance, and even when you do spot them it is often only a glimpse. Here at Strumble Head you still mostly see just a fin and part of the body, but the other problem, a lack of reliability, is assuaged. The head is regarded by some as simply the best place in Britain, or even in Europe, to see a harbour porpoise. They are here all year round.

The porpoise is the smallest of Britain's cetaceans – the collective term for whales and dolphins. On a fine day, when the sea is like a mill pond, you can make out the small, low, blunt triangular fin quite easily. The animals are lethargic and slow-moving, a complete contrast to the dynamic bottle-nosed dolphin, which also occurs here regularly. The dolphin is bigger and has a somewhat sickle-shaped, backwards-pointing fin. It is more sociable than a porpoise, usually in pods.

Amazingly, there are other species here, too, which are quite regular, at least in the late summer. Risso's dolphins are larger than a bottle-nosed dolphin, with a grey colour with pale scar lines, and they have stubby 'noses', lacking the beak of most dolphin species. They occur off Strumble Head in small groups, not usually moving very fast. Finally, you might also see the short-beaked common dolphin, smaller than a bottle-nosed dolphin, with pale, almost yellow flanks.

And if your luck is really in, a minke whale is also a possibility, bigger than them all and recognised by its regular 'blows'.

This parade of sea mammals doesn't even include the grey seals which are found around the head regularly, and can be seen breeding on the nearby beaches, with the creamy-white pups born in the late autumn.

How do you reach this miraculous place? It is well signposted from the A40 at Fishguard and the drive is then a meander along minor roads. They lead to a car park opposite the lighthouse, which is on an island, Ynys Meicel – there was once a footbridge across the gap for the lighthouse workers. From the car park walk down to the disused War Department building below the road on the right. This has now been renovated as an observatory, looking conveniently out to sea some 70ft above the waves. Rarely is there nobody there, and watchers are often armed with telescopes. They will gladly point out the birds and sea mammals.

The seabirds are just as special, and sometimes easier to see. There is always something around, even if it is only a marauding great black-backed gull. Cormorants, shags and gannets are here year-round, fulmars, kittiwakes, guillemots and razorbills are offshore in the summer, and from March to October there are usually Manx shearwaters about. These, however, are not what the regulars hope for. In stormy conditions in the Irish Sea, onshore winds blow such exciting birds as Leach's petrel, great shearwater and Sabine's gulls closer to shore. Most birders begin their observations at first light, the best time.

Of course, seeing such exciting pelagic birds, which spend their non-breeding seasons far out in the oceans, is a matter of luck and the weather. However, even on a quiet day there will also be birds such as choughs and peregrines.

After an hour or two your eyes might be strained by all the concentration, in which case the Pembrokeshire Coast Path lies both to the west and east. It is a fine walk indeed, in either direction, but if you come here only for a stroll you are certainly missing something.

Seasonal highlights

Spring
Guillemot, razorbill, kittiwake

Summer
Bottle-nosed dolphin, Risso's dolphin, Manx shearwater

Autumn
Minke whale, Leach's petrel, Sabine's gull

Winter
Chough, grey seal, shag

All year
Harbour porpoise, great black-backed gull, peregrine

Bottle-nosed dolphin

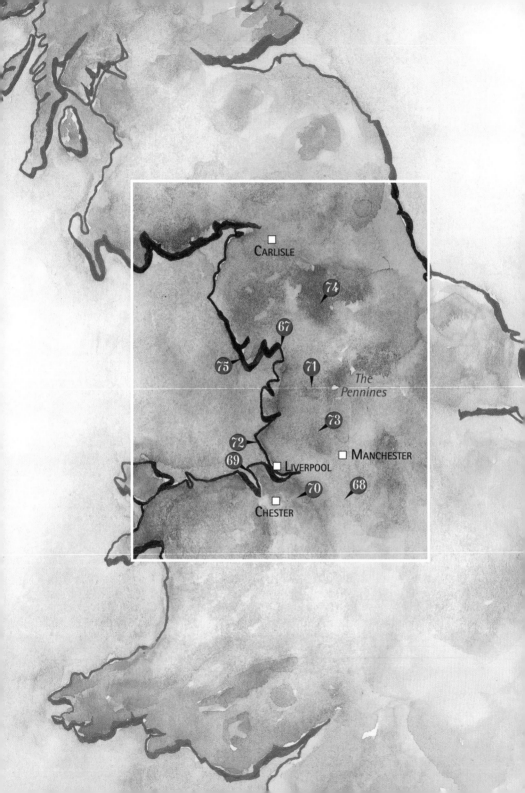

CARLISLE

74

67

75

71

The
Pennines

73

72

69

□ MANCHESTER

□ LIVERPOOL

70

68

CHESTER

Northwest England

67 Arnside Knott

Great wildlife and spectacular views

The Promenade, Arnside, Carnforth, Cumbria LA5 0DE

Grid ref SD455787

Directions From Milnthorpe go west on the B5282 to Arnside Promenade

Lunch stop The Wheatsheaf at Beetham, Beetham, Cumbria LA7 7AL

It is almost unreasonable how good the Arnside and Silverdale area is for wildlife. This lump of land on the corner of Morecambe Bay, squeezed between the Lake District to the north and the Forest of Bowland to the south, is blessed with top sites for all sorts of things. To be honest, if you are in the area, you can take your pick of Leighton Moss for birds, or Gait Barrows and Silverdale for flowers. If you want a bit of everything – and who doesn't? – then Arnside Knott, a quick trudge up from Arnside village, is probably your best bet.

A good way to start this walk is to park your car on the seafront at Arnside. That way the fabulous views from the top of the 520ft hill will unfold more slowly and satisfyingly, even though the locals say you shouldn't look back until you've reached the top!

Whatever happens, your walk should be constantly interrupted by wildlife. Even before you have started, in fact – the seafront here is the mouth of the River Kent, which drains into Morecambe Bay, the best estuary for birds in Britain in terms of sheer numbers. There are a couple of wader roosts along here, one just north of the railway viaduct, and this area is also noted for gulls. But this is a digression. There will be birds on the sands if the tide is out – and the viaduct across the river is quite impressive.

From the promenade, turn left on Silverdale Road and follow the signs to Arnside Knott. The path will take you up through Red Hills Wood, a mixture of sessile oak, holly, rowan, hazel and yew, where you might hear the 'pit-choo' call of a marsh tit, one of its more northern locations. Nuthatch and great spotted woodpecker also occur here, and you might spot a roe or fallow deer.

The trees thin out and, as you ascend, a grassland is unveiled, but not your everyday grassland. These hills are made up of limestone, with the rocks sticking out in some places, pavement-like, and with lots of scattered yew and juniper. This is a highly unusual habitat and it makes Arnside Knott very special for wildflowers, including orchids. Masses of early purple orchids cover the ground in May, soon to be followed by common spotted orchids, fragrant orchids and fly orchids, and later on gems such as dark red helleborine.

There are many other wildflowers here, too, including some major rarities such as Teesdale violet in one of its few British localities, and blue moor-grass, which is confined to upland limestone. Wild service tree and small-leaved lime grow here at their northerly limit in Britain.

The biggest natural history draw, though, is the butterflies. Arnside Knott is one of the best places to see them in the whole of Britain. Alongside a range of common species are a number of much rarer ones. Here you can find the Scotch argus at its most southerly station, one of only two sites in England. It isn't a very impressive butterfly – like a very dark meadow brown that skips low over the tussocks – but in June and July enthusiasts will be flocking here to see it. Its larva feeds on the blue moor-grass. Among other scarce butterflies is the northern brown argus, another fussy eater that likes tall, unimproved grassland, its caterpillar feeding on common rock-rose.

The most challenging species here are the fritillaries, of which there are three species, all of them nationally scarce. On warm summer days these big orange butterflies come past at express pace, their engines heated to turbo by the sun. Dark green fritillary is the commonest, while the fast-declining high brown fritillary is outnumbered at least five to one. The pearl-bordered fritillary, not quite as big as the other two, is found on the woodland fringes. Even if you don't find these, though, there are plenty of other, more common species to enjoy in this treasure trove.

On any day at Arnside Knott you will be tempted to keep your head down watching invertebrates and looking for plants. You can get wondrously lost in this activity, and wander off on the many different paths that criss-cross this small area. Don't forget to look up and admire the view, however. Even on a grey day you can see the shoreline of Morecambe Bay, and usually the hills of the Lake District to the north. This means that, even when the butterflies are not flying, the view is still well worth the walk.

Seasonal highlights

Spring
Early purple orchid, Teesdale violet, blue moor-grass

Summer
Scotch argus, dark red helleborine, fritillaries

Autumn
Yew, rowan

Winter
Gulls, waders, hazel catkin

All year
Wild service tree, lime, roe deer

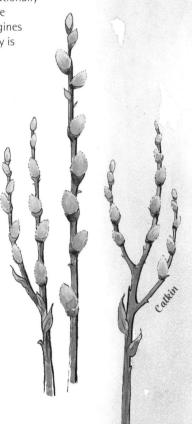

catkin

68 Danes Moss

Raised bog with a wild atmosphere

Woodhouse End Road, Gawsworth, Macclesfield, Cheshire SK11 9QS

Grid ref SJ902701

Directions In Gawsworth turn right off main road at Church Lane and follow Woodhouse Lane out of town; bear right into Woodhouse End Road and park at sharp corner

Lunch stop Harrington Arms, Church Lane, Gawsworth, Macclesfield, Cheshire SK11 9RJ

Not many of the folk of Macclesfield will be aware that they are almost sitting on a raised bog. However, Danes Moss, about 2 miles south of the town, is just that. Next to a landfill site, it is a classic case of a small, special location with a wild atmosphere lying astonishingly close to human settlement. Now looked after by the Cheshire Wildlife Trust, and newly upgraded to allow people to walk a circuit and enjoy its charms, it is the largest bog of its kind in the county. It can be accessed from the small town of Gawsworth, with its attractive churches and fishery (park along Woodhouse End Road at about SJ902701) or from the towpath of the Macclesfield Canal (SJ910706).

Danes Moss had a fascinating birth. A glacier gouged out a depression in the earth and this filled with water and then vegetation. With no drainage, when plants died they slow-cooked to form peat and became acidic. Over time the peat built up above the water table to create a so-called 'raised' bog, fed by rainwater, and immensely thick in places. Bogs are very nutrient-poor, and thus only a small community of specialised plants occur here.

One of the joys of Danes Moss is its diversity of one of these specialised plants, sphagnum moss. These are the wonderful spongy mosses, green and fulsome, that you can pull up and squeeze – although on a nature reserve this isn't recommended. There are no fewer than six species here, four of which are characteristic of different parts of bog formation, an indication of the variety of conditions present.

On the whole, bogs excite botanists and entomologists the most, and a circuit of the new paths and boardwalks should occupy them for hours. Besides the bonanza of sphagnum, which is an all-year phenomenon (indeed, mosses as a group are at their best in mid-winter), there is an excellent range of other plants. There is an important population of bog myrtle, with its delightful sweet scent (and apparent use as an insect repellent), while cranberries grow alongside cross-leaved heath. Dotted about are round-leaved sundew, an insectivorous plant with sticky leaves, marsh cinquefoil and Labrador tea, a naturalised plant related to the rhododendron, with clusters of white blooms. There are also two species of cottongrass, with flowers that look like white fluffy flags.

Cottongrass

Of all the animals that occur at Danes Moss, those that receive the most attention from local enthusiasts are the dragonflies. As one leaflet enthusiastically puts it, 'the dragonfly numbers are so high that they come and land on visitors', and indeed on a sunny day in July or August the place is heaving with them, so much so that you can hear the rattle of high-voltage wings. The chief attraction is the black darter, Britain's smallest dragonfly (as opposed to damselfly). At rest it holds its wings open and flat, while damselflies hold theirs closed or partially closed over the back. This dinky species flourishes most in acid bogs with lots of mosses. It is quite elusive, whereas you can hardly miss the wide-bodied emperor dragonflies and southern and brown hawkers, nor the four-spotted chaser, which abounds here. Dragonfly enthusiasts will enjoy finding emerald, large blue, azure and blue-tailed damselflies. The broad-bodied chaser and common darter make up the remainder of the tally of these summer and autumn beauties.

Of course, there are other highlights. Trapping on site has revealed an excellent range of small mammals, such as shrews, while badgers and brown hares breed and, for what it's worth, there are grey squirrels in the woodland. And, although the sky above rarely appears thick with birds and the pools have a habit of looking empty, the nature reserve has a respectable list of 75 or so species. The most reliable are woodland staples such as green woodpecker, and scrub-lovers such as willow warbler and bullfinch. However, the reed bunting does breed on the bog itself. The hobby sometimes visits in summer to feed on the dragonflies.

Danes Moss is a fine example of a site that, with good management, has been transformed from a decent wildlife location into an excellent one, with the removal of encroaching scrub and extension of the wet areas. It shows what can be done, even on the urban fringe.

Seasonal highlights

Spring
Orange-tip, bog myrtle, willow warbler

Summer
Black darter, Labrador tea, green hairstreak

Autumn
Cranberry, brown hawker, common darter

Winter
Cottongrass, ducks

All year
Several sphagnum moss species, badger, reed bunting

69 Dee Estuary
Two unmissable experiences

Dee Lane Slipway, South Parade, West Kirby, Wirral, Cheshire CH48 0QG

Grid ref SJ210867

Directions North end of Marine Lake; parking is limited on Parkgate promenade but there is free parking at Old Baths car park (CH64 6RN), north end of The Parade, and Wirral Country Park car park on Station Road (CH64 6QJ)

Lunch stop Irby Mill, Mill Lane, Greasby, Cheshire CH49 3NT

The River Dee rises in Snowdonia, flows east to Chester and discharges into a wide estuary, the left-hand cleft of the two on the coast between Wales and England; the other is the Mersey. As it disgorges into the Irish Sea it provides some first-class wildlife habitat, despite the many towns that have been built along the coast. In this area, there are two experiences that you simply shouldn't miss, each in a different place and both very different in themselves.

The first is a visit to offshore, uninhabited Hilbre Island and its sister islets Little Eye and Middle Eye, which is a real adventure involving walking over the sands from West Kirby jetty at low tide. It is impossible not to feel a thrill as you contemplate the wide expanse before you from the jetty, knowing that in a few hours it will be inundated by sea water. And it isn't an adventure to undertake lightly. Although they are only a mile offshore, it takes an hour or so to reach the first island, Little Eye, and you must start your walk at least three hours before high tide. There is no food, fresh water or any facilities available, despite the houses on Hilbre itself, so you must take provisions with you. The walk will become downright dangerous, into pools and quicksands, if you don't follow the correct, well-marked route – out to the left of Little Eye and then round to the others. Walking out here feels deliciously outside normal comfort zones – a rare treat.

Field vole

The wildlife is the icing on the cake. The pools in the sand and the rock pools between islands are a delight for sea creatures, while as you approach Little Eye you might well hear the moaning calls of grey seals, which haul out here on

West Hoyle sandbank. In the winter thousands of waders, brent geese and ducks, as well as gulls, use the mudflats, making the Dee one of the most important estuaries for birds in the country (in the top 10 in Europe). The number of waders is impressive, such as 20,000 oystercatchers and 20,000 dunlins, yet to the casual visitor it just seems as though waders are swirling everywhere.

On Hilbre Island itself the well-camouflaged turnstone, using its short bill to overturn stones and other debris among rocks and seaweed, is always present, and another speciality in the winter is the purple sandpiper, which shares the turnstone's habitat but has a longer bill and uses it for probing.

The three islands are of red sandstone and more substantial than they appear from a distance; the cliffs of Hilbre are 55ft high and it is 12 acres in extent. One of the buildings is used as a bird observatory, particularly in the autumn when rarities often turn up on this exposed coastline – 270 species, an astonishing total, have been recorded in all. Some brave birders visit during gales, when the cliffs are a good vantage point for seabirds, including the rare Leach's petrel.

Yet this place has everything for the adventurous wildlife-lover, in any conditions. From lazy summer days to fierce autumn storms, the fact that the islands can only be reached by foot across the sands makes them special. On a fine day, the views are often spectacular, across to the Lake District and even the Isle of Man.

For the second experience, just as remarkable in its way, you must position yourself at Parkgate Marsh, near Neston down the coast, on a rising spring tide. On a few days each year, depending on the weather, the water rises over the marsh much higher than usual, and the spectacle is fantastic. If this happens in autumn or winter, thousands of wading birds are pushed close to the Parkgate promenade and give incredible views. At the same time, raptors such as short-eared owls, sparrowhawks and merlins close in as birds try to settle and find they cannot. On very high tides animals that are usually concealed are flushed into the open, even onto the car park. These include birds such as water rails and, more unusually, small mammals such as field voles, water shrews and weasels. Even moles have been spotted as they flee the rising water. It's a truly remarkable sight.

Seasonal highlights

Spring
Terns, swallow, dunlin

Summer
Gulls, grey seal, rock pools

Autumn
Field vole, seaweed, Leach's petrel

Winter
Purple sandpiper, short-eared owl, knot

All year
Cockle, oystercatcher, turnstone

70 Delamere Forest

A place of peace and solitude

Forest Centre car park, Linmere Cottages, Delamere, Northwich, Cheshire CW8 2JD

Grid ref SJ549704

Directions At Delamere turn left following signs just before the station

Lunch stop The Fishpool Inn, Fishpool Road, Delamere, Northwich, Cheshire CW8 2HP

This is a place where a time machine would be an interesting add-on to a day out. You could turn up at the Linmere car park, flick a switch and a very different horizon would open out. Gone would be the car park, café, entrance to rope climbing and cycling and the other accoutrements of the modern-day outdoors. Go back a thousand years and you would be in the ancient forest of Mara, and instead of conifers the wood would be of oak. The landscape around would have been bogs and lakes, quite similar to parts of Scotland or even Scandinavia. In the midst of the landscape wild boar and deer would be roaming, the latter hunted by wolves, which are thought to have persisted in the area until the 14th century.

Reed bunting

Of course, it doesn't look anything like that now, and you would be excused for thinking that the forest has been tamed and abused. Visit on a sunny day and remain near a car park and it looks overwhelmed. But the truth is that some parts of the area have survived almost intact. And, better still, something of what was lost has been restored by conservationists. The meres and moors of Cheshire and neighbouring counties have been viewed kindly in the last few decades, and much has been done to preserve the habitats and promote their value.

One of the first beneficiaries of the restoration has been Blakemere Moss. The mere was drained in the 19th century and planted with Scots pine. However, in 1992 the Forestry Commission and partners decided to recreate the wetland habitat, first by felling all the trees and then by flooding it. The project has been a remarkable success, and more 're-wetting' has been carried out since

Seasonal highlights

Spring
Adder, marsh marigold, tree pipit

Summer
White-faced darter, black-headed gull, yellow iris

Autumn
Common sundew, siskin

Winter
Treecreeper, goldcrest, crossbill

All year
Quaking bog, Scots pine, willow tit

then. There is even a black-headed gull colony here, sometimes with a few Mediterranean gulls thrown in among them. It is easy to walk around the mere and see virtually no other people.

Another innovative project is one of the few dragonfly reintroduction programmes ever carried out. The rare white-faced darter, a classic creature of northern bogs, used to occur in the Delamere Forest area, but became extinct in 2003. Larvae are being gathered in Shropshire and Staffordshire and translocated to a donor site in the forest to see whether they can become established again. Keep a careful lookout for these colourful and elegant insects.

One or two parts of the forest have remained intact, of which an example is Black Lake, in the west of the area. This is a rare example of a quaking bog, in which the bog vegetation floats on a mat above water, and if the surface is disturbed it moves or 'quakes', or makes ripples. Here sphagnum mosses anchored by sedges occur, and there is a large colony of the intriguing insectivorous plant the common sundew. It is an excellent hotspot for dragonflies and it has a rather strange, brooding atmosphere. By the way, it wouldn't be a good idea to try to walk on this particular bog.

One of the best parts of the forest for wildlife is Hatch Mere, in the north of the forest close to the village of the same name. A kettle lake gouged by glaciation and fed by rainwater, it is flanked by woodland and is a good general wildlife area. Great crested grebes breed here and reed and sedge warblers breed in the surrounding reed swamp, along with reed buntings. Lesser reedmace grows among the reeds, and waterside plants such as marsh marigold and yellow iris provide a dash of colour.

The pine woodlands are not as good for wildlife as the rest of the area, but crossbills and siskins occur here and there, along with much commoner birds such as great spotted woodpeckers, treecreepers and goldcrests. In summer tree pipits breed in the open areas of young plantations, and redstarts in the deciduous sections. Willow tits are widespread, while lesser redpolls breed where there are birch trees and range widely.

Delamere Forest is an easy place in which to find peace and solitude. As the years pass, it is likely to become better and better for wildlife, too.

Marsh marigold

71 Dunsop Valley

Birding in the remote Forest of Bowland

Dunsop Bridge car park, Dunsop Bridge, Clitheroe, Lancashire BB7 3AZ

Grid ref SD660501

Directions Minor roads through the villages of Bay Horse, Dolphinholme and Abbeystead lead down to Dunsop Bridge

Lunch stop Parkers Arms, Newton-in-Bowland, Lancashire BB7 3DY

Dunsop Valley is part of the Forest of Bowland, a remote area in northeast Lancashire. It doesn't look anything like a forest; it is a landscape of upland fells and moors, with some coniferous plantations and other trees in the valleys. Historically, a 'forest' was an area set aside for hunting, and it's from this that the name derives.

This is rugged country. The Forest of Bowland is designated as an Area of Outstanding Natural Beauty (AONB), but the beauty is bleak and elemental rather than bountiful. The area receives very few visitors, particularly in comparison to the Lake District and Peak District, and it is harder to see everything, with many private areas and comparatively few public footpaths. It is perfect, though, for those who are happy to use their feet to get up to see some fabulous views and rare wildlife.

Any number of places in the forest are ideal for wild walking, and it doesn't take long to find yourself in a suitably lonely spot. However, the Dunsop Valley is a perfect location for seeing much of what the Forest of Bowland has to offer, together with a good parking spot in the village of Dunsop Bridge. You can even start your wildlife viewing by feeding the ducks in the vicinity of the eponymous stone bridge. Two public footpaths go north up the valley either side of the river, but they soon converge at a bridge not far up. Dunsop Bridge itself is a picture postcard village set in a wide valley with fields and deciduous trees. In the winter there can be many thrushes and finches here. The whole walk is principally a bird location.

The 'path' is actually the private road to Whitendale. It follows along the beck, where dippers and grey wagtails breed and are resident, joined by common sandpipers in the summer, with their piccolo-like alarm calls. The rushy fields are the habitat for waders such as redshank, lapwing and oystercatcher, all of which will noisily pester you if you are close to their nests. Up above you the hills grade from green into the sort of pink wash typical of the moorland, except in August and September when the whole top is flushed with purple. The sides soon become steeper as you enter a patch of coniferous woodland. Although

Seasonal highlights

Spring
Wheatear, common sandpiper, lapwing

Summer
Hen harrier, tree pipit, wheatear

Autumn
Purple heather, skylark, stonechat

Winter
Brambling, thrushes

All year
Peregrine, short-eared owl, merlin

largely barren for wildlife, these woods do hold goldcrests, siskins and sometimes common crossbills, too.

But the interest is in the upper moors. The path gets tougher once you have forked right to Whitendale, and tougher still if you decide to brave the path on to Dunsop Fell, to the east of this stunningly remote village. But if you can, you should. This is where it gets lonelier, and more thrilling; but don't be foolish if the weather is closing in. It's uncompromising countryside.

These moors are where the most celebrated wildlife can be found. Chief among the attractions is the hen harrier, a bird at the centre of controversy. It used to do well here, in its only remaining breeding site in England, but harriers eat some grouse and the predators have been disappearing. You can still see them, and maybe up here the effort of walking will mean you deserve a meeting with these ghosts of the moors, the male as white as a gull but gliding low over the heather or bog, head down looking for small birds and mammals.

It isn't the only bird of prey here. There are short-eared owls, which fly low over the moors on buoyant wings, their flight wavering and floating. They are seeking mostly voles. Peregrines drop by and merlins, too, which make their living by chasing small songbirds, such as the super-abundant meadow pipits, skylarks and tree pipits. There are other species potentially on its menu, and yours. Stonechats breed on the heather, whinchats by the bracken and ring ouzels in the cloughs (ravines). Northern wheatears, plump robin-like birds with white tail flashes, make their nests in holes in the rocks, often at ground level. And, of course, among all the other birds is the red grouse, darling of the moorland landowners.

These moors are rare habitats, although they don't look it up here. They are fragile, too, and again they don't look it. Human beings are also fragile in this location, and that feeling is good.

Peregrine falcon

72 Formby Point

Squirrels and toads in the dunes

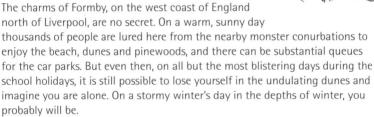

Red squirrel

Victoria Road, Formby, Liverpool L37 1LJ (Squirrel Reserve)

Grid ref SD274082

Directions At Formby follow signs to Freshfield station then National Trust car park

Lunch stop The Pheasant Inn, 20 Moss Lane, Hightown, Liverpool L38 3RA

The charms of Formby, on the west coast of England north of Liverpool, are no secret. On a warm, sunny day thousands of people are lured here from the nearby monster conurbations to enjoy the beach, dunes and pinewoods, and there can be substantial queues for the car parks. But even then, on all but the most blistering days during the school holidays, it is still possible to lose yourself in the undulating dunes and imagine you are alone. On a stormy winter's day in the depths of winter, you probably will be.

Few parts of England are blessed with such riches in terms of wildlife as this, the Sefton Coast. Birders come here for the waders on the beach and rare seabirds; mammal-watchers come unequivocally for the red squirrels; herpetologists are delighted with a potential hat-trick of goodies; botanists come for the dune-slack orchids and other treats. There are rare moths, ferns, and even a famous liverwort. There are even superb fossils on the beach. It is a place to come as a birder and leave as an admirer of sedges, or vice versa. This is a place where it pays to be distracted and to wander where you will.

First, though, to the practicalities. The affluent town of Formby is not especially large and has two stations not far from the beach (Freshfield and Formby), so you can get here easily by public transport. You can park for free in some parts of town. Most people still use the designated car parks, such as the National Trust one, and pay if they aren't members. However, once here the whole area is free to access.

The most famous wild residents of the area are the red squirrels, which, at the time of writing, form the southernmost mainland population in England. These animals live in the pinewoods on the dunes, and the best place to see them is the Freshfield Squirrel Reserve, reached from the National Trust car park on Victoria Road. The animals are beautiful and tame; indeed, you can even buy nuts to feed them from the warden's office. They are at their smartest in the

Spring
Natterjack toad, sand lizard, great crested newt

Summer
Common tern, dune helleborine, round-leaved wintergreen

Autumn
Gannet, shearwater, storm petrel

Winter
Sanderling, grey plover, gulls

All year
Red squirrel, seashells, fossil footprints

winter, when their ear tufts have just regrown; in summer, they can look distinctly scruffy.

The three cold-blooded stars of Formby are the natterjack toad, the sand lizard and the great crested newt. The sand lizard and natterjack live for most of the year in the dunes, but while the sand lizard is active during the day, the toad comes out at night. The best way to appreciate the latter is to come between April and July on a warm, damp evening, and listen beside a breeding pool for their strange wheezy croak, which can become quite a chorus when many males are together. The sound has given this amphibian the local names of 'Bootle organ' and 'Birkdale nightingale'. The animals croak from shallow, ephemeral pools which are dotted about the site if there has been enough rain. The great crested newt is found in the larger ponds, but is difficult to see.

Birders who visit will be anxious to get to the magnificent sandy beach beyond the dunes. At low tide between October and March, thousands of waders will be feeding out on the mud; at high tide they roost just south of Formby Point, at Taylor's Bank by Cabin Hill. Numbers can be very impressive: there are tens of thousands of knots, thousands of dunlins and bar-tailed godwits and hundreds of oystercatchers, grey plovers, redshanks and sanderlings. In the late summer many hundreds of common terns may congregate here, while westerly gales in the autumn may blow storm-driven seabirds within view of the point: species such as Leach's and storm petrels, shearwaters and gannets.

The intertidal zone is rich in the usual shells, washed-up seaweed and other strandline flotsam. Here, however, you can indulge in a quite different kind of beachcombing. The sand is eroding sediment laid down in the Mesolithic and Neolithic eras between 8,000 and 5,000 years ago, and quite often footprints are exposed. These have included those of deer, wolves, aurochs (a now extinct wild cattle) and humans. Make sure you take a look at these if some are around.

Coming back inland, it is worth noting the superb dune flora. There are orchids on the dunes and slacks, including the rare dune helleborine, green-flowered helleborine and marsh helleborine, and some of the other flowers include round-leaved wintergreen and grass of Parnassus.

Space doesn't permit much detail about the flora, nor the mosses, moths or butterflies. The fact is, if you visit, there won't be space in the day to appreciate it all.

73 Longworth Clough

A series of ecological suburbs

Longworth Lane, Egerton, Bolton, Greater Manchester BL7 9PU

Grid ref SD702147

Directions At Egerton town centre go left on Longworth Road, over River Croal and fork left onto Longworth Lane

Lunch stop The Royal Arms, Tockholes Road, Tockholes, Lancashire BB3 0PA

This is a part of the country where almost everywhere is on the outskirts of somewhere; in this case, Longworth Clough is on the edge of Egerton, on the flanks of Bolton, which these days is almost contiguous with Manchester. The towns of Chorley and Blackburn lurk close by. Yet this is a remarkably peaceful spot, which many of the local residents have never visited, if they know it exists at all. You can truly be alone with the birdsong and follow the trails in peace, appreciating this corner of the West Pennine Moors.

A 'clough' in the north of England is a steep-sided ravine, and in this case it slopes down to Eagley Brook. There used to be a mill here, but not any more, and now the river is a spot for seeing dippers and, sometimes, kingfishers. The clough itself has a surprising mix of habitats formed over its Carboniferous sandstones and shale, among them woodland and acid grassland. The most unusual feature, though, is the complex ground water; there is a network of springs and streams all the way up the clough, resulting in marshy areas of several different types. This leads to a good display of different plants and, in turn, excellent general biodiversity.

The area is open access, and most visitors approach it from the eastern end and cross a bridge over the brook, following it up to the edge of the woods. These woods hold a decent range of birds, and if more people decided to check the area out the list would undoubtedly grow. Good species that breed here or have bred here in the past include tawny owl, woodcock and wood warbler, while garden warbler and tree pipit have been heard singing in the scrubby areas. Great spotted woodpeckers, long-tailed tits, jays

Long-tailed tit

Seasonal highlights

Spring
Tree pipit, marsh marigold, buttercup

Summer
Sedges, great horsetail, common spotted orchid

Autumn
Tormentil, siskin, bog asphodel

Winter
Kingfisher, grey squirrel, alder

All year
Acid grassland, jay, long-tailed tit

and nuthatches are also almost guaranteed on a visit, and siskins often fly over.

Longworth Clough is a Site of Special Scientific Interest (SSSI), largely because of the complicated ecology caused by the springs and flushes. One spring can have quite different plants and flowers around it in comparison to another close by. Every corner is different and you will keep coming across new things. This isn't the place for all the detail, but if you look carefully you might spot several types of different woodland, with fragments of alder/ash and birch/oak and even a section where the alder has an understorey of sedges.

Some of the flushes under the trees have large stands of the impressive great horsetail, some reaching a great height, their fronds quite similar to horses' tails or perhaps ostrich feathers. These evergreens are primitive plants: mini-versions of the ones that dominated the Carboniferous landscape prior to the dinosaurs, at just the time the bedrock of this area was formed. On other flushes are blooms such as marsh marigolds, buttercups and common spotted orchids.

Near the top of the slope the area opens out into Oak Field, on the other side of the road from Delph Reservoir – a plateau of acid grassland where again there are flushes of ground water. Here you can find very acidic mires with plants such as bog asphodel, cottongrass and several types of sphagnum moss. If you are a fan of sedges (and, let's face it, who isn't?) you will have a field day in the wet areas here, looking for carnation sedge, common sedge, bottle sedge and even white sedge to add to the cottongrass, which is also actually a sedge. There are several interesting rushes, too.

All this may be too much for some people, but the fact is that Longworth Clough is a site of great variety – of flowers, trees, birds, butterflies and many invertebrates. In some ways you could almost see the place itself as a series of ecological suburbs, all on the outskirts of each other.

Long-tailed tit

74 Smardale Gill

Teeming with butterflies, birds and flowers

Beck Lane, Smardale, Kirkby Stephen, Cumbria CA17 4HG

Grid ref NY740082

Directions Ignore the sign for Smardale hamlet and cross the disused railway, turn immediately left and then left again for the car park

Lunch stop The Black Swan, Ravenstonedale, Cumbria CA17 4NG

This glorious walk is situated in eastern Cumbria, near the town of Kirkby Stephen on the edge of the Pennines. The walk takes you along the disused Stainmore Railway which once ran between the junction at Tebay to the west and Darlington to the east. So, you could say that this 'off the beaten track' walk is actually along a beaten track.

The path will take you down through a ravine ('gill') cut out by a river, Scandal Beck, with steep, wooded sides. Around the embankment there are limestone grasslands and damp flushes, while above looms open moorland. To add to the mixture, the route crosses over the very impressive and rather shapely Smardale Gill Viaduct, and further down is an old bridge that was originally built for packhorses. Whatever time of year you visit, the views are always stirring and the route, which begins on high ground and then descends, is relatively undemanding, although uneven in places. Even without any wildlife sightings it would massage the soul.

But this area teems with butterflies, birds and wildflowers. The section of track between Smardale village and Newbiggin-on-Lune is 3.5 miles of National Nature Reserve looked after by the Cumbria Wildlife Trust. On a summer's day, in particular, there is lots to see, some of it rare and localised.

You can approach the walk from north or south. Most people park in a car park near Smardale village at NY740085 and walk down, but you can also start from Low Lane in Newbiggin and walk up. There is little to choose between the approaches, but if you start at the top you can do a circuit by crossing over Smardale Bridge and returning over Smardale Fell.

Assuming a start by Smardale village, you quickly descend into the steep-sided ravine, which is largely covered with ash and birch trees, with some oak, wych elm and rowan and, these days, some cleared areas. The flowers under this canopy are impressive and colourful, and include bluebells, primrose and wild garlic in the spring. It is also an excellent spot for ferns such as lady fern. Among the masses of dog's mercury look for the inconspicuous and uncommon herb-paris, with its four leaves each at right angles to the other. In spring, birds will be jamming in these woodlands. Listen for redstart and pied flycatcher among the commoner birds. Ravens breed nearby and the sound of their croaking is a feature of the walk. If you are lucky you might catch sight of a red squirrel, which at the time of writing still hangs on here.

The scenery opens out once you reach the viaduct, and as it does so the emphasis of interest will shift. This is one of the best places for butterflies in Cumbria and, with more than 20 species on the list, the variety is exceptional for the north of England. The biggest draw is the skittish Scotch argus, for which this is one of the best places in Britain, and one of only two sites in England (the other is Arnside Knott, page 180). It isn't a particularly beautiful butterfly, being mainly chocolate-brown with burnt ochre bands near the edges of the wings. In the sunshine, it has a reputation for flying incessantly without many pauses. Another equally awkward customer is the dark green fritillary, which itself tends to fly very fast, leaving little impression but an orange blur. Meanwhile, the other scarcity is northern brown argus, a very small butterfly related to the blues, but brown above. It also flies fast, but at least it sometimes stops to feed on nectar on flowers.

If the butterflies drive you to distraction, the flowers along the railway line, on the embankment and down by the beck will be the perfect antidote. In early summer there is a heady mix of the rare, the beautiful and both. One of the very best is the bird's-eye primrose, which has lilac-pink flowers with a yellow centre. Orchids are plentiful, with an abundance of fragrant orchid and rather less bountiful greater butterfly orchid and a few fly orchids. The bloody cranesbill, with its showy bright mauve flowers, dominates the trackside, while other good but less ostentatious species include grass of Parnassus and common wintergreen. The melancholy thistle, tall but with mournfully drooping flowerheads, is a classic northern plant.

Beyond the viaduct you will see much the same things and, if you are short of time, it makes sense to return as soon as you reach the packhorse bridge. It is well worth the short detour to see this 18th-century stone bridge, a Grade II listed construction. If nothing else, this gives the best view up through the dale.

Seasonal highlights

Spring
Bird's-eye primrose, bloody cranesbill, redstart

Summer
Dark green fritillary, northern brown argus, Scotch argus

Autumn
Grass of Parnassus, lady fern, melancholy thistle

Winter
Raven, treecreeper

All year
Buzzard, sparrowhawk

Bluebell

75 Walney Island

Stunning views and priceless wildlife

West Shore Road, North Walney, Barrow-in-Furness, Cumbria LA14 3UE

Grid ref SD171699

Directions At Barrow-in-Furness go over Jubilee Bridge onto Walney Island; follow minor roads to North Walney and Earnse Point

Lunch stop The Crown, North Scale, Walney Island, Barrow-in-Furness, Cumbria LA14 3RP

Walney Island, just off the coast from Barrow-in-Furness, is 11 miles long, narrow, flat and windswept. Never more than a mile wide, it has been described as the windiest place in lowland England, and proof of its exceptional draughtiness is easily seen in the abundance of wind farms that have mushroomed off its coast, and the windsurfers who are drawn to its beaches. Despite being heavily built up in the centre – Vickerstown is just an extension of Barrow – both its southern and northern tips are given over to nature reserves. The southern tip has a bird observatory and hides for which a permit is required; the northern tip is a National Nature Reserve with a somewhat wilder aspect. Both are well worth a visit, but for the purposes of this book we head north.

You park at Earnse Point (SD170700), on the west side of the island just beyond the village of North Walney, and then you must walk, although it is hardly anything but a delight. The National Nature Reserve begins just under a mile along the coastal track. The reserve starts close to the end of Walney Island Airport, which is private land, and extends to the tip near the sands of the Duddon Estuary. There are three colour-marked trails to follow, and at the time of writing the paths are being improved. There is a bench to sit on about halfway round the circular route.

This northern tip of Walney Island is a mixture of dunes, vegetated shingle, meadows, so-called 'dune heath' and, offshore, saltmarsh and mudflats. Despite being on this low island close to industry, the views are stunning, mainly because they are dominated by the Langdale Fells in the nearby Lake District, with the Duddon Flats in front. At times this view is so beautiful that you have to force yourself to look at plants and animals.

Walney Island is a terrific spot for birdwatching and botanising, which means that you alternate between checking the sky and sea and looking at your feet, but both bring rich dividends. As ever, birdwatching is wonderful all year round, and the surrounding Duddon Estuary is internationally important for redshanks and knots and nationally important for a host of other things, including sanderlings, the waders that run very fast in between breaking waves, feeding in the backwash. You can easily while away sweet hours watching the waders, ducks and geese here, just doing their thing. You cannot fail to notice the tri-coloured shelduck, a big whitish species with a long greenish neck and a chestnut breast band. Offshore, red-breasted mergansers and eiders dive for fish, while pintails join the commoner wildfowl on the saltmarsh. Winter brings predators, and this part of the island is good for short-eared owls.

The plant list includes plenty of rarities, but one is particularly interesting because it is unofficially called the Walney geranium. It is sadly only a pale pink version of bloody cranesbill, but was discovered here for the first time and is sometimes called var. *lancastriense*, even though Walney is now in Cumbria! The unusual habitats will make a plant-lover very happy indeed. There are several uncommon orchids, such as northern marsh and coralroot orchid and both marsh and dune helleborines, mainly found in the wet areas around the dunes (slacks). Also here is yellow bartsia, round-leaved wintergreen and seaside centaury, an attractive combination of yellow, creamy-white and pink. There is also an excellent shingle flora with such classy flowers as sea rocket, sea kale and Ray's knotgrass, while the dune grasslands support lady's bedstraw, wild pansy and common restharrow. It is unusual to find heathland flowers on sand dunes, but in patches here several heathers grow.

Despite the profusion of birds and flowers, Walney Island is perhaps most famous for a quite different resident, the natterjack toad. The immediate area holds almost a quarter of the British population of this rare, dune-loving animal. It is hard to see, hiding away in holes in the dunes by day, but it hunts on the surface at night and, in spring and summer, lays eggs in the shallow pools and slacks. North Walney would be special even without this and other rarities; with them it is priceless.

Seasonal highlights

Spring
Natterjack toad, knot, sea duck displays

Summer
Viper's bugloss, pyramidal orchid, green hairstreak

Autumn
Sea kale, shells, marsh helleborine

Winter
Eider, pintail, sanderling

All year
Shelduck, redshank, sand dunes

Natterjack toad

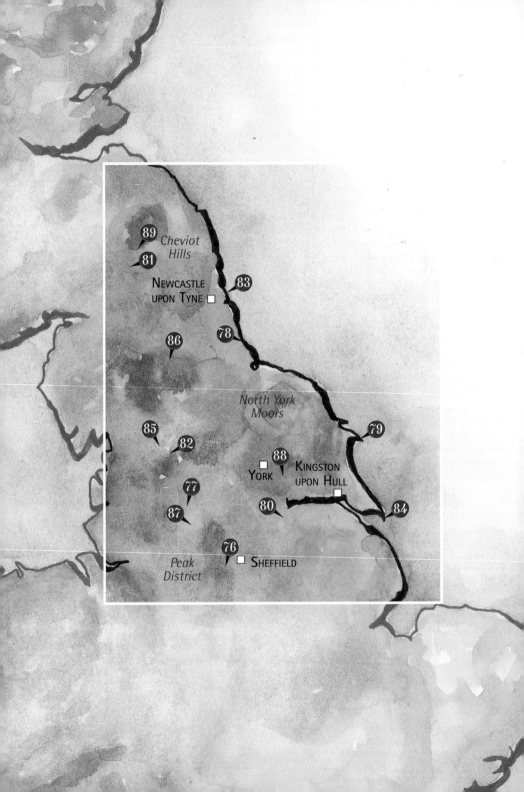

89 Cheviot
Hills

81

NEWCASTLE
UPON TYNE   83

78

86

North York
Moors

85   79

82

88
York   KINGSTON
UPON HULL

77
80   84

87

76
Peak   SHEFFIELD
District

Northeast England

76 Blacka Moor

A rare treasure in the steel city

Hathersage Road, Sheffield S17 3BJ

Grid ref SK277805

Directions Follow A625 southwest out of Sheffield past Brick Houses (becomes Hathersage Road); park just before junction with A6187

Lunch stop Riverside Herb Centre, Castleton Road, Hathersage, Sheffield S32 1EG

This miraculously wild-feeling place is so close to Sheffield, Britain's fourth-largest city, that it could almost be a suburban park. Blacka Moor has the city breathing down its neck, yet it retains the ruggedness of a much more remote area, far from civilisation. It lies just inside the boundary of the Peak District National Park and this, rather than nearby Sheffield, defines its identity.

In this unlikely setting Britain's largest land animal lives and breeds. Nobody knows the origin of the isolated herd of red deer here, but the local explanation is that they escaped from the Chatsworth Estate in Derbyshire, about 15 miles away, which is not so far as the deer runs. This big game animal rubs shoulders with the human visitors, seemingly well accustomed to intrusion, but also retaining its secretive nature. It is perfectly possible to visit Blacka Moor and miss seeing a red deer completely, yet at other times you will simply come upon them, either in the mixed woodland or on the open moorland.

Red deer

Red deer coexist here with Britain's only other native deer, the roe. The reds are tall, straight-backed deer with a long muzzle and ears; they have a subtle cream rump, a brownish tail and are often found in herds, especially the hinds. The roe, on the other hand, is a much more solitary animal. Smaller than the red deer, it has a stark whitish oval or kidney-shaped rump and no obvious tail. Bucks have small antlers not much longer than the head, while red deer have huge antlers and the stags are famous for locking horns in the autumn. They aren't quite the only large grazing animals on Blacka Moor.

The Sheffield and Rotherham Wildlife Trust allows Highland cattle to graze here too, in the warmer months, to keep the vegetation down.

Much as the red deer are the most celebrated residents of this unusual reserve, it is equally important for its breeding birds, which are plentiful. The woodland, which is mixed with conifers (pines and larch) and deciduous trees (oak, birch, rowan), holds a good range of common birds. Willow warblers are particularly common in summer, uttering their sweet, gently falling cadence from the edge of the wood, where the trees begin to thin out to leave open moorland. Cuckoos are still common, despite declining in many parts of Britain. And on the moorland itself you can easily find three relatives of the robin: the stonechat, whinchat and wheatear. The stonechat will probably be perched on gorse or heather, the whinchat probably on bracken, and the wheatear is likely to be on the ground, although none of this is guaranteed. Curlews still breed nearby and might be heard. In the winter, Blacka Moor is an excellent place for the 'winter thrushes', redwing and fieldfare. About 90 species have been recorded in all.

There are plenty of other attractions, not least the utterly sumptuous heather, which drenches the undulating landscape in purple in the autumn, tastefully offsetting the green leaves and brilliant red berries of the rowan trees. A visit is delightful just to enjoy the colours. On a smaller scale, there are many adders and common lizards, and the reserve is also noted for something smaller still, the bilberry bumblebee. This is a northern insect, often found as high as 3,300ft in Scotland. It prefers areas with a mixed landscape of heather, which it visits, but also woodland with an understorey of bilberry. It is a small bumblebee with a particularly obvious orange-reddish abdomen. This is outstanding moorland, beloved of the locals and with much wildlife to impress the visitor. Easily accessible, with two car parks next to the A625 Hathersage Road (Stony Ridge and Piper Lane), which runs along the western part of the site, it is a rare treasure in the Steel City.

Red deer

77 Broadhead Clough

Fairy clubs and a woodland bog

Cragg Road, Mytholmroyd, Hebden Bridge, West Yorkshire HX7 5FB

Grid ref SE007251

Directions From Mytholmroyd go left (south) on B6138 to just before Dauber Bridge

Lunch stop The Alma Inn, Cottonstones, Sowerby Bridge, West Yorkshire HX6 4NS

Did you know there was such a thing as a woodland bog? Not many people do, and very few have ever been to one. If, however, you are ever passing Mytholmroyd, in the Calder Valley of West Yorkshire, just such an oddity lies a few minutes out of town. It is a hidden spot, visited by few people, and you can only get there by foot. It is a damp but curious part of overlooked Britain.

Plenty of people do know the B6138 road from Mytholmroyd south towards Cragg Vale, however. Road cyclists will recognise it as the longest continuous ascent in the whole of England, a lung-bursting 6 miles. Well, it so happens that this road passes by Broadhead Clough, although you can't see it as you go. You have to stop and then walk up a track to the entrance. If you set off by car from Mytholmroyd, park carefully at the end of the first mile, just where the houses give way to fields, and before Dauber Bridge. A footpath points right to Frost Hole; follow this steeply uphill for a quarter of a mile and then fork left on the concrete road and it will lead you to the entrance of this Shangri-La. You can pat yourself on the back for just getting here.

The clough itself is a broad valley beneath looming Bell House Moor to the west and Erringden Moor to the

Spring
Cuckoo, wood horsetail,
heath spotted orchid

Summer
Sedges, cottongrass,
common cow-wheat

Autumn
Waxcaps, fairy clubs,
earth tongues

Winter
Mosses, lichens

All year
Woodland bog, oak, alder

north. The sides are mostly wooded, but there are also portions of acid grassland and typical South Pennine moorland,
so the site is quite varied, something that becomes even more obvious if you examine the flora at your feet. But first of all, just revel in the quietness of the place. You are well off the beaten track here.

It doesn't take long to find the famous woodland bog – your sinking boots will locate it before you do. A woodland bog is simply that, a wet peaty area below tree cover. Underneath the oaks and alders the ground is characteristically wet, usually with large patches of sphagnum moss, the ultimate bog plant. These sometimes occur among the roots and, not surprisingly, from time to time the trees will be undermined and fall to the ground, where they add to the peat. Apart from the sphagnum, those who are in the know will enjoy seeing a good range of other plants on the woodland bog, such as wood horsetail, common cottongrass (an incongruous sight under tree cover) and a range of sedges including remote sedge and smooth-stalked sedge. The rest of us can just admire this curious juxtaposition of bog and tree cover, especially if we are used to seeing miles and miles of open bog land in the rest the Pennines.

There is plenty more of interest here. The grassland contains still more sedge species, if you like that sort of thing, and more conspicuous plants such as bracken, bilberry and common cow-wheat, a yellow bloom that is much more attractive than it sounds. Mycologists will delight in the grassland fungi in summer and autumn, which includes waxcaps, earth tongues, pink gills and fairy clubs – these sound more like cake recipes than mushrooms! There is also some 'normal' woodland and some typical open moorland, the latter with heather, heath spotted orchid and cranberry, among other widespread moorland plants.

In the summer, the area is good for birds, so visitors can enjoy the sweet sound of birdsong as they try to extricate their boots from the sylvan mire. There is usually a cuckoo singing in the late spring, while curlew breeds on the nearby moors. Tree pipit, redstart and wood warbler have all bred in the past, although none seems to be entirely reliable these days. These, though, are add-on pleasures, all of them being common elsewhere. The main glories lie at your feet.

78 Castle Eden Dene

The Jungle of the North

Oakerside Dene Lodge, Stanhope Chase, Peterlee, County Durham SR8 1NJ

Grid ref NZ427393

Directions From Peterlee go past college, turn right at roundabout on Passfield Way and left on Durham Way; follow round until Stanhope Chase on right

Lunch stop The Royal George, The Village, Old Shotton, Peterlee, County Durham SR8 2ND

This place is nicknamed 'The Jungle of the North' by the locals, and when you see it you will immediately realise why. It is a deep cleft taken over by rank and rich vegetation. In the narrower parts the trees are ancient, gnarled and tangled, the soil is heavy and the sides are steep, clayey and unstable. There are hidden corners everywhere, damp and shaded. Nothing much has changed in this deep ravine for thousands of years, literally. The cleft, which runs for 3.5 miles inland down towards the North Sea, was originally formed by post-glacial meltwaters carving a path through the magnesian limestone. And here their work has remained for 10,000 years, almost intact, useless for building on or any kind of development, a remnant of the wildwood in the cellar of Peterlee New Town. It is sandwiched between the urban centres of Middlesbrough and Sunderland yet retains its primeval essence – miraculous indeed.

Overall the dene is quite a large site, with open areas, even grassland and scrub, at each end, and the narrowest, steepest section in the middle. There is a visitor centre on Oakerside Drive, Peterlee, near the Oakerside entrance, where you can park and enjoy a small pond and garden, with a range of 'wild' flowers. There are other entrances dotted about; Gunner's Pool Bridge spans an impressive gorge, and an elegant railway viaduct goes over the eastern end, near the sea.

Much of the woodland is ash and wych elm, with oaks, sycamores and some areas of planted conifers. One its most unusual features is the large amount of yew cover; this is the furthest north this tree grows naturally in Britain. Many individuals are old and multi-branched, and some are collapsing as the sides of the gorge periodically give way. They add a dark, magical atmosphere to the cleft. Under the deciduous trees is a thick and extensive understorey of hazel, dogwood, spurge laurel, spindle, privet and guelder rose, making this a good place to test your shrub identification skills.

The spring brings an impressive carpet of woodland-floor blooms. Bluebells are here in number, with the white nodding heads of wood anemone carpeting

Seasonal highlights

Spring
Wild garlic,
garden warbler,
herb-paris

Summer
Bird's-nest orchid,
northern brown argus,
Blomer's rivulet (moth)

Autumn
Whitethroat, hoverflies,
clouded yellow

Winter
Grey wagtail, hart's
tongue fern, brambling

All year
Yew, ash, wych elm

some places. But the truly dominant ground flower is wild garlic (ramsons), which is abundant, clothing the ground in fresh green and white, and suitably smelly. Overall the dene is exceptionally good for flowers, not only the woodland variety, but also plants that grow in rock crevices and, at the extreme ends, limestone grassland. Among the unusual species found in the woodland are bird's-nest orchid, herb-paris, lily-of-the-valley and round-leaved wintergreen. Giant horsetail is found in wetter areas.

The woodland until recently provided refuge for red squirrels, but these have now been replaced by greys. The latter are at least easier to see, especially if you follow the marked Squirrel Trail. Foxes, badgers and roe deer hide away here, and on summer nights bats flit across the narrow paths.

The bird list is very impressive: over 200 species, but it should be mentioned that a good many of these have been seen from the eastern end of the ravine, where it opens out and looks over the sea. In the wood itself there are typical birds such as nuthatch, treecreeper, green and great spotted woodpeckers, redstart, tawny owl and sparrowhawk. At this seaward end, there is a pebble beach where little terns have bred, and quite extensive hawthorn and blackthorn scrub where migratory birds regularly make a grateful landing after crossing the North Sea. Many rarities have been seen here, including wryneck and waxwing. The brook that runs through the dene, Castle Eden Burn, meanders to the sea at this point and also creates a semi-permanent pool just inshore, providing another type of habitat. The grassland in this section is good for the rare northern brown argus, a butterfly whose food plant is common rock-rose, the latter being plentiful here. This is just one of the profusion of invertebrates that occur in this place.

All in all, this is an exceptional area for wildlife and a remarkably well preserved part of our ancient heritage. Be warned: at times the area acts out its wildness and landslips make the paths impassable. Take good boots, take good care and enjoy the jungle.

Brown argus butterfly

210

79 Flamborough Head

Seabird city with a spectacular rush hour

North Landing, North Marine Road, Bridlington, East Yorkshire YO15 1BJ

Grid ref TA238719

Directions From Bridlington take the B1255 to Flamborough and beyond to North Landing

Lunch stop The Seabirds Inn, Tower Street, Flamborough, East Yorkshire YO15 1PD

It might seem odd that this book is sending you to a city, but then Flamborough Head is a different sort of city: a seabird city. On the chalky cliffs of the Flamborough peninsula the breeding birds are packed together more tightly than in an urban centre. The invisible thoroughfares, taking the birds fishing out to sea and then back to the cliffs, are so congested it is always the rush hour. The noise is as endless as the hub of human activity and the smell is as bad as industrial waste. There are conflicts, bad temper, life and death. There is even a dangerous underclass of predators. And here on the cliffs, at the times when the birds have mostly gone in winter, the sea and the wind replaces the squeals of the birds. This place is magnificent, but in truth it is rarely peaceful.

Flamborough sticks out 6 miles into the North Sea just north of the town of Bridlington, East Yorkshire. At its tip the cliffs are about 200ft tall, but on the north side of the peninsula, Bempton Cliffs rise to 400ft. This 4-mile stretch plays host to more than 200,000 pairs of seabirds between April and July, of a wide variety of species. There are about 40,000 pairs of kittiwakes, a very noisy gull with clean black wing-tips, 60,000 guillemots, 15,000 razorbills, 6,000 gannets and about 1,000 puffins, as well as herring gulls, shags, cormorants and fulmars. The guillemots and razorbills look rather like flying penguins, with their upright stance, white bellies and black upperparts, while the gannets are huge ivory-white seabirds with a 6ft wingspan; their wing tips are black and their heads butterscotch coloured. All have their niches on the cliffs. The puffin, everybody's favourite, is slightly more difficult to see, but few visitors in the correct season will leave disappointed. The herring gulls and great black-backed gulls often cause the smaller birds trouble.

This seabird spectacle is one of the most accessible in England. You just turn up and look at them, parking at Bempton Cliffs or North Landing; the longer walk from Flamborough Head is also delightful. The farmland around the head is private, but there are public footpaths along all the cliffs. All three car parks

Seasonal highlights

Spring
Grasshopper warbler,
guillemot, thrift

Summer
Puffin, northern marsh
orchid, rock pools

Autumn
Harebell, skuas,
shearwaters

Winter
Gulls, cormorant, shag

All year
Gannet, fulmar, jackdaw

mentioned have facilities. On cold winter days there might not be anyone about.

It isn't all seabirds. The farmland is good for tree sparrows and skylarks, with sedge and grasshopper warblers around the scrubby areas. Joining the seabirds on the cliffs are jackdaws, rock pipits and peregrine falcons. Even the pigeons are interesting here; they bear striking similarity to their distant ancestor, the rock dove, which breeds on tall cliffs, although few are pure-bred.

You might think that this is a 'summer-special' site, but the good news is there is always something to see, even in the depths of winter. And not just gulls, as you might expect. Gannets and fulmars are here all year round, as are cormorants, shags and, to some extent, guillemots, although all of these are in reduced numbers. Puffins are absent between August and April, so it is important, if you wish to see these birds, not to come too late in the summer. The skylarks and pipits of the clifftop fields don't abandon the place either, and on a calm January day you

could easily hear a lark singing. In the autumn many migratory birds pass through, some on the land and some over the sea. It is a superb spot for shearwaters and skuas, right from August through to October. In the autumn landbird rarities are often present. There is an extensive programme of ringing and study carried out by the Flamborough Bird Observatory.

Although the birds are more obvious than anything else, Flamborough does offer other interesting animals and plants. On the clifftop, colourful flowers such as thrift, harebells and both pyramidal and northern marsh orchids can be found. At South Landing beach, there are quite superb rock pools. Even adults will find the different-coloured seaweeds, the shrimps, seashells and small fish captivating. All in all, the area is one of the best places in Britain to see a lot of great wildlife very easily.

Puffin

80 Humberhead Peatlands

Four bogs near Goole

Grange Road, Moorends, Doncaster, South Yorkshire DN8 4NA

Grid ref SE702159

Directions From Thorne turn left on Marshland Road into Moorends, then right at Grange Road; park near end

Lunch stop Kings Chamber, Selby Road, Thorne, South Yorkshire DN8 4JE

Humberhead Peatlands is the posh name for four bogs near Goole in Yorkshire, not far from the Humber Estuary. The four constitute the largest area of raised bog in lowland Britain, an impressive wilderness the size of 3,000 football pitches. It was once much larger, but is still a substantial National Nature Reserve, notable especially for its birds and insects.

The four bogs are Thorne Moors, Goole Moors, Crowle Moors and Hatfield Moors, the first three being joined together, while Hatfield Moors is a little to the south, separated by the M180 motorway. The moors formed on the underlying clay deposits here about 3,000 to 4,000 years ago, forming a dome of peat which rose above the surrounding catchment, hence 'raised' bog or mire, and kept wet with rainwater. The four bogs have all been cut for peat and drained to some extent, and all are now being gradually restored. The area contains a good mix of different habitats including lakes, marshes, scrub, heath and deciduous woodland.

For the visitor, the peatlands are a superb place to get away from it all and see raised bog for miles around under wide skies. They can, though, be a difficult place to see the best wildlife. Birds, especially, move freely around, something that is harder for a human visitor to do. It is worth persevering, though, and the two parts of Humberhead Peatlands have superb paths and trails that you can walk along. It is a truly wild, often lonely, place.

The best way to see the northern three moors is to park at Moorends, north of Thorne, picking up the Peatlands Way by parking in Grange Road and following the brown signs onto the track. The trail takes you out onto the moor and eventually to a metal observation platform where you can look for such birds as marsh harrier, merlin and, if you are lucky, hen harrier, which comes here to roost. The moors are also excellent for wildfowl. Hatfield Moors are best reached off the A614 along a track opposite Boston Park Farm (SE6704). There is a complex of lakes right here where you immediately begin to look for wildfowl and waders. Lapwings, little ringed and ringed plovers breed in the peatlands and such birds as greenshank and black-tailed godwit pass through. In the winter a feature of both areas is the visiting herds of whooper swans and pink-footed geese. Cranes have been recorded several times recently, and for a few years a small number of bluethroats bred.

The other main ornithological gem is the nightjar, a nocturnal bird that breeds here in nationally important numbers (90 pairs recently, about two per cent of the British population). These birds trawl the skies for night-flying insects such as moths and beetles, and the males make a peculiar hollow and highly atmospheric 'jarring' sound on summer nights. Another summer visitor is the hobby, which feeds on the abundant dragonflies.

Both Thorne Moors and Hatfield Moors are exceptionally good places for creepy-crawlies, the former being the richest site in the whole of northern England, and the best raised mire in Britain. Amazingly, 5,000 species of insects have been recorded in the two moors, which amounts to nearly a quarter of the entire British total and is only exceeded by three other sites in the country. You aren't going to see many of them, of course, but these totals do reflect what an important site this is. Six of the species don't occur anywhere else in Britain: step forward the mire pill-beetle *Curimposis nigrita* and the ground beetle *Bembidion humerale* as two examples, both of which are also rare throughout Europe.

Other highlights include a very strong population of adders, together with some good bog plants such as bog rosemary, cranberry, round-leaved sundew and an abundance of cottongrasses of two species.

This is one area that is much richer than its overall appearance suggests. It repays repeated visits at all times of the year.

Seasonal highlights

Spring
Cottongrass, black-tailed godwit, damselflies

Summer
Rare beetles, nightjar, large heath

Autumn
Cranberry, hobby, bog rosemary

Winter
Pink-footed goose, whooper swan, hen harrier

All year
Sphagnum moss, lapwing, cross-leaved heath

Cottongrass

81 Kielder Forest

Scandinavian-style lake and forest

Bakethin Nature Reserve, Lakeside Way, Hexham, Northumberland NE48 1HD

Grid ref NY630926

Directions Follow south shore of Kielder Water past Leaplish Waterside Park; at west end of lake, park near viaduct

Lunch stop The Pheasant Inn, Stannersburn, Falstone, Hexham, Northumberland NE48 1DD

If ever a site didn't deserve to be in a book about getting away into the wild, then surely the Kielder Forest is it. Nothing hereabouts is natural. Kielder Forest is the largest forestry plantation in Britain and the biggest entirely planted forest in Europe. Many of the harvested trees are Sitka spruces, which come from North America, so aren't even native. Kielder Water is the largest artificial reservoir in England by capacity, although Rutland Water has a longer shoreline. When constructed in 1975-81 it submerged farmland, a school and a railway. Even the surrounding moorland, priceless nowadays for its rare upland breeding birds, is a far cry from the broadleaved forest that would once have covered the area. Therefore, even the feeling of getting away from it all, easy in the forest, is in a way fake, stemming from big projects by large industries.

Of course, the site is in this book because very little in our crowded islands is genuinely natural, and Kielder is just a very big example of what happens everywhere. And besides, it offers some great walking and superb wildlife in scenery that resembles the lake and forest regions of Scandinavia. A walking trail, Lakeside Way, extends about 26 miles around the shore. The region is well developed as a tourist site, with generally good facilities.

Such a large place (250 square miles) needs a starting point for wildlife-watching, and the Bakethin Nature Reserve, run by the Northumberland Wildlife Trust, is ideal, because it offers a genuinely rich all-round site that also showcases the local specialities. So, for example, it is full of common frogs, while also offering the visitor a chance to see an osprey. The 346-acre reserve is found right on the northwest corner of Kielder, alongside Kielder Burn as it flows into Bakethin Reservoir. It is only a short distance from the tourist sites of Kielder Castle and the salmon hatchery, both of which are worth a look.

A recommended walking trail begins in the viaduct car park by Butteryhaugh Bridge. If you are here early in the morning, keep your eyes peeled as you walk left along the burn and cross the bridge, because otters can be seen here at

Osprey

quiet times of day; they can also be seen all around the lake shore. The trail leads along a road and then an old logging track, cutting back along the old viaduct of the inundated railway. The Scots pine/Norway spruce woodland is good for roe deer and, if you are very sharp, you might see a red squirrel in the treetops. However, these are much easier to see in other parts of Kielder, not least the bird hide by the castle. Look especially for lovers of coniferous woodland such as siskins and crossbills, the latter specialising in taking seeds from cones of spruce and, to a lesser extent, pine. Goldcrests and coal tits are also abundant.

Kielder Forest is famous for its birds of prey, and the viaduct section is one of many good lookout points. Apart from buzzards, which are common, you might be fortunate enough to see a goshawk, for which Kielder is a major stronghold. They are big versions of the sparrowhawk, the bird of prey that often snatches tits from the bird feeders, yet these are buzzard-sized, their long tails making them distinctive. They feed on mammals such as squirrels as well as birds. Merlins also breed on the surrounding moors and can sometimes be spotted, as can peregrine falcons.

These days, though, the bird that everybody wants to see is the osprey. These fish-eating raptors first nested on Kielder Water in 2009, and at the time of writing there are three pairs, raising nine young. Ospreys are summer visitors, so you can only see them between April and August, when they will perform their spectacular talons-first plunge-dives into the water to catch fish several times a day. They are easiest to see at Leaplish Waterside Park, along the southern shore of Kielder Water, where telescopes are set up to see the nest (June to August).

The nesting ospreys are a magical part of the Kielder experience, but also symptomatic of the site. The birds breed here, but it has taken the construction of artificial nesting platforms to get them to do so. Once again, despite the appearance of wildness, all is not as it seems.

Seasonal highlights

Spring
Common frog, barnacle goose, merlin

Summer
Osprey, otter, trout

Autumn
Siskin, pink-footed goose, crossbill

Winter
Goldeneye, goosander, whooper swan

All year
Sitka spruce, goshawk, red squirrel

217

82 Malham Cove

Water running under the pavement

Chapel Gate, Malham, Skipton, North Yorkshire BD23 4DG

Grid ref SD899626

Directions From Skipton follow minor roads to Malham; if car park at visitor centre is full, park on side of road towards Kirkby Malham

Lunch stop The Lister Arms, Malham, Skipton, North Yorkshire BD23 4DB

This wonderful site doesn't qualify as the quietest or most neglected in this book. In fact, it is often full of tourists. However, the trippers usually just walk to the cove and back again, so only the determined or more intrepid climb the seemingly endless steps up the western side to the limestone pavements on top. Once you get here, peace isn't so far away.

The area might be a tripper-trap, but you've got to come. Only a mile down a well-worn track from the tea-shop-infested village of Malham in the Yorkshire Dales, the cove is soaring in its sheer magnificence, the towering limestone cliffs forming a huge amphitheatre of rock. It looks impressive now, but go back to just after the last Ice Age and this was a massive waterfall clearing meltwaters from glaciers, a chute of epic proportions. The arched shape is caused by the centre of the waterfall being eroded more rapidly than the sides. The limestone is porous and full of caves and, rather pathetically when you think about it, a river, Malham Beck, now emerges from the bottom instead of the top. This stream originates from Malham Tarn, and dives underground at Water Sinks, a little short of the cove.

If you visit the cove from late March to July, you are likely to bump into a wildlife viewing spectacle without even trying. Since 1993, pairs of peregrine falcons have been nesting on the cliffs, and the RSPB has recently set up viewing areas where you can watch the birds through telescopes (currently Saturday to Wednesday, 10.30am to 4pm). There is usually at least one bird sitting on the cliff face, while, if you are lucky, you might witness the other, usually the male, bringing in a catch for the female and/or the young. The peregrine is the world's fastest flyer (112mph at the very least) and dives upon pigeons and other birds, often breaking their neck on impact – a remarkable if brutal sight.

Several other species of birds breed in the rocks. The habitat is right for little owl, and up until very recently there was a tree where one sat to be admired reliably. Otherwise it's up to you (or the RSPB spotter) to find this well-

House martins

camouflaged bird. Much easier to see are the house martins and swifts. These birds are of particular interest because they usually nest on buildings. Here, though, they are breeding on entirely natural cliff sites; the swifts use crevices, while the house martins build their famous cup-shaped mud nests that adhere to the rock faces. While on the subject of birds, look out for green woodpeckers feeding on ants on the grassy slopes, and for dippers and grey wagtails along Malham Beck.

There are about 400 steps from the base of the cove to the top, but if you have the energy it is always worthwhile – if only for the view of Malham and beyond, which is particularly fulsome and stunning. However, from a natural perspective, the climb brings you onto the limestone pavement, an intriguing treasure trove of plants and flowers. Here you will learn all about clints and grykes, and you'll be the better for it.

Limestone pavements are so named because they consist of a series of slabs with gaps between them, like a pavement. The slabs or blocks are called clints, and on the surface of these grow flowers that like the sun and normally thrive in open habitats such as grassland. The vertical gaps between the slabs, however – the grykes – are typically humid and sheltered, and the plants that grow inside these are typical of shaded areas, even woodland. On these pavements, then, you can find plants of completely different habitats rubbing shoulders with each other. To give an example, the clint flowers occurring here are those such as common rock-rose and wild thyme, while the gryke-loving flora includes woodland plants such as bloody cranesbill, wood sorrel, dog's mercury and a wide range of ferns, including the rigid buckler fern that is confined to these pavements.

Having paid homage to the buckler fern and company, the choice is yours – solitude on the top trails or a return to the tea shops. Both are thoroughly agreeable options.

Seasonal highlights

Spring
Peregrine, house martin, dog's mercury

Summer
Green woodpecker, swift, bloody cranesbill

Autumn
Rigid buckler fern, wild thyme, common rock-rose

Winter
Buzzard, raven, grey wagtail

All year
Magnificent cliff amphitheatre, dipper

83 St Mary's Island

A magnet for day-trippers of all kinds

The Links, Whitley Bay, Tyne and Wear NE26 4RS

Grid ref NZ350750

Directions From the A1058 coast road continue to the seafront; turn left and head through the village of Cullercoats to Whitley Bay

Lunch stop The Harbour View, 1–3 Beresford Road, Whitley Bay, Tyne and Wear NE26 4DR

The lighthouse on the top of St Mary's Island, near Whitley Bay, is one of the most photographed spots on the northeast coast. What the numerous visitors to this delightful spot don't often realise when they come is just how good it is for wildlife, too. It attracts thousands of passers-by, and not all of them human.

Take the famous grey seals, for instance. They can be seen here for most of the year, but they don't breed or raise young on the rocks of the island; they are visitors from the Farne Island colonies 40 miles to the north. So, in a sense they are just as much day-trippers as the crowds of people. The seals use the rocks as a 'haul-out' as it is known, a place to rest for a while during feeding expeditions and other business.

Haul-outs are very important to these animals for their overall health and energy conservation, and unfortunately this sometimes leads to problems with disturbance. People get curious and edge too close, panicking the sea mammals off the rocks. A seal watch has been set up and visitors are asked to give the seals a respectfully wide berth. Anyhow, there is a lookout shelter from which you should obtain good views.

While the seals draw the attention of the general public, many other forms of wildlife make use of the island and the nearby St Mary's Wetland, a small adjacent area of freshwater pools. In particular, wading birds use the whole place for roosting and feeding, some in nationally important numbers. Purple sandpiper, turnstone, sanderling, redshank and golden plover are all here between July and March or April, and loaf on the rocks, the wetland or the clifftop grassland. Terns often visit during fishing trips from the Farne Islands or Coquet Island, and a good mix of species is often found in mid to late summer, including a lot of Arctic terns and a few of the rare roseate tern. This tern has a delicate pink flush to its breast. Arctic terns pass by on their way to the Antarctic region for the winter.

It is hardly surprising that wading birds are drawn to the coast here, because the mud, seaweed and rocks are a haven for a fabulous range of creatures.

Seasonal highlights

Spring
Common frog, Sandwich tern, gannet

Summer
Roseate tern, kittiwake, moths

Autumn
Golden plover, barnacle goose, Manx shearwater

Winter
Purple sandpiper, eider, oystercatcher

All year
Grey seal, rock-pool life, turnstone

Sunny days may see dozens of human families out on the rocks, with buckets, spades and enthusiasm, thrilling to the sight of crabs, shrimps, winkles, sea anemones and small fish. It is one of the best rock-pooling sites in the northeast of England, if not the whole country.

St Mary's Island itself is one of those exciting places that is cut off at high tide. Most of the time it is easily reachable by foot across a causeway but twice a day it is a real island. Check the tide times posted in the car park carefully. If the island is accessible, it has good facilities including a small museum in the lighthouse. There is an entrance fee and you can climb the 137 steps to the top, from which the view is ravishing.

Much work has been done recently to look after the wetland by the car park for St Mary's Island, and don't neglect the grassland at Curry's Point and on the walk towards Crag Point and Seaton Sluice. As well as providing refuge for passing birds, the wetland has breeding common frogs, lapwings, mallards and coots, and ducks such as gadwall drop in. Several pairs of grasshopper warblers breed in the waterside reeds and scrub, alongside the commoner birds such as whitethroats and sedge warblers. The cliff grassland, meanwhile, has a decent flora and attracts a couple of rare moths: the coastal dart and the lyme-grass moth.

Let's face it, not many visitors to St Mary's Island are there for the moths! But they do show what a rich and varied wildlife manages to coexist with the flocks of humankind that inhabit this superb piece of coastline.

Common frog

84 Spurn Point

Wonders at the end of the road

Spurn Road, Kilnsea, Hull, East Yorkshire HU12 0UH

Grid ref TA417158

Directions Go south from Kilnsea; no vehicular access to Spurn Point

Lunch stop The Camerton, Main Street, Thorngumbald, East Yorkshire HU12 9NG

The peninsula at Spurn is not one of the most scenic sites in this book, but it nonetheless has an otherworldliness about it which is attractive and unmistakable to a visitor. It is also, arguably, the best site in Britain for birdwatching, at least on the mainland, and is a great place to observe the antics of people with binoculars. Spurn is a magnet for rarities, and on a good day, especially in autumn, the excitement on the peninsula is palpable.

Spurn Point is 32 miles southeast of Hull or, strictly speaking, Kingston-upon-Hull. Go east along the A1033 to Patrington, then southeast on the B1445 to Easington and onward to the minor road to Kilnsea. You can park here or continue to the Bluebell Café where there is a car park and visitor centre, or to Warren Cottage, where the old bird observatory is still based (there is an additional new one in Kilnsea). You can take your choice, although there are plans afoot for a new visitor centre which might change these arrangements. Once here you are at a major hub in the birding world, with its military-style nicknames for tiny landmarks – the Triangle Field, the Canal Zone, Sammy's Point, the Narrows and so on – yet it is also a place where it is easy to find lonely beaches and solitude.

Spurn Point protrudes 3.5 miles into the mouth of the giant Humber Estuary, the huge cleft on the east coast that drains one-fifth of all England. The Point itself is made up from hard glacial deposits that don't easily erode, and around these form unstable sand dunes connected to the mainland. The coastline of shifting sands is dynamic and unpredictable. A severe storm surge in 2013 washed away a section of the peninsula, including the access road to the Point below the old observatory, and these days this breach is covered by high tides and the road is no longer used for traffic. When visiting, keep an eye on the tide times to make sure you aren't cut off.

The area is largely open access and so you can walk at your leisure. The mix of habitat includes the dunes, the North Sea and beach (the rare little tern breeds nearby), the saltmarsh on the landward side, some chalk grassland, some fresh water, and stands of bushes and trees, the latter providing cover for

migratory birds. None of it is especially pretty, unless you are a small bird desperate for a suitable spot to refuel after a long migratory journey.

Spurn Point attracts birds for two reasons. It is a peninsula that becomes narrower and narrower, so a southbound bird following the coastline will be funnelled towards the spit of land. At the same time, northbound coasting birds will make landfall here once they have crossed the Humber. Finally, in autumn, when the winds are from the east, this part of the coast catches the massive surge of birds that fly south down the coast of the near Continent. If you add these factors together and combine them with the great variety of habitats in a small area, you can begin to imagine why up to 300 species can be seen here in a single year.

Although many rare birds drop in, with something good present on just about every single day of the year, the biggest excitement is on autumn mornings. Many species make local movements in the first few hours after dawn, still visibly migrating in the daylight. At the Narrows, at first light, streams of birds such as chaffinches, meadow pipits, snow buntings and rarities such as Lapland buntings and Richard's pipits may fly almost overhead, calling as they do so, with all kinds of species involved. Once this has died down you can visit the ringing station at Warren Cottage to see what has been trapped: birds such as redstarts, flycatchers and yellow-browed warblers. It is also worth looking over the sea to see what is passing, maybe a skua or a shearwater or two. This truly is birding heaven.

There is other wildlife, too. The observatory records moths and butterflies, which can be spectacular – the hummingbird hawk-moth is one of the regular migrants. Grey seals and dolphins (even whales) are sometimes seen offshore, while good plants live on the shingle, dunes and saltmarsh, such as pyramidal orchid.

But all these occur in plentiful supply elsewhere. For birds, Spurn is simply out of this world.

Hummingbird hawk-moth

Seasonal highlights

Spring
Little tern, ringed plover, orange-tip

Summer
Hummingbird hawk-moth, terns, pyramidal orchid

Autumn
Migrant birds, migrant moths

Winter
Brent goose, dunlin, bar-tailed godwit

All year
Tree sparrow, meadow pipit, seals

85 Stainforth Force

Where salmon leap and spawn

Stainforth, Settle, North Yorkshire BD24 9QD

Grid ref SD820672

Directions Just west of Stainforth village

Lunch stop The Lion at Settle, Duke Street, Settle, North Yorkshire BD24 9DU

Everybody loves waterfalls, but this one is special. Not only is it set within the glorious countryside of the Yorkshire Dales, next to an attractive village, but you can also witness one of nature's compelling dramas here in the autumn. There is a load of wildlife in the immediate area. And, if you haven't had your fill, there is another excellent 'secret' waterfall nearby.

Stainforth Force lies close to its namesake village and is beloved by locals and tourists alike as a beauty spot, where the adventurous dip and swim. In October and November, though, it doubles as a front-row seat for watching leaping salmon; in fact, people occasionally swim at the same time as these majestic fish are trying to negotiate the rapids. This probably isn't a good idea among these slippery rocks and deceptively deep pools, bearing in mind that it's autumn and it must be perishing cold, too. And besides, you can get so close to the salmon that it sometimes feels as though you could touch them anyway. The fish perform best after periods of rain.

The salmon run is, of course, one of nature's great journeys. The fish start as eggs upstream in the quiet early reaches of the river (here it's the Ribble), hatching in the spring. They grow for a year or so before heading downstream for a brief stop in estuarine waters and then the open sea, some reaching the waters off Greenland, where they remain for between one and four years. Big, muscular fish now, they find their home rivers in a way we don't fully understand, although sea currents, the stars in the night sky and the earth's magnetic field all play a part, as well as the 'smell' of the familiar river. The leaping is close to the end of their journey, the last act of this extraordinary life cycle, when the exhausted fish spawn in the same spot where they, too, began life.

You reach the falls – there are several small drops and one big one – by parking in Stainforth and following the B6479 north before crossing left over the railway line and following the track over the packhorse bridge, built in 1675. Turn left, and shortly the Force is with you. The area is quite wooded, so look out for birds in the trees.

Once you have spotted a salmon, there are other options to delight the visitor, not least Catrigg Force, which lies to the east just off the Pennine Bridleway. The stroll takes you uphill along a wide track, where in summer there are birds such as northern wheatear and lapwing. You don't see the waterfall at first, only a sign to the left, which takes you steeply down through a lovely wooded valley to Stainforth Beck. The falls themselves are hidden away but surprisingly impressive, two of them each with a 20ft drop, too much for a salmon to handle. Apparently the composer Edward Elgar found inspiration at this spot, and it isn't difficult to see why.

The gorge is good for woodland birds such as redstarts, while if you spend enough time near these rushing torrents anywhere hereabouts you are certain to see a dipper. These remarkable aquatic birds, which can swim underwater, often breed behind waterfalls, which is one of the safest places any bird can nest, well out of reach of predators. Grey wagtails should be equally as common. Both species can be seen all year round.

You could go straight back down to Stainforth, but the Dales countryside will have got to you by now, and there are plenty of paths to delay your return to civilisation, up to Catrigg or down to Langcliffe, where there is, incidentally, a fish ladder at the weir, where again you might spot the long-distance travellers. Whatever effort you expend today, theirs will be the greater.

Seasonal highlights

Spring
Redstart, buttercup, common twayblade

Summer
Common sandpiper, violet oil beetle, lapwing

Autumn
Salmon, harebell, black knapweed

Winter
Dipper, grey wagtail

All year
Waterfalls, raven

86 Upper Teesdale
Ice Age relics and plunging water

Bowlees Cottages, Newbiggin, Barnard Castle, County Durham DL12 0XE

Grid ref NY908281

Directions From Barnard Castle head northeast to Middleton-in-Teesdale and Bowlees

Lunch stop The Crown, Mickleton, Barnard Castle, County Durham DL12 0JZ

Some parts of the country are simply more richly blessed with nature than others, and in this respect, few can compete with the hallowed ground of Upper Teesdale, in the west of County Durham. In the distant past, 295 million years ago in the Carboniferous period, large intrusions of magma seeped through the limestone bedrock to form a layer of dolerite called the Great Whin Sill. This mix of rocks, through which flows the magnificent, rushing River Tees, has given rise to a remarkable landscape characterised by crags and thundering waterfalls. The varied geology, which also includes the very rare sugar limestone – so named for its white, square-lump appearance – has created a botanical treasure house in the heart of the moody Pennine landscape, one of the finest in all of Britain. It is a place to be overpowered by the majesty and diversity of nature.

The most famous sights of Upper Teesdale are its waterfalls, and it is worth coming to see these even without the flowers, birds and other wildlife delights. They provide a year-round element to the site's attractions, being at their fiercest after rain in autumn or winter. High Force is the most impressive, a thundering brute of a waterfall that seems to squeeze through the gaps in its crag with a roar of effort, angriest in early spring when the snow starts to melt in the fells above. Low Force is a gentler, more 'contented' waterfall further downstream in a more open landscape, while Cauldron Snout, quite some way west below the dam of Cow Green Reservoir, is a set of powerful rapids.

For a few weeks in the summer, from late May until the end of July, Upper Teesdale explodes with wildflower magic, and botanists travel here from far and wide to gorge on the rare and the beautiful. You don't need to be a specialist to enjoy the sight of orchids on the limestone verges and banks, and colourful public blooms such as the meadow cranesbill, globeflower and melancholy thistles, the latter nodding distinctively. But to rave about Teesdale with the best of them, you need to get among botanists, perhaps joining a tour, or at least looking at the best sites with a wildflower book in your hand.

Upper Teesdale has acted as a refuge for Arctic-alpine plants ever since the Ice Age. As the ice retreated north, the warming land of northern England became less and less suitable for cold-adapted species. Here, though, the late springs, snowmelt and suitable geology have frozen the flora in time, so to speak, and the subsequent traditional management of hay meadows on the limestone has been kind to all the flowers. In a small area, ideal ecological conditions and resistance to mechanisation have created this wildflower haven.

Black grouse

Thus, here at Teesdale you trip easily over the rarities. Pay a visit to the meadow at Widdybank Farm for Scottish asphodel and Alpine bartsia, and to steep Cetry Bank just below the farm for yellow saxifrage, the quarry at Bowlees for St John's-worts and lady's mantles. And whatever you do, don't miss the climb up on to Cronkley Fell, part of which is along the Pennine Way. You pass through the largest juniper wood in Britain, and then at the top reach the sugar limestone area where the prizes include hoary rock-rose and Alpine meadow-rue. One of the most colourful gems, the spring gentian, also occurs here. It is the classic alpine plant, the tubular flowers of surreal deep blue, growing in small patches. You can hardly take your eyes off such a sight, but do lift them and enjoy the surrounding Pennine landscape.

The joys of the Teesdale spring don't end with the flowers, or the views. Upper Teesdale also happens to be a superb site for rare breeding birds; indeed, it holds one of the densest concentrations of waders in the country. The key species are lapwing, curlew, redshank and golden plover, and all are handsome and all are noisy. Dippers, grey wagtails, common sandpipers and goosanders all breed along the River Tees; there are raptors such as merlin in the hills and the woods resound to the songs of redstarts, wood warblers, pied flycatchers and tree pipits.

For many, though, the ornithological highlight is the display ground ('lek') of black grouse on Langdon Common. These handsome birds are in severe decline in the UK, yet here they are still common. Every morning and evening from early spring into autumn the males gather here to display and attract the attention of females, who visit, choose their favourite performer, mate and leave. The spectacle is visible from the road at dawn and dusk. On a good day, there will be skirmishes and bubbling, cooing calls, and much commotion at the appearance of a female. It's as entertaining as a television blockbuster.

And that, indeed, could refer to the whole Upper Teesdale experience.

Seasonal highlights

Spring
Black grouse, ring ouzel, spring gentian

Summer
Arctic-alpine flowers, waders, willow warbler

Autumn
Juniper, rock whitebeam, late flowers

Winter
Goosander, red grouse, peregrine

All year
Magnificent waterfalls, sugar limestone, powerful rapids

87 Wessenden Moor

The heart of the Dark Peak

Station Road, Marsden, Huddersfield, West Yorkshire HD7 6AP

Grid ref SE046118

Directions From Marsden, follow signs to station; alternatively park just off A635 along Wessenden Head Road (SE077075)

Lunch stop The Olive Branch, Manchester Road, Marsden, Huddersfield, West Yorkshire HD7 6LU

Wessenden Moor is not the richest wildlife spot in this book, but if you do see something, there is a high chance that it will be interesting, and perhaps not common. Situated in the Dark Peak, this is uncompromising moorland, magnificent and inspiring to some but intimidating and desolate to others. You will never be overwhelmed with wildlife sightings here, but if you like a sense of wilderness and stark beauty, this will make up for that.

There are two ways to reach Wessenden Moor. You can jump straight in by parking just off the A635 on Wessenden Head Road and following the path down towards Wessenden Head Reservoir. An enjoyable alternative, if you have time, is to begin in the town of Marsden and walk; the advantage of this is a chance to enjoy the transition between the busy Pennine settlement and the steadily increasing isolation as you make your way up onto the moors. Park at Marsden Station (paying), make your way up Station Road, bear right to keep the impressive St Bartholomew's Church on your right. Go through the tunnel beneath the A62 (noisy), past the sports ground, go over the roundabout and follow the marked footpath through the mill until, quite suddenly, you are at the foot of Butterley Reservoir dam. From here it is 210 steps to the water level, and the end of civilisation – for now at least.

The path follows the water company road past Butterley and Blakeley Reservoirs; listen out for the piccolo-like calls of common sandpipers in summer. At the end of Blakeley, turn right on the Pennine Way to cross Wessenden Brook and ascend steeply up towards Blakeley Clough and the open moor, or carry on, also on the Pennine Way, past Wessenden Reservoir and complete your reservoir set at Wessenden Head. Either way, you will be engulfed in the moorland atmosphere. The wind and wild sounds will make Marsden seem far away.

Wessenden Moor is a mixture of heather moor, bare peat and blanket bog. The peat has been laid down for 9,000 years and is very thick. Apart from the heather, look out for several berry-bearing plants: bilberry (which you can harvest and eat in the autumn), crowberry and cloudberry. The former is a

shrubby evergreen with lots of tiny pink flowers along its stem. It can never decide what colour its berries should be; they start green then go pink, purple and end up black. The cloudberry has raspberry-like fruits, except that they are orange.

There are many excellent birds to see and hear on the moorland, including one that is unequivocally always reddish-purple. The red grouse is common here and you sometimes flush them from the heather, causing them to blurt out their loud 'go-back' call. On spring mornings this is translated into an atmospheric display call, uttered in a brief display flight. Curlews are here, too, with their gorgeous liquid bubbling and, if you are very lucky, you might also hear the needle-sharp, melancholy call of the golden plover. Together with the seemingly endless, rather mechanical 'sip-sip-sip' of the meadow pipit, you truly have a chorus to remember. Skylarks occur in places, too.

Although difficult to see, one of the star species of this part of the Pennines is a small, rather plain finch known as the twite. It is related to the more colourful linnet but has a more cereal-coloured face without any white patches, and certainly no brilliant crimson on the breast, as the linnet does. It is shy and retiring and difficult to see, so it would be a major coup if you came across it.

One of Wessenden Moor's most famous inhabitants is also one of its most elusive. The mountain hare is the only hare or rabbit certainly native to Britain, the others having been deliberately introduced: the rabbit by the Normans and the brown hare probably by the Romans. The mountain hare is well adapted to harsh upland conditions, not least by turning white in the winter, with the only black on the tips of its ears and tail. The Pennine winter isn't reliably snowy, however, so these mammals sometimes stick out like a sore thumb when they turn white but the moors remain damp and brownish-purple. However, even when they are conspicuously white these mammals can still lead enthusiasts a merry dance. They are largely nocturnal and hide away during the day in the heather. To see them you need luck, and plenty of patience. But in a place like this, time stands still anyway.

Mountain hare

88 Wheldrake Ings

Genuinely ancient landscape

Ings Lane, York, North Yorkshire YO19 6DE

Grid ref SE694444

Directions From York, take the A19 southeast and follow signs to Wheldrake; follow Main Street to Church Lane east out of village, reserve is on left after sharp right-hand bend

Lunch stop St Vincent Arms, Sutton-upon-Derwent, York YO41 4BN

Wheldrake Ings is part of an ancient landscape. It isn't just the appearance that is timeless – many places in the UK look like they have been there forever – it is the reality. For hundreds of years, people have worked these watermeadows along the Upper Derwent River in the traditional way, cutting rather than ploughing and, mercifully, refraining from using pesticides and herbicides. This gentle land management has continued to the present day, meaning that the area is exceptionally rich in flowers, insects and all other wildlife.

It is a Yorkshire Wildlife Trust reserve encompassing 388 acres of flood meadows, riverbank, reedbeds and a large permanent pool. Despite the fact that it is only 8 miles from the city of York, and is well known locally for its wildlife, it is never crowded here and you often have one of the hides to yourself. It is elemental, flat and very quiet. In contrast to almost everywhere else nearby, you strain your ears in vain to hear the roar of traffic.

The area is celebrated for many things, not least the flood meadows, which in summer burst with colour and profusion. Some parts of the site may contain as many as 25 species of flowers in a single square yard. A very unusual plant assemblage known as the 'great burnet/meadow foxtail community' occurs on part of the site, the great burnet being a tall herb with a globular purple flower head, and the foxtail being a grass. There is less than 3,707 acres of this community in the whole of Britain, of which Wheldrake Ings is a major contributor. You cannot fail to see this community as you pass, and look out too for marsh marigolds, meadowsweet, cuckoo flower, yellow rattle and ox-eye daisies, among a host of others.

The site is fantastic for birds, and whatever season you visit you will see an excellent range of species and often big flocks too. In the summer, it is an astonishingly good place for breeding wildfowl and

Ox-eye daisy

Spring
Garganey, marsh marigold, cuckoo flower

Summer
Great burnet, corncrake, dragonflies

Autumn
Lapwing, little egret, bees

Winter
Swans, geese, roosting gulls

All year
Greylag goose, tufted duck, otter

waders. The former include greylag goose, shelduck, mallard, gadwall, shoveler, tufted duck, a few wigeon, teal and pochard and even the very rare garganey, although the last named is a secretive duck and you would be fortunate to see it. Waders include many lapwings, flocks of which appear on the newly cut meadows in late summer, plus curlew, redshank and snipe. In recent years little egrets have begun to breed, and, formerly an exceptional rarity, great egrets have been sighted with increasing frequency.

Some of the rarest breeding birds at Wheldrake Ings are unfortunately almost impossible to see, although you can hear them well enough. The site is famous for hosting a few singing male spotted crakes, which presumably hang on to breed when the silent females turn up. Recently corncrakes have also been heard every year, in perfect habitat for them, and the open grassland sometimes holds quail, too. All of these secretive birds, along with the much commoner and more numerous water rail, tend to make their advertising calls at night, the spotted crake sounding like the lash of a whip, the corncrake like a comb running over a matchbox and the water rail like a squealing pig. The quail makes a soft 'wet-me-lips' call. Together with the reeling of grasshopper warblers, the various ducks' calls and the noisy chorus of reed and sedge warblers, the nocturnal chorus can be pretty remarkable.

The change that comes with winter is profound. The meadows become progressively more flooded with normal amounts of rainfall and there is much extra open water. This attracts large numbers of wildfowl – up to 40,000 use the Lower Derwent Valley as a whole. Many of the ducks mentioned above are here in much greater numbers, except for garganey, which is a summer visitor. Arctic-breeding swans and geese winter in small numbers, mainly whooper swans and greater white-fronted geese. The open water is a perfect habitat for roosting gulls, and thousands come into the reserve on winter evenings.

The site is reached by turning off the A19 south of York to Wheldrake. Go through the village and on towards Thorganby, where you very quickly encounter a sharp right-hand bend. Just after the bend is a tarmac road left down to the reserve, where you park by the river. Your adventure begins as you cross the bailey bridge and follow the footpath. As well as muddy tracks, there are boardwalks through the reeds, and even a tower hide. Those are the modern trappings of a nature reserve. The rest is timeless.

89 Whitelee Moor

A blanket bog in the isolated uplands

Carter Bar, Jedburgh, Northumberland TD8 6PT

Grid ref NT698068

Directions From Newcastle upon Tyne take A696 then A68 to Carter Bar

Lunch stop Simply Scottish, 6–8 High Street, Jedburgh, Northumberland TD8 6AG

Red grouse

Many a visitor stops on the A68 at Carter Bar to take a picture as they reach the England–Scotland border on their way between Newcastle and Melrose or Edinburgh. Back in 1575 it was the scene of one of the last armed confrontations between the Scots and the English, the so-called 'Raid of the Redeswire', with a small loss of life and a Scottish victory. Coming here, you wonder why anybody would choose to fight over such a place. It is now, as it was then, an isolated upland pass at 1,371ft, surrounded by miles and miles of boggy moorland, within the undulating Cheviot Hills. It is mostly peaceful between nations now, but the countryside is harsh and difficult.

Carter Bar is the main entrance point for one of Britain's key upland nature reserves, Whitelee Moor. A gate at the car park leads to a very wet and boggy public footpath, which starts along the border and eventually follows the contours of a high and steep ridge. The heart of the moor is inhospitable and the track is hard to follow, a sort of heaven for the adventurous. Another track to the south runs through the north of Redesdale Forest, by Catcleugh Reservoir, but this soon deteriorates, too. Wildlife-watching is most definitely a challenge.

Whitelee Moor is, perhaps, one of those very important places where the wildlife is protected by the elements as well as the title of National Nature Reserve. A host of interesting birds breed on it, and as an active blanket bog it is

also botanically special. The bog plants include such staples as sphagnum moss, which is everywhere. Bog asphodel, cloudberry and both common and hare's-tail cottongrass are other distinctive plants, while the early marsh orchid blooms in a few places. Recently, much effort has been expended by the Northumberland Wildlife Trust into restoring the structure of the peat and preventing run-off into the River Rede. They have been putting in logs of coir, a neutral waste product that comes from coconuts. The coir stabilises the gullies and prevents erosion of the peat. In this way, the River Rede remains pristine and a good habitat for the rare freshwater pearl mussel, which is common in its clean shingle beds.

The birds of Whitelee Moor are a select band of upland species, many of which are declining in Britain. They include species you are likely to run into, such as whinchat, and those that are much harder to see, such as the predatory merlin, a small falcon that specialises in hunting small songbirds such as skylarks, meadow pipits and linnets. The merlin is just one of the many birds of prey that breed on the moor or nearby, the others being sparrowhawk, kestrel, buzzard and peregrine falcon. Hen harriers also visit.

The other prominent birds are waders, especially the rare golden plover, with its melancholy dirge, and the dunlin, which makes a song like the loud blast from a referee's whistle. Red grouse are common, and black grouse sometimes visit from nearby Scotland.

One of the curiosities of Whitelee Moor is the herd of feral goats, currently numbering around 50 animals. Goats are not native to Britain, but there are herds in parts of the country that might have been living wild for centuries. The origin of the Cheviot goats is not known for sure, but they have certainly been at large for over 100 years and probably much longer. Their shaggy coats, backward-pointing horns and dirty white and black/brown colour makes them easy to distinguish from the roe deer that also occur hereabouts, and the sheep and cattle that are set loose to keep the vegetation down. The goats are usually seen in the southwest of the reserve, close to Kielderhead.

Goats are not the only mammalian treat. Otters are also found here along the River Rede, although, as ever, they are secretive and difficult to see. However, you can at least try to glimpse them by watching quietly from the road at dusk; it would be foolish indeed to wander across the moor in the darkness in search of wildlife or anything else.

Seasonal highlights

Spring
Early marsh orchid, palmate newt, adder

Summer
Ringlet, dunlin, northern eggar (moth)

Autumn
Merlin, buzzard, cloudberry

Winter
Freshwater pearl mussel, black grouse, peregrine

All year
Red grouse, wild goat, otter

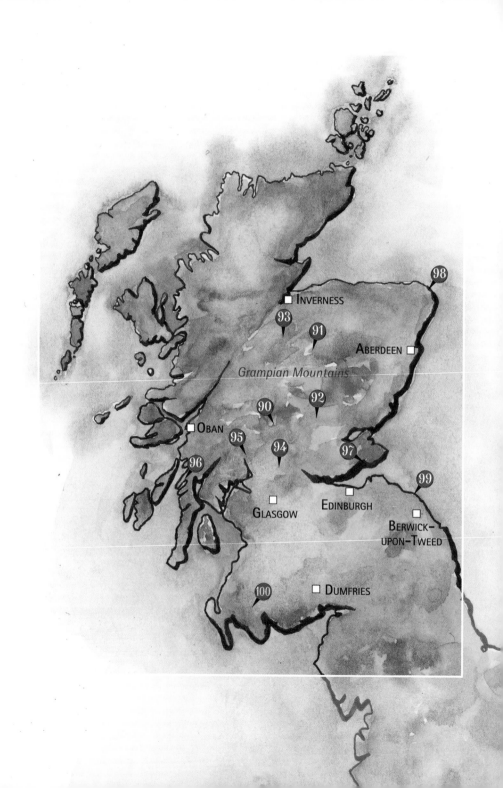

Scotland

90 Ben Lawers

The mountaintop rock-garden

Ben Lawers car park, Killin, Perthshire FK21 8TY

Grid ref NN608378

Directions Along the north shore of Loch Tay to Edramucky, turn right to car park

Lunch stop The Old Smiddy, Main Street, Killin, Perthshire FK21 8XE

If you were to ask a botanist which single site they would most like to visit in Britain, there is a good chance that this would be it. Ben Lawers has been famous for its wildflowers for more than 200 years. It also has special birds, butterflies and mammals. Add in the fact that it is easy to reach by road, has good accommodation and facilities and is not very far from many of the big Scottish cities, and you might ask yourself why you have never been there.

This mountain is the tenth highest in Britain, at 3,984ft. It is the tallest in the Central Highlands and is closely surrounded by six other peaks over 3,000ft – the so-called Munros. It is, however, very different from most other Scottish mountains in ways that affect its flora. The key feature is the schist rocks that push through the main bedrock formations high up towards the summit. The schists, which release minerals to create base-rich soils, are at a higher altitude than on other equally tall Scottish mountains, and it is these, together with the long periods of snow cover and the wind chill, that lend these slopes affinities more with Arctic-alpine regions than with other parts of the UK. The mountain is thus a refuge for many plants that are normally found a lot further north or on much higher ground.

The season is late here, and snow is sometimes still about in June or even July. The upper slope 'hanging gardens', as enthusiasts call them, are nevertheless as colourful and flowery as any garden rockery. From the vivid blue of the snow gentian to the sky-blue of the Alpine forget-me-not, the yellow of the mountain pansy and the white of the mossy saxifrage and pink moss campion, the blooms are vivid but small, and often in cushions. It really does look and feel akin to the rock gardens of the mountains of Central Europe.

There is a mind-blowing list of rarities on the mountain, of many different kinds: saxifrages, willows and lots of sedges and rushes, from the obscure to the stunning. They begin at the car park above Edramucky, where there is a nature trail and some areas have been fenced off from sheep and red deer browsing, mainly for the preservation of mountain scrub and willows. Follow the burn uphill and there will be starry saxifrage, grass of Parnassus and Scottish asphodel. Once the schists begin on the ridge there are many different rare saxifrages and the delight never stops all the way to the summit.

All this time you spend botanising, the rest of the wildlife world will distract you. It might be a peregrine overhead, a fluttering small pearl-bordered fritillary or mountain ringlet passing by, or even a mountain hare bursting from cover. Dippers and grey wagtails breed along the burns, red grouse are in the heather, and, near the summit, those hardy grouse, ptarmigans, eke out a living. A golden eagle might even pass overhead, although these are commoner on the northern side of the mountain. Black grouse occur nearby.

Much as general botanists will be enraptured by Ben Lawers, those who study the lower plants really will think they are in heaven. The damp flushes and snowmelt areas provide habitat for a wealth of mosses and liverworts, and as for the lichens – well, this is the best montane site in Britain. An incredible 600 species have been recorded, which is almost unimaginable. No fewer than 20 of these have not been seen anywhere else in Britain.

Of course, all this richness is in a location of stunning scenery. The mountain overlooks Loch Tay, and near the top you can see as far as Loch Lomond to the southwest and the Cairngorms to the north. The nearby summits are glorious, especially when snow-capped, as they so often are. A winter trek around here is beautiful, but you should take due care. Birds such as ptarmigans will be around, but they are a good deal tougher than you are; they roost on the snow.

And under that same snow, preserved by the chill, the glories of Ben Lawers await another season of growth.

Seasonal highlights

Spring
Rare willows, ring ouzel, alpine forget-me-not

Summer
Mountain ringlet, Arctic-alpine plants, snow gentian

Autumn
Red grouse, grey wagtail, red deer

Winter
Mosses, liverworts, golden eagle

All year
Lichens, ptarmigan, mountain hare

Alpine forget-me-not

91 Ben Macdui

A first-rate runner-up

Cairngorm Ski Area, Aviemore, Cairngorms PH22 1RB

Grid ref NH989060

Directions Off B970 to Coylumbridge look for signposted minor road to Glenmore and ski centre

Lunch stop Ptarmigan Restaurant (top of funicular railway), Cairngorm Ski Area, PH22 1RB

Heather

For a high mountain, Ben Macdui (4,295ft) keeps a low profile. While most people can probably remember that Ben Nevis is the tallest mountain in Britain, how many remember the name of the second highest peak, only 130ft or so lower? And who bothers to climb Ben Macdui when you can get a significantly long way up Cairngorm, Britain's sixth-highest mountain, with no effort at all by using the funicular railway, and indulge in a coffee at the Ptarmigan Restaurant? In the summer you cannot leave the immediate vicinity of the viewing area at the top of the railway, so to get to nearby Ben Macdui is an effort that many shirk.

So, although this mountain is in the heart of the Cairngorms National Park, it qualifies as an underrated, off-the-beaten track location. There are days when you reach the summit and genuinely don't see a soul, yet it is only 4 miles from the foot of the railway at the Cairngorm ski centre, at Coire Cas. The hike is reasonably easy to do on a summer day.

The Cairngorms massif contains the highest, coldest and snowiest plateau in Britain, and the wildlife fits the profile. On an average day you won't see many species of anything, but most things you do see are interesting. Take the birds, for instance. On the top plateau you should run into two species that are very difficult to see breeding elsewhere in Britain: the dotterel and the snow bunting. The dotterel is a wader, related to the lapwing, which is drawn to plateaux. It is a colourful but subtle mixture of grey, white, green and glorious chestnut, the female being more colourful than the male. It is renowned for its tameness, and is the only bird of its kind you will see up here.

The other special bird is the snow bunting, a phenomenally hardy songbird that breeds further north, in Greenland, than any other comparable species. It breeds near the summit and, in winter, is sometimes found down at the car park. Ptarmigans, possibly the world's hardiest species, are quite easy to see an hour or so's walk from Coire Cas; before that you might see red grouse on the moors on the walk up. The ptarmigans appear when the vegetation thins out and it is rockier. Listen out for the ptarmigan's advertising call in spring, which sounds as though the bird is retching – with such a meagre diet of twigs and other plant material, you couldn't blame it. The ptarmigan is famous for moulting several times a year to blend with the changing background, from golden-yellow in summer to greyer in autumn and pure white in winter.

Another inhabitant of the high tops is the mammal equivalent of the ptarmigan, its coat moulted with the seasons: greyish-brown in summer and pure white in winter. However, while the ptarmigan retains a black tail and a tiny patch of black between the bill and the eye, the mountain hare shows black tips to its ears. These tough creatures, that don't even retreat to holes at night, are common at this elevation.

On the slopes or summit of Ben Macdui, you might find yourself crossing paths with another exceptionally hardy animal, the reindeer. These were native to Britain during the last glaciation 8,000 years ago, but are long since extinct. However, a highly managed, semi-tame population of 50–100 has free rein to wander on these hills. They are often seen on the road to the ski centre car park.

From Coire Cas it takes an hour on the well-marked route to get up high enough to see the best birds and animals, steadily climbing through the moorland. However, in summer you should be able to spot several good flowers on the way. Not surprisingly, there are some rare species in such an extreme environment, best seen in June and July. You can, in fact, turn off the main track to Ben Macdui and instead head up no more than a mile towards one of the so-called 'northern corries', Coire an t-Sneachda (Snow Corrie), to witness a superb selection of Arctic-alpine flowers, among them roseroot, alpine lady's mantle and globeflower. Cranberry also grows here. However, getting up towards the topmost cliffs and ridges will yield still more specialities. Look out for moss campion, alpine and highland saxifrage, hare's-foot sedge, curved wood-rush and green shield-moss.

Indeed, if you finally make the summit of Ben Macdui, some of these flowers – and even the birds – will literally be at your feet. They may be the only company you have.

Seasonal highlights

Spring
Ring ouzel, wheatear, lady's mantle

Summer
Dotterel, globeflower, rare mountain flowers

Autumn
Cranberry, meadow pipit, heather

Winter
Mountain hare, raven

All year
Snow bunting, reindeer, ptarmigan

Overleaf: Ben Macdui

92 Falls of Braan

Colourful fungi and leaping salmon

Hermitage car park, Old Military Road, Dunkeld, Perthshire PH8 0HX

Grid ref NO012421

Directions At Little Dunkeld carry on past A923 (to Dunkeld over bridge), turning left into car park after about a mile

Lunch stop Meikleour Arms, Meikleour, Perthshire PH2 6EB

Salmon

The Victorians knew a thing or two about designing curious and beautiful places. The Hermitage at Dunkeld, north of Perth, owned by the National Trust for Scotland, is just such a creation. A visitor here will be immersed in a largely artificial landscape which doesn't pretend to be wild or untouched; and yet somehow the place just 'works' as a wildlife location.

One of the major attractions of the site is the River Braan, particularly the spectacular Falls of Braan. In the autumn salmon leap along these falls, especially in October and November. Set to a backdrop of fiery autumn colour, this is a glorious location in which to see the mighty fish reach the end of their epic journey. But, in fact, all isn't quite what it seems. The Braan is not a genuine wild salmon river. There are managed hatcheries upstream, so these fish began life in the care of humans. They carried out their journeys to the sea and back, alright, but the reality is that the falls produce too much of a barrier and the salmon cannot leap them; they eventually give up and lay eggs a little downstream. But does it matter? As a spectacle, it is still thrilling and the instincts of the fish are as real as any other. It is absolutely worth seeing, the best viewpoints being from St Ossian's Hall and the bridge.

The other curiosity of the Hermitage is its magnificent tall trees, some of which are among the loftiest in Britain. But again, this is not a true natural spectacle. The trees concerned are Douglas firs, which are native to western North America, where they compete with redwoods as the tallest conifers in the world. The only real Scottish connection is that they are named after Scotsman and botanist David Douglas. But they are still an impressive spectacle. The tallest here is just over 201ft, putting it fourth on the list of individual British trees, all of which are also Douglas firs (the tallest is at Stronardron, Argyll, and measures just over 209ft). The Hermitage Fir is still about the height of 15 double-decker buses piled on top of one another, so it makes an awesome sight.

Of course, the wild animals around here are not aware that their surroundings are artificial. The red squirrels use what trees they can, and can be seen along the Braan Walk (park in the National Trust for Scotland car park). The goldcrests that nest high up in the firs are content to use foreign branches – Britain's smallest bird in its largest tree. The wildlife makes do. In truth, Britain is such a modified place ecologically that it isn't much different here to everywhere else.

You can therefore come here and visit neighbouring Tay Forest Park (Craigvinean) with a clear conscience. There are many peaceful walks and gems to enjoy, some easy to see and some very difficult indeed. In the latter category, pine martens occur, but they are incredibly hard to see. It is worth taking a walk at dawn or dusk and remaining as quiet as possible. These sleek and beautiful predators are specialised for hunting in trees, but they spend much time on the ground too and can sometimes be seen running across forest tracks. The same applies to another local – the elusive black grouse.

In the category of being hard to miss, the spring display of flowers at the Hermitage woodlands begins early, in February, with snowdrops, and progresses on to dog's mercury, wood sorrel, wood anemone and, finally, bluebells. The walk is also excellent for mosses, liverworts, lichens and ferns, although identifying these will be much more difficult than finding them. On the river itself, dippers are also easy to see. These are extremely hardy birds that sing in mid-winter (the phrases are quite similar to a simple version of a song thrush) and breed by February. Coincidentally, crossbills, which occur in the pine trees in this area, may also be nesting at this strange time, if their favoured conifer seeds are ripening.

Dunkeld is a damp, mild part of Scotland and, besides the mosses already mentioned, the climate also greatly favours fungi. There are an impressive 270 species recorded on the National Trust property.

Indeed, colourful fungi, stunning autumn leaves and leaping salmon are good reasons to come here at this time. But in this peculiarly British curiosity, there is always something to enjoy.

Seasonal highlights

Spring
Dog's mercury, wood sorrel, wood anemone

Summer
Osprey, grey wagtail, ferns

Autumn
Salmon, black grouse, fungi

Winter
Goldcrest, crossbill, snowdrop

All year
Douglas fir, red squirrel, pine marten

93 Findhorn Valley

Where goats and golden eagles dare

Coignafearn Lodge, Inverness, Inverness-shire IV13 7YB

Grid ref NH709178

Directions Turn left at Findhorn Bridge down valley signposted Coignafearn

Lunch stop Carrbridge Kitchen, Main Street, Carrbridge, Aviemore PH23 3AS

You've probably heard that there are golden eagles in Scotland. Many people, though, dismiss the possibility of ever seeing one for themselves, even during a holiday in the Highlands. After all, it isn't as though you can simply drive up to somewhere, look up in the sky and see one, can you? Or is there some mythical place where this happens?

Well, perhaps not every time. But go down the valley of the River Findhorn, into the area known locally as Strathdearn, and you will end up at what is a good candidate for the car park at the end of the universe, at Coignafearn. And then check the ridges and sky. Do this for long enough and you'll see a golden eagle. And since this is one of the best places for raptor-watching in Scotland, there might well be somebody else making the same pilgrimage, and more pairs of eyes increase the chances.

The Findhorn Valley is reached by turning off the A9 15 miles south of Inverness (or 12 miles north of Aviemore), near the village of Tomatin. Just south of the village is Findhorn Bridge, and from there it is 10 miles to Coignafearn along the narrow but well-paved road. Even if you are here for an eagle fix, you shouldn't hurry. There are oystercatchers and common gulls at the bridge, along with common terns. The eagles will wait.

They don't have many traffic problems here, so you can afford to take in the countryside and slow right down if you need to. Locals will appreciate it, though, if you don't block the road. After a while you will come across the turning to Farr on your right, and then a mile after that there is a particularly good spot where a small river flows into the Findhorn. This is the best place to look for the birds of fast-flowing streams, particularly dipper, grey wagtail and, in summer only, common sandpiper. In the autumn, you might see salmon, not leaping but laying their eggs. Check the hills, too, for any silhouettes. Buzzards will probably be here, so take a good look at their shape and be prepared for something different.

The road continues into the valley and the scenery is magnificent, if somewhat haunting. By the time you park the car it will feel thrillingly remote.

Red kite

A private estate begins here but it is possible to walk for many miles along the valley and feel utterly alone. Don't go too far unless you are well equipped, even in summer. In the autumn and winter, be careful all the time. Drink this in, though, for the solitude is not likely to be a familiar feeling. And sharpen those senses. Use a pair of binoculars and scan all the ridges. Unless it is raining or snowing you will soon see something. The golden eagle is much bigger than a buzzard, and it has a longer, rather straight tail and a surprisingly protruding head. What you might notice above all, though, is how it is so serenely controlled and imperious. Buzzards have quick, stiff wing-beats; those of the golden eagle are slower. Both birds hold their wings up in a V. If it is blowing a gale, hardly unusual here, the golden eagle still manages to fly around.

One of the eagle's prey species is the mountain hare. The Findhorn Valley is as reliable for this animal as it is for eagles, and you are likely to see one simply by walking around on the paths and tracks. They can be flushed from the heather moors. The same applies to red grouse, which are also common. Both of these hardy species remain right through the winter months, but while the mountain hare's fur turns white, the red grouse remains reddish-purple.

There are also herds of red deer in the valley, and you would be most unlucky not to see some. They are at their best, of course, on autumn mornings during the rut, when the stags may be roaring all day, sounding as if they are suffering from a severe bout of indigestion. If your luck is in, you might also pick out herds of wild goats.

But most people come principally for the eagles. It's fair to say that the majority are successful, although for some it is a test of patience. Mind you, tarrying here among these hills, with wheatears, ring ouzels and cuckoos calling, could not be called hardship. Some dots in the sky become buzzards, peregrines or kestrels, sparrowhawks, ravens or even goshawks. Hen harriers occur, as do merlins and red kites. It is an impressive list of what are, essentially, bridesmaids.

Seasonal highlights

Spring
Common gull, cuckoo, red grouse

Summer
Common sandpiper, wheatear, short-eared owl

Autumn
Red deer, salmon

Winter
Buzzard, sparrowhawk, raven

All year
Golden eagle, mountain hare, wild goat

94 Flanders Moss

Mosses, moths and reptiles

Thornhill, Stirling, Stirlingshire FK8 3QT (car park)

Grid ref NS647978 (car park)

Directions From Thornhill village go left (south) on B822 for 1.25 miles

Lunch stop The Inn at Kippen, Fore Road, Kippen, Stirlingshire FK8 3DT

Flanders Moss is a large raised bog in the valley of the Upper Forth, just to the west of Stirling. If you don't like bogs you can stop reading, but you will be missing out. This is a very special place, with an atmosphere all its own: peaceful and full of wildlife.

The site lies in the Carse of Stirling, and once was just one of many bogs that covered much of this part of Scotland. So many have been drained, cut for peat and otherwise destroyed that Flanders Moss is now one of the largest (2,125 acres) and most intact bogs in Britain, or even in Europe. It has been here for 8,000 years, beginning life as an estuary – an extension of the Forth – with hills on all sides. The thick clay of the estuary formed a plug which, when the site became landlocked, acted like the plastic on the bottom of a pond, preventing drainage and allowing peat to build up. The piles of peat, fed only by rainwater, have grown upwards at 1mm a year, and now you can just see the slight domed shape of the bog above the level plain.

Bogs have all sorts of good attributes, and here on Flanders Moss it is easy to see them in one short visit. You access this National Nature Reserve (run by Scottish Natural Heritage) by turning off the B822 between Kippen and the village of Thornhill. A small road takes you down to a car park, a boardwalk and, recently added, a magnificent tower platform, which gives elevated views over the reserve.

The boardwalk, only half a mile long, takes you into the nitty-gritty of the bog. It is here that you can admire the sphagnum mosses of many different species, all spongy and wondrously green or brown. Several rare species occur, indicating

Common lizard

that this is a truly intact site. Other plants show off their habitat allegiance: bog rosemary, bog myrtle and bog asphodel. Common cottongrass is everywhere, and there are also several species of orchids, such as lesser butterfly orchid. The distinctive white blooms of Labrador tea are here, a species of rhododendron. Its origin in Britain is obscure, and it is possible that the seeds were brought across the Atlantic on the feet of birds.

In summer the bog is a renowned place for dragonflies and damselflies. It marks one of the southernmost stations in Britain for the northern emerald, a metallic dark green dragonfly with green eyes. The common hawker, generally misnamed, really is abundant here, and other good species include the gold-ringed dragonfly and the black darter.

Lepidoptera are well represented and, although such butterfly goodies as small pearl-bordered fritillary and large heath are found, Flanders Moss has long been known as a hotspot for moths. It is notable for the Rannoch brindled beauty (not quite as stunning as it sounds) and for the day-flying argent and sable, which looks just like a small black-and-white butterfly. However, moth enthusiasts, particularly those from southern England, will also salivate at the prospect of Manchester treble-bar, northern eggar, shaded pug, great brocade, silvery arches, map-winged swift and round-winged muslin. Commoner heath-loving moths include the delightfully named true lover's knot, the emperor and birch mocha.

Another set of creatures that do very well at Flanders Moss are reptiles. Adders are common but difficult to see, while common lizards are very difficult not to see. They bask all over the boardwalk from spring through to mid-autumn, and even run through your legs when you are standing watching something else.

The tower offers the chance to see some of the bog's birds, although you generally need to make an effort to see much. Snipe, curlew and reed bunting breed within the wet areas, while both meadow and tree pipit are found in open and scrubby habitats respectively. The meadow pipit is the host for the cuckoo, which is common hereabouts. Another interesting breeding bird locally is the osprey, which fishes in the Lake of Menteith to the west of the reserve. In the winter, there are hen harriers and wildfowl, including a flock of pink-footed geese, but it can be difficult to see much at this season. Winter is the time for moody skies and subtle colours – and for looking forward to the summer.

95 Inversnaid

A trip to Scotland's rainforest

Inversnaid Hotel, West Highland Way, Stirlingshire FK8 3TU

Grid ref NN337088

Directions From Aberfoyle, go left (north) on B829 to its end, then left on minor road to Inversnaid

Lunch stop The Forth Inn, Main Street, Aberfoyle, Stirlingshire FK8 3UQ

The foliage is dense, the atmosphere is moist and everywhere the rocks, trunks and branches are adorned with copious hanging vegetation. Does this sound familiar from somewhere? Well, they call the woods of Inversnaid 'Scotland's rainforest' and you can see why. At least the 'rain' part is usually accurate; this is one of the wettest parts of the UK.

It isn't as remote as the jungle, being not a great distance from Glasgow, but it is still well off the beaten track. Owned and managed by the RSPB, Inversnaid is on the 'other' side of Loch Lomond to the one most people visit, where the A82 takes you up to Glencoe and on to the west coast of Scotland. So instead, to get here you must take the A81 to Aberfoyle and then drive west on the B829 for 12 miles before turning down to this dead end, albeit a lovely one with a splendid waterfall, a hotel and a pier. A ferry does cross to the busy side, but you are highly unlikely to find this place crowded.

The nature reserve has two main features: the sessile oak wood 'rainforest' on the steep slopes above the lake, and moorland higher up. You can explore the woods on a nature trail; follow the West Highland Way path north along the shore of the loch as far as the boathouse, and the trail will turn into the woods and up to a couple of delightful viewpoints before looping back down. If you feel energetic you can reach the moorland by parking a little way up the road at Garrison Farm and following the Upland Trail. Both are glorious walks, with quite different wildlife.

The sessile oak woodlands are as important for their range of mosses, liverworts, ferns and fungi as anything else, all of these 'lower' plants thriving in the damp conditions. They make a visit well worthwhile in the autumn, along with usual seasonal colours. Just recently there has been a grumble in this jungle about the conflict between these treasured plants – which have few

Seasonal highlights

Spring
Wood warbler, redstart,
pied flycatcher

Summer
Red-breasted merganser,
twite, ferns

Autumn
Fungi, whooper swan,
goldeneye

Winter
Profusion of mosses,
liverworts, lichens

All year
Waterfall, feral goat, pine
marten

champions – and the local population of feral goats, which have inhabited these hills for a long time. The trouble is, goats eat almost anything, including rare lichens that have taken years to develop. The RSPB tried to institute a cull, but in the end the population will be kept in check by a contraceptive device shot as a dart. It is amazing what goes on in Britain's quiet corners.

Most people visit in the spring and summer, when these woods are alive with birds and their songs. The sessile oak woods are particularly well known for a trio of species – the redstart, wood warbler and pied flycatcher – that flourish here. The redstart and pied flycatcher nest in tree holes, but oddly the wood warbler nests on the ground. All these are insectivorous and, let's face it, there is plenty of food in this part of Scotland. The midges, for their part, would agree with that statement.

While enjoying the woodland, make sure that you check the shores of the lake, too. You have the chance of seeing interesting ducks and, occasionally, divers as well. The goosander is a large duck that dives under the water and swims after fish, yet, remarkably, it nests in holes in trees. Its close relative the red-breasted merganser is also a fish-feeder, but it nests among rocks on the shoreline. Both species occur at Inversnaid year-round and, in autumn and winter, whooper swans and goldeneye might also be seen in these sheltered waters.

Back on dry land, where the woodland thins out towards the top of the ridge, you might just glimpse one of a small population of black grouse that hangs on here. These are most easily seen at dawn, a tall order unless you are staying nearby. Otherwise the moor itself holds a small population of twite, a small finch related to the linnet. This species isn't easy to find, but you cannot miss meadow pipit, and some of the larger birds up here such as raven and buzzard. With a lot of luck, you might just see a golden eagle, too.

Some mention should perhaps be made of the other mammals on the reserve, besides the famous goats. Red and roe deer occur, but others, such as the pine marten, are extremely elusive. It is just possible that true wildcats might hang on – the mixed habitat is good for them – but you would be incredibly lucky to see one. The Scottish outlaw Rob Roy is alleged to have had a hideout near here, and nobody could find him, so what chance do you have to find a cat?

You can try, though. Wildlife-viewing is all about trying. And if you are going to search for animals, you could hardly choose a more scenic spot in which to do so.

96 Knapdale

Beavers, otters and extraordinary beauty

Knapdale Scottish Beaver Trail, Lochgilphead, Argyll and Bute PA31 8PS (nearest post code)

Grid ref NR737852 (NR790910 Taynish car park)

Directions From Lochgilphead head north on A816 for nearly 2 miles, west on B841 to Bellanoch and south to car park

Lunch stop Tayvallich Inn, Tayvallich PA31 8PL

Just two hours' drive from Glasgow, Knapdale is situated at the northern end of the Kintyre Peninsula, roughly opposite the tip of the island of Jura. It is a region of *cnaps* and *dalls*, meaning steep rocky ridges interspersed with, literally, low lying fields, with lochs and lochans. It is very sparsely populated. Since the 1930s much of the land has been planted with conifers, but there are also some precious acreages of almost untouched ancient Atlantic woodland, which is full of wildlife, and some bogs. The animals that you can see here are as Scottish as haggis – red squirrels, ospreys, pine martens, eagles and perhaps even a few remaining wildcats. Or, at least, all are except one – the beaver. Knapdale is now famous as the site where these rodents have been reintroduced to the wild.

Native beavers disappeared from Britain about 400 years ago and it was perhaps high time to get them back after we had persecuted them to extinction, especially since they have a positive effect on biodiversity, with all their construction and damming work. So, from 2009, the official reintroduction of the Eurasian beaver began here. And these days, you can come and see how they are doing yourself.

If you take the A83 at Tarbet, at the northern tip of Loch Lomond, the road eventually wends its way onto the Kintyre Peninsula at Lochgilphead. If you take the turning here for Oban, then turn off and follow the road for about 5 miles towards Tayvallich, you will soon see Barnluasgan Information Centre on the left. This marks the beginning of the Beaver Detective Trail, a 3-mile walk that

Beaver

will certainly enable you to see signs of beavers, and perhaps these elusive creatures themselves. The best chance of an encounter is at dawn or dusk.

It takes 20 minutes to get to Dubh Loch, where the beavers are stationed (there are four families in Knapdale). You will easily see the gnawed trees, cut into pencil-tipped ends, and the areas flooded by the animals' activity. The beaver dam itself is next to a pontoon where Dubh Loch connects to Loch Coille-Bharr. If you do see the beavers, they will be low in the water, just revealing their head – you often notice the large V of their wake first. In alarm, they slap the water with their tails.

There is a walk round Loch Coille-Bharr where you might see crossbills and siskins and even glimpse a red squirrel. For another excellent walk, retrace your steps to the car park, carry on towards Tayvallich and then, just after the village, turn left for Taynish National Nature Reserve and follow the track down to the parking area. If you thought the previous site was scenic, this one is another order of beauty entirely.

Instead of commercial forestry, here there is broadleaved woodland of the most ancient kind – spore tests show that it has been here for at least 6,000 years, since the end of the last Ice Age. The flora of so-called 'lower plants' is incredibly rich: mosses, lichens and ferns festoon just about every surface, be it

inert rock or living trees, their growth aided by the exceptionally damp, mild climate – 61 inches of rainfall a year. An incredible 250 species of mosses and liverworts grow here, which is a quarter of the entire British tally. There are 500 species of lichens – an extraordinary number – and 300 species of flowering plants, too, among them the rare narrow-leaved helleborine.

Yet, really, the delight is in the atmosphere of these woods, seething with life. In the spring the birdsong is almost deafening, with blackcap, willow warbler, garden warbler, cuckoo, wood warbler and redstart all contributing, along with the commoner birds.

This wooded sweetness isn't all. There are boggy mires, grasslands and the shores of Loch Sween and Linne Mhuirich to enjoy. The grasslands hold nationally important numbers of the rare marsh fritillary, while there is a very good chance of seeing otters along the shore.

Now imagine that – seeing otters and beavers on the same day! If that's your goal, you must come to Knapdale.

Seasonal highlights

Spring
Narrow-leaved helleborine, wood warbler, redstart

Summer
Marsh fritillary, ferns, osprey

Autumn
Crossbill, fungi, blackcap

Winter
Lichens, mosses

All year
Beaver, otter, red squirrel

257

97 Largo Bay

Sea ducks, sand dunes and land snails

Kincraig, Leven, Fife KY9 1HB

Grid ref NO469005

Directions 1.25 miles beyond Balchrystie on A917, turn right to Kincraig

Lunch stop The 19th Hole at Earlsferry, 5 Links Road, Earlsferry, Fife KY9 1AW

Largo Bay is on the northern shore of the Firth of Forth, to the east of Kirkcaldy. It lies in a delightfully quiet, almost tourist-free zone of pretty but perhaps unremarkable countryside. It is mostly flat, with low hills, and many of the villages are colourful. St Andrews, where some people apparently play golf or go to university, is 10 miles to the north.

If nothing else, it is worth coming here for the wide, sandy beach, which is stunning throughout the year. You can park either side of the bay's sweep, either at Leven Links in the west, Kincraig (by the caravan park) in the east, or in the middle at the village of Lower Largo. The Fife Coastal Path goes all along this coast, so you have no chance of getting lost, in contrast to Lower Largo's most famous son, Alexander Selkirk, of *Robinson Crusoe* fame.

Among wildlife enthusiasts, Largo Bay is most famous for its sea ducks. The term 'sea ducks' is used to distinguish between ducks you might see on freshwater ponds, like mallards, and those that spend part of their lives in coastal waters. A good many freshwater ducks don't dive, but all the sea ducks do, and because many of them feed on bottom-living animals, they prefer shallow and sheltered coasts. Largo Bay fits their requirements well, and for many years has been a favoured spot to look for them. These ducks include the eider, which is the one from which feathers are still harvested in some parts of the world to make duvets. Eiders have huge, triangular bills which they use to crush mussels and other shellfish. Another abundant one here is the common scoter, which is much smaller and, in the males at least, is all black (the females are brown with a pale cheek); its relative the velvet scoter – bigger and with a heavier bill to crack those beleaguered sea creatures, occurs in smaller numbers. Still another is the beautiful long-tailed duck, a most tasteful mixture of white, grey, brown and black, with

Cowslip

males having a long, wispy tail. Ruddon's Point, a low, rocky cliff at the east end of the bay, near Kincraig, is famous as the best place in Britain to see a rarity, the surf scoter. The fact that it comes all the way from North America to winter at Largo Bay says it all.

The flocks of sea ducks are most abundant in the winter; only a few eiders and common scoters remain in summer to loaf about. Joining the masses from October to March is an enviable range of other birds, mostly using the shallow waters to catch fish. These include red-throated and black-throated divers, and several species of grebe, sometimes including the very scarce red-necked grebe. Add in the wading birds that use the sand and rocks, such as oystercatchers and curlews, and the regulars at Largo Bay amount to a very impressive cast. If you go as far as Kincraig, you can enjoy the birds while dangling from the chain walk that has been on these cliffs since 1923 – but take due care and only go at low tide.

The wildlife charms of Largo Bay extend well beyond the birds. Just to the east of Lower Largo is Dumbarnie Links, a reserve of the Scottish Wildlife Trust, which preserves an outstanding area of sand dunes and lime-rich grassland. In spring and summer this is excellent for flowers, beginning with carpets of cowslips in spring, followed by such delights as meadow cranesbill, common and greater knapweed, the gorgeous viper's bugloss and, at its northern limit in Britain, houndstongue. There are also 30 species of grass, although this may not cause any influx of tourism.

The reserve is remarkably good for invertebrates, including an excellent variety of land snails and an astonishing 1,100 insects. Admittedly many of these are flies, but there is also a highly respectable list of butterflies, among them the uncommon dark green fritillary.

Largo Bay provides a superb location for a walk of almost any length. And when you've finished, you can always go and play golf...

Seasonal highlights

Spring
Cowslip, flies, butterflies

Summer
Houndstongue, viper's bugloss, grasses

Autumn
Gulls, curlew, oystercatcher

Winter
Scoters, grebes, divers

All year
Eider, land snails, seashells

98 Loch of Strathbeg

Where wild geese thrill spectators

Starnafin, Crimond, Fraserburgh, Aberdeenshire AB43 8QN

Grid ref NK056580

Directions From Crimond follow signs to loch and visitor centre

Lunch stop Albert Hotel, 75 Queen Street, Peterhead, Aberdeenshire AB42 1TU

It wouldn't be an exaggeration to say that the sight and sound of thousands of geese flying across the sky at twilight is one of the most thrilling wildlife spectacles in the world. Yet remarkably few people are aware that Britain is one of the top places to see this happening. Even fewer are aware that anybody can turn up to witness the event. And, incredibly, it is all free of charge!

One of the finest goose displays in the country takes place at the Loch of Strathbeg, north of Aberdeen, every winter morning and afternoon between September and March. In September, there may be as many as 80,000 pink-footed geese involved, as well as 10,000 greylag geese and smaller numbers of barnacle geese and white-fronted geese. There are smaller numbers in mid-winter, but still thousands of birds.

The geese spend the day on the nearby fields feeding, spread out over a wide area, but at night they retreat to the safer waters of the loch, where predators cannot reach them. It is the commuting movements, at dawn and dusk, that are so magnificent. Not everybody moves at once, so for a while skeins of geese, often in perfect V formations and other patterns, criss-cross the darkening skies, often against a background of the setting sun, eventually settling down. It is a social event, and every goose calls to the others. The sound of thousands of birds, the pink feet making 'ang-ang' and musical 'wink-wink' noises, is as stirring as the sight, and the voices together coalesce into a kind of roar. It is pure wildlife magic.

At the loch, the RSPB has enabled its Tower Hide to be used by anybody at any time, so you can simply turn up at the visitor centre, walk for 10 minutes and obtain a panoramic view of the action. If this was human theatre, you'd pay a fortune. But it isn't even theatre; it is life in the raw.

If a drama occurs at the Loch of Strathbeg every winter night, nothing could quite compare to the awesome, terrible events that originally led to the loch being formed. The loch was once a lagoon with a permanent outlet to the North

Geese

Seasonal highlights

Spring
Willow warbler, little gull, dune flowers

Summer
Common tern, mute swan, dark green fritillary

Autumn
Goose flocks, greenshank, ruff

Winter
Pink-footed goose, merlin, ducks

All year
Tree sparrow, lapwing, beachcombing

Sea, and next to it was a village, Rattray, with a harbour. However, one day, back in 1720, a storm of epic proportions cut off the seaward channel at a stroke by blowing tonnes of sand across it, and at the same time inundated Rattray under dunes. The loch has been landlocked ever since.

As it turned out, these violent events created something special. At 556 acres, the Loch of Strathbeg is Britain's largest dune lake, and the habitat around includes scrub and marshland, with extensive reedbeds. It attracts a phenomenal number of birds and other animals, many of which are rare and localised. For example, the only bittern that winters in Scotland comes here, and in 2016 a pair of little gulls nested: the first time the species has ever fledged chicks in Britain. In the winter, there are hundreds of wild ducks, and many predators, such as peregrine, hen harrier and even white-tailed eagle at times. Otters use the reserve, one of more than 20 species of mammals that have been seen. In the summer, a large colony of black-headed gulls and common terns use the lake's island, right in front of the visitor centre, and the flowers in the dunes to the seaward side of the loch are at their best. In autumn, many migrant waders pop in, and on the sea at nearby Rattray Head all manner of exciting seabirds pass by. And that is without mentioning the beach, with all its sea life.

The whole area is easy to work. The visitor centre is free, and is reached by turning off the A90 at Crimond, north of Aberdeen between Fraserburgh and Peterhead, and following the brown signs. There are two other hides, the Fen Hide and the Bay Hide, accessed through Crimond Airfield. You can see the loch from the south on the way to Rattray Head, accessed on a minor road to the south of Crimond.

You might see much that is unusual or rare here, but still none of it will compare to the thrill of the wild geese.

99 St Abb's Head

Designer habitat for seabirds

St Abb's Head National Nature Reserve, B6438, Eyemouth, Berwickshire TD14 5PL

Grid ref NT913674

Directions From Coldingham turn left on B6438 to visitor centre

Lunch stop Ebb Carr's, Harbour, St Abbs, Berwickshire TD14 5PW

Scotland provides habitat for a very high percentage of Britain's seabirds, and on the east coast, just north of Berwick-upon-Tweed, the abundance begins. Just 12 miles north of the border, St Abb's Head boasts around 60,000 breeding birds. Some of these might wander south to fish off the English coast at times, but no matter, they nest on Scottish soil – or on Scottish rock.

St Abb's Head is a large outcrop of volcanic larva formed 400 million years ago, and it abuts sedimentary rocks at its northern edge at Pettico Wick. Weathering has made its edges jagged, with many coves and offshore stacks – designer seabird habitat. In the peak months of May to mid-July, the cliffs reverberate with the wails, grunts and moans of the various species, as well as the crashing waves, making it a compelling place to visit. Two of the main seabirds are guillemots and razorbills, both members of the auk family, which stand upright on the rock faces. Guillemots nest on narrow ledges, packed like sardines, while razorbills tend towards broader ledges, often with an overhang. Both species lay just the one egg; that of the guillemot is individually marked with spots and squiggles so that the parents can recognise not just their egg, but also their nest site. Kittiwakes also breed in large numbers but, in contrast to the auks, they build a cosy nest of mud and grass, albeit one with a sheer drop on the side; the nests occasionally give way. These species share the cliffs with fulmars, shags and herring gulls. Shags often nest much lower down, close to the sea and sometimes in caves. There are also a few pairs of puffins at St Abb's Head, but these can be very difficult to see.

Most of the activity on the cliffs quietens down in autumn and winter, but gannets and fulmars are always around, and other birds spend the season offshore, among them common

Northern brown argus

scoters and red-throated divers. In the autumn exciting migratory seabirds such as skuas and shearwaters pass south down this coast.

Cliff-nesting seabirds and butterflies might seem an unusual combination of specialities, but St Abb's Head is famous for its colony of the rare northern brown argus. These are small butterflies related to the blues, although the wings are brown rather than blue, even in the male. Here in Scotland this butterfly has a distinctive white spot on its forewing, making it very easy to identify, which is just as well, because the common blue butterfly occurs here too. The argus larvae feed on the common rock-rose.

To see the butterflies you first need to reach the visitor centre and car park, a mile out of Coldingham along the B6438. From here walk along the coastal path for about a mile until you come to a fenced-off area, which is the butterfly reserve. The fences are there to prevent the sheep from over-grazing on the rock-rose, and on the adult butterfly's favourite feeding plants, wild thyme and bird's-foot trefoil.

Speaking of flowers, the grasslands on the clifftops contain a great variety, sometimes as many as 20 species per square yard. The rock is acid in parts and mineral-rich in others, and if you add in salt-resistant maritime species it makes for a good display. Species to look out for in summer include thrift, purple milk-vetch and tormentil.

St Abb's Head also has one decidedly peculiar quirk for a clifftop site: a freshwater lake, Mire Loch, surrounded by dense gorse bushes and birch trees, providing cover for migrant birds. The loch has decent fish populations, including eels, perch and sticklebacks, while frogs and toads croak from the margins in spring.

St Abb's Head provides a magnificent setting for wildlife-watching. Remarkably, it lies only 4 miles away from the A1, the great trunk road to the north from England. Even here, just a short distance north of the border, the wildlife heart of Scotland is already beating.

Seasonal highlights

Spring
Common toad, guillemot, razorbill

Summer
Northern brown argus, grayling, puffin

Autumn
Tormentil, common rock-rose, migrant birds

Winter
Shag, cormorant, gulls

All year
Gannet, fulmar, gorse

Overleaf: St Abb's Head

263

100 Wood of Cree

Scotland's largest ancient woodland

Newton Stewart, Dumfries & Galloway DG8 6RJ

Grid ref NX381708

Directions From Newton Stewart go north through Minnigaff; turn left past Monigaff church, continue on C50 for 3 miles to car park

Lunch stop Creebridge House Hotel, Minnigaff, Newton Stewart DG8 6NP

You don't normally go to woods to see an otter, but this gorgeous RSPB reserve to the west of Dumfries has a car park next to the River Cree, along a stretch where several females hold territory. A viewing platform looks over a pool where sightings are regular, if not routine. If you are successful, it certainly starts your exploration of southern Scotland's largest ancient woodland with a bang.

The Wood of Cree cloaks a hillside of rushing torrents, with the Cordorcan and Pulhowan Burns tumbling down into the valley. In places the woodland floor is a jumble of mossy boulders, with lichens on the trees and ferns in the gullies. It is thought that this small area has been under continuous tree cover for 5,000 years. As such, it is a forest rich in just about everything: plants, birds, invertebrates, mammals – you name it.

There is a time of year, usually in early May, when this wood is carpeted with millions of bluebells. There are so many, indeed, that this spot is regularly included in the list of Britain's top 10 bluebell woods – and they aren't just in the wood, either, but also on the adjacent open ground. It is a sensational display and, well, what can you say about carpets of bluebells? They just make you happy to be alive. Here, combined with the fresh air and the rushing torrents of enthusiastic rivers, it is hard not to feel joyful.

Not surprisingly, the richness of the wood attracts birds. One of the area's specialities is the willow tit, which generally likes damp woods. This is a bird that has been in serious decline in Britain for some time, and over large swathes of the south of England it has literally become locally extinct. These are smart little birds, mostly a neat brown, creamier below, and with a smart black cap and bib. Generally unobtrusive, they give a very nasal 'zee-zee-zee' call as if they were holding their nose while calling.

Willow tits occur year round in the reserve, along with buzzards, great spotted woodpeckers, treecreepers, tawny owls and, along the Cree, barn owls. In summer their numbers are swollen by a profusion of colourful, noisy summer visitors. Pied flycatchers, redstarts and wood warblers – all classic lovers of sessile oak woodlands – shout it out with garden warblers, blackcaps and chiffchaffs, not to mention chaffinches, blackbirds, song thrushes and robins. The jumble of sounds gives you a headache trying to identify them all. Meanwhile, in the more open areas on the edge of the moorland, the willow warblers are joined by tree pipits, which have a delightful song flight, lifting off from a branch, rising up to moderate height, then gliding down to a perch with wings and tail raised. It is a song and a display, a two-for-the-price-of-one package designed to impress females and rivals.

Otter

Even after the fullness of summer, the area is still worth a visit. Leaf fall makes the birds easier to see, and autumn is the time when the local red squirrels are most in evidence, searching for winter food supplies. These delightful mammals also moult into their winter coat, making their ear tufts in particular look much more obvious. This is a good time to look for the reserve's other mammals, not just otters but also roe deer and, on rare occasions, pine marten. The reserve also has a rare breeding bat, the Leisler's bat, and six other commoner species.

Once winter has set in, the nearby pool is worth a check for visiting whooper swans, goldeneye and teal. The hillside roars with the sound of rushing torrents.

While the Wood of Cree is ancient and wild, it is not a wilderness. There is a good car park, some limited wheelchair access and five well-marked trails to follow, not all of them among trees. And it is also a work in progress. Recently a six-year project to plant native trees and connect this wood with other fragments in the same area ended; the idea was to create a 12-mile network from Newton Stewart to Glentrool. The RSPB bought land on the nearby Moor of Barclye and in all has planted nearly a quarter of a million new trees.

These plantings won't begin to look like the surrounding woodland for at least 50 years. But when a wood has been around for 5,000 years already, that doesn't seem very long.

Seasonal highlights

Spring
Bluebell, pied flycatcher, wood warbler

Summer
Leisler's bat, redstart, sessile oak canopy

Autumn
Red squirrel, roe deer, robin song

Winter
Whooper swan, goldeneye, teal

All year
Otter, willow tit, barn owl

Index of species

Further reading

AA. *The Pub Guide 2017*, AA Publishing, 2017.

Conlin, A et al. *Where to Watch Birds: North West England and the Isle of Man*, Christopher Helm, 2008.

Couzens, D et al. *Britain's Mammals*, WildGuides, 2017.

Dudley, S et al. *Watching British Dragonflies*, Subbuteo Natural History Books, 2007.

Gartshore, N. *Best Birdwatching Sites: Dorset*, Buckingham Press, 2011.

Hall, K and Govett, J. *Where to Watch Birds: Somerset, Gloucestershire and Wiltshire*, Christopher Helm, 2004.

Hamlett, G. *Best Birdwatching Sites: Scottish Highlands*, Buckingham Press, 2014.

Harrap, S and Redman, N. *Where to Watch Birds in Britain*, Christopher Helm, 2010.

Harrap, S. Harrap's *Wild Flowers*, Bloomsbury, 2013.

Harrison, G et al. *Where to Watch Birds in the West Midlands*, Christopher Helm, 2007.

Lang, D. *Britain's Orchids*, WildGuides, 2004.

Lowen, J. 52 *Wildlife Weekends: A Year of British Wildlife-Watching Breaks*, Bradt Travel Guides, 2013.

Moores, R. *Where to Watch Mammals: Britain and Ireland*, Christopher Helm, 2007.

National Trust. 2016 Handbook, National Trust, 2016.

Newland, D. *Discover Butterflies in Britain*, WildGuides, 2006.

Newland, D et al. *Britain's Butterflies*, WildGuides. 2012.

Packham, C et al. *Nature's Calendar: A Month-by-Month Guide to the Best Wildlife Locations in the British Isles*, Collins, 2007.

Smith, P. *Wilderness Weekends: Wild Adventures in Britain's Rugged Corners*, Bradt Travel Guides, 2015.

Somerville, C. *Britain and Ireland's Best Wild Places: 500 Essential Journeys*, Penguin, 2011.

Stathers, K (ed). *Wildlife Britain: Over 1000 of the Best Wildlife Sites around Britain*, Think Books, 2007.

Taylor, D et al. *Where to Watch Birds in Kent, Surrey and Sussex*, Christopher Helm, 2009.

Thomas, A and Francis, P. *Best Birdwatching Sites in Sussex*, Buckingham Press, 2003.

Unwin, B. *Best Birdwatching Sites: North-East England*, Buckingham Press, 2012.

Wildlife Trusts. *Wildlife Walks: Great Days Out at Over 500 of the UK's Top Nature Reserves*, Think Publishing, 2008.

Image credits

The Automobile Association wishes to thank the following photographers and organisations for their assistance in the preparation of this book.

Front Cover: Tomas Burian/Alamy Stock Photo
Back Cover: Helen Hotson/Alamy Stock Photo

16 Chris Cole/Alamy Stock Photo; 23 geogphotos/Alamy Stock Photo; 29 Stephen Spraggon/Alamy Stock Photo; 40 Kathy Hancock/Alamy Stock Photo; 46 Eye Ubiquitous/Alamy Stock Photo; 51 James Adler/Wildlife Trust; 56 David Chapman/Alamy Stock Photo; 58 David Chapman/Alamy Stock Photo; 63 Jenifer Bunnett/Alamy Stock Photo; 71 robertharding/Alamy Stock Photo; 81 Graham Custance/Alamy Stock Photo; 87 Tony Watson/Alamy Stock Photo; 93 Courtesy of The Essex Wildlife Trust; 96 Meibion/Alamy Stock Photo; 108 AA/C Jones; 116 Michelle Yates/Alamy Stock Photo; 127 AA/T Mackie; 130 Alastair Balderstone/Alamy Stock Photo; 136 Tracey Whitefoot/Alamy Stock Photo; 150 radnorimages/Alamy Stock Photo; 156 The Photolibrary Wales/Alamy Stock Photo; 166 Nature Photographers Ltd/Alamy Stock Photo; 176 CW Images/Alamy Stock Photo; 187 Alan Novelli/Alamy Stock Photo; 192 David Chapman/Alamy Stock Photo; 196 Courtesy of The Wildlife Trust; 204 Design Pics Inc/Alamy Stock Photo; 212 AA/D Clapp; 219 chris joint/Alamy Stock Photo; 224 A.P.S. (UK)/Alamy Stock Photo; 231 adam taylor/Alamy Stock Photo; 236 Courtesy of The Wildlife Trust; 244 AA/M Hamblin; 249 DP Landscapes/Alamy Stock Photo; 256 John Peter Photography/Alamy Stock Photo; 264 Elizabeth Leyden/Alamy Stock Photo

Every effort has been made to trace the copyright holders, and we apologise in advance for any unintentional omissions or errors. We would be pleased to apply any corrections in a following edition of this publication.